W9-BTM-542

Baseball Immortal

DEREK JETER

A CAREER IN QUOTES

Danny Peary

CO-AUTHOR OF THE BESTSELLING
TIM M^cCARVER'S BASEBALL FOR BRAIN SURGEONS AND OTHER FANS

PAGE STREET
PUBLISHING CO.

PAGE STREET
PUBLISHING CO.

First published in 2015 by
Page Street Publishing Co.
27 Congress Street, Suite 103
Salem, MA 01970
www.pagestreetpublishing.com

Distributed by Macmillan, sales in Canada by The Canadian Manda Group.

18   17   16   15   1   2   3   4   5

ISBN-13: 978-1-62414-162-1
ISBN-10: 1-62414-162-5

Library of Congress Control Number: 2015942390

Cover and book design by Page Street Publishing Co.
Author photo by Mark Hartley

Printed and bound in the United States.

Page Street is proud to be a member of 1% for the Planet. Members donate
one percent of their sales to one or more of the over 1,500 environmental and
sustainability charities across the globe who participate in this program.

FOR SUZANNE, ZOË, AND JULIANNA.
THEY ARE THE BEST WIFE, DAUGHTER, AND
GRANDDAUGHTER IN THE LAND, AND YOU
CAN QUOTE ME ON THAT.

"PASSION IS THE GENESIS OF GENIUS."

—GALILEO

CONTENTS

Introduction

A picture might be worth 1,000 words, but I believe 100,000 words can paint a revealing portrait of any person, including the face of baseball for two decades, Derek Jeter, who in his own way was as protective of his privacy as Greta Garbo, Howard Hughes, and J.D. Salinger, and frustrated journalists by refusing to say anything they considered personal or controversial during his entire career. Yet in retrospect he provided them (and us) with as many intelligent and quotable statements as any athlete not named Ali. The many Jeter quotes in this book, mixed with those about Jeter by hundreds of individuals in and out of baseball, give us a true, unique insight into this extraordinary ballplayer, showing us that we didn't have to wait until he retired to understand who he was throughout each of his 40 years. He was to be found in the words, including his own, all along.

"YOU JUST COULDN'T HAVE WRITTEN A BETTER SCRIPT IF YOU'D BEEN IN HOLLYWOOD."

—DEREK JETER

— ONE —

The Education of
a Ballplayer

"I have been playing baseball as long as I remember."

—**Derek Jeter**, *Game Day*, **2001**

"[Derek Jeter] was raised in a loving but very disciplined household by his
mother, Dorothy, an Irish-American accountant, and his father, Charles, an
African-American substance-abuse counselor. Charles and Dorothy met when they
were both serving in the military and stationed in Europe . . . Charles became the
kind of man many would consider a role model—a solid student and a gifted athlete,
he put himself through college at Fisk University in Nashville, Tennessee, where he
played for the school team . . . He lacked the resources to launch a major league
career, and later he happily settled into family life with Dorothy near her New Jersey
hometown of West Milford. Derek was born on July 26, 1974, [in the Chilton
Memorial Hospital] in the New Jersey town of Pequannock."

—**Robert Craig**, *Derek Jeter: A Biography*, **1999**

"When he was four, his family moved from West Milford to Kalamazoo,
[Michigan,] a city of 75,000, so that his father, Charles, could pursue his doctorate
at Western Michigan University. The family first lived in the Mount Royal
Townhouse Complex near the college."

—**Brian Costello, about the complex where the Jeters lived for six years,**
New York Post, **July 11, 2011**

"The blue, split-level home [at 2415 Cumberland Street] is where Jeter's journey to baseball immortality took off. . . . Jeter was molded here on this quiet Midwestern street. The arm that would eventually rocket throws to first base first threw balls off the side of the house until one of his parents came out to play with him. The swing was developed with thousands of practice cuts on a hitting contraption set up in the one-car garage. The endless confidence was developed in a house where the word 'can't' was banned, where his and his [younger] sister, Sharlee's, achievements were hung on the family room's Wall of Fortune."

—Brian Costello, *New York Post*, July 11, 2011

"[Until he was thirteen] Derek and his sister, Sharlee, continued to spend summers in West Milford, N.J., at the home of his grandparents, William and Dot Connors. Jeter may have inherited his athletic prowess from his father . . . but he acquired his love of the Yankees from his grandmother. . . . Dot would tell Derek about the time she went to Yankee Stadium, a few days after Babe Ruth's death in 1948, to walk past the slugger's casket at home plate and pay her respects."

—Kelly Whiteside, *Sports Illustrated Presents: The Champs! 1996 New York Yankees: A Special Collector's Edition*, November 13, 1996

"The Yankees games were on television. . . . My grandmother watched a lot of them, so I just watched with her. It started with my grandmother. Pretty much since the time I started watching baseball, I was a Yankee fan."

—D.J.

"Dorothy was one of fourteen children, so Derek spent his early years surrounded by a huge extended family, many of whom were avid Yankee fans."

—Robert Craig, *Derek Jeter: A Biography*, 1999

"My uncle used to have season tickets and . . . we used to go to the games all the time."

—D.J., who was six when his grandmother took him to his first game at Yankee Stadium, which he said looked bigger than any place he had ever seen

"All his cousins would still be sleeping, and he would say, 'C'mon, Gram, let's throw.' He wanted to be a pitcher then. I was his catcher. Even as a little kid his throw would almost knock me over."

—Dot Connors, Derek's maternal grandmother

"IN HIS BEDROOM, A FULL YANKEES UNIFORM HUNG ON THE WALL, SIGNIFYING THE DREAM."

—BRIAN COSTELLO, *NEW YORK POST*, JULY 11, 2011

"At home, Derek wore a Yankee cap and T-shirt."

—Robert Craig, *Derek Jeter: A Biography*, 1999

"When Derek was a kid, two of his most prized possessions were a gold Yankees medallion and a blue Yankees windbreaker."

—Kelly Whiteside, *Sports Illustrated Presents: The Champs! 1996 New York Yankees: A Special Collector's Edition*, November 13, 1996

"Legend has it that at the age of five, Derek told everybody he would someday be the Yankees starting shortstop. They laughed then."

—Keith Olbermann, *Fox Sports*

"It was never a matter of wondering whether it would happen. I always knew it would."

—D.J., about his insatiable desire to grow up and play shortstop for the New York Yankees

"My dad had been shortstop when he was in college, and you know, when you're a kid, you want to be just like your dad."

—D.J.

"I used to go watch him play in a softball league. He was probably my first role model. . . . He says he was better than me."

—D.J.

GROWING UP WITH SPECIAL PARENTS

"I could talk about my parents for a year and still not be able to thank them enough for helping me fulfill my dreams."

—D.J., *The Life You Imagine*, 2000

"What kind of influence did my parents have on my life? Well, they had the most influence. These are the people who are closest to me."

—D.J.

"My upbringing was like *The Cosby Show*. We had fun, always did a lot of things together. My parents were involved in everything my sister and I did."

—D.J., to Michael Silver, *Sports Illustrated*, June 21, 1999

"Derek Jeter will tell you that what many people consider to be his gifts—his generosity, his compassion for others, his humility, his self-assurance, and his formidable athletic skills—were furnished by his parents."

—Robert Craig, *Derek Jeter: A Biography*, 1999

"We weren't allowed to use the word *can't*—'I can't do this, can't do that.' My mom would say, 'What? No.' She's always positive."

—D.J.

"Ever since I was young, I said I wanted to [be a major leaguer], and they said, 'As long as you work hard, you can do it.'"

—D.J., about how his parents encouraged him to pursue what others believed was a foolish dream, 2014

"If I wanted to be a doctor, my family would have helped me be a doctor."

—D.J., to Jennifer Flake, *Kalamazoo Gazette*, December 30, 1993

"My parents always told me, 'There's always going to be someone that's better. But there's no reason why someone should outwork you. That's just an excuse.'"

—D.J., recalling how he wasn't allowed to make excuses to Seth Mnookin, *GQ*, April 2011

"I looked up to my parents because they were very successful in what they wanted to do. I was lucky; I didn't have to look far for role models."

—D.J., PBSKids.org "It's My Life"

"[Derek's father] Charles Jeter had grown up in Montgomery, Alabama, without a father—an experience that he later said, 'Made me want to be there for my kids. . . . It's important to have a male role model.'"

—Robert Craig, *Derek Jeter: A Biography*, 1999

"[Dad] used to beat me at everything we played. . . . I was going to afternoon kindergarten, and we used to watch *The Price Is Right*. Now, I'm five years old [and don't know prices]. And he used to beat me at the Showcase Showdown and send me to school."

—D.J., to Ed Bradley, *60 Minutes*, September 25, 2005

"I think my dad was teaching me lessons. Things don't come easily. People aren't just going to let you get your way. I mean, people aren't going to say, 'Here, you can have this.' You have to work for it."

—D.J., to Diane K. Shah, *Playboy*, June 2004

"His father never belittled his guesses, or his ideas, but quietly stressed that a person will have advantages and disadvantages in playing any game. You must never use your disadvantages as an excuse when you lose, his father explained. . . . Charles Jeter would beat young Derek at checkers, Scrabble, pool, basketball, and every other game they played. He knew that, when Derek finally did win at some game, the victory would mean more."

—Clifford W. Mills, *Derek Jeter*, 2007

"I was 13. I thought I was ready to finally beat him in one-on-one [in basketball]. . . . So I challenged my father to play at Western Michigan one day and shocked him. . . . My father was right. All those years of losing to him didn't matter when I finally won. It made the wait worth it. . . . Dad had to clean the bathrooms for a month after that to pay off our bet."

—D.J., *The Life You Imagine*, 2000

"Once every year the Jeters would draw up a contract with [Derek and Sharlee], detailing what was expected from each in the coming year—in school, in athletics, within the family, and even in their interaction with friends. For Derek, participation in baseball, the activity he cherished most, was a reward for meeting these expectations."

—Robert Craig, *Derek Jeter: A Biography*, 1999

"Your role models should teach you, inspire you, criticize you, and give you structure. My parents did all of these things with their contracts. They tackled every subject. There was nothing we didn't discuss. I didn't love every aspect of it, but I was mature enough to understand that almost everything they talked about made sense."

—D.J., quoted by Larry Dobrow and Damien Jones, *Derek Jeter's Ultimate Baseball Guide 2015*, 2015

"First of all, we want them to do well academically. [Derek's] a serious student, and we're serious about his education. And we want them to be involved in things. The contract outlines study hours, curfew, and participation in school activities."

—Charles Jeter, Derek's father, to Mike McCabe, *Detroit Free Press*, 1992

"Derek got into his share of trouble, kid trouble. He was grounded; privileges were taken away. But Derek has tunnel vision. He's focused. He knew that if he broke the rules, there would be consequences, and he accepted that and moved on. Now, Sharlee, she was a negotiator."

—**Dorothy Jeter, Derek's mother**

"Derek had goals, but he knew if he wanted to play in the Little League all-star game or go to baseball camp, he better come home with a 4.0, he better have his behavior intact, and he better make curfew, or he wasn't going anywhere."

—**Dorothy Jeter, who was pleased with her son's 3.82 grade point average at Kalamazoo Central High and his membership in the National Honor Society, quoted by Robert E. Schnakenberg, *Derek Jeter: Surefire Shortstop*, 1999**

"I always used to get in trouble [in school] for talking too much. When it was time for parent-teacher conferences, I remember that I was always embarrassed about what my parents would hear about me!"

— **D.J., PBSKids.org "It's My Life"**

"It's a little different when your dad is a drug and alcohol abuse counselor. . . . I'm not saying I'm any better than anybody else. I've just been educated on that, and there are side effects, too. Eventually, I think you're making a deal with the devil."

—**D.J., on why he left high school parties early when his classmates were drinking, and why as an adult he would create a foundation to combat substance abuse among teenagers, February 19, 2009**

"I'VE ALWAYS HAD . . . THE MENTALITY THAT I NEVER WANTED TO EMBARRASS MY PARENTS."

—D.J. TO MATT LAUER, *TODAY*, SEPTEMBER 30, 2014

"My dad never put pressure on me. He always said, 'If you want A, B, or C to happen in your life, you have to do certain things. He was tough on us in school. We had to sit down and do our homework for an hour every night. Even if we didn't have homework, we had to sit down and do something school related for an hour. Obviously it worked. I got good grades."

—D.J., to Diane K. Shah, *Playboy*, June 2004

"By my senior year, the most depressing clause in the contract was curfew. It was the only clause I ever zealously fought against. [My girlfriend] Marisa had a later curfew than I did, and that got embarrassing. . . . For a guy who never had a curfew when he was growing up, my father was unrelenting."

—D.J., *The Life You Imagine*, 2000

"Jeter's parents provided him with the tools and a road map to navigate situations that would challenge his core beliefs in times of adversity and peer pressure."

—Wayne G. McDonnell Jr., *Forbes*, August 31, 2012

"Oh, by the way, my father is black and my mother is white, a biracial coupling that is a lot more interesting to other people, from the stares we used to get to the questions we still get, than it is to us. So you can add gutsy to the list of adjectives that describe my mom and dad—gutsy to make sure their love conquered all, including bouts with bigotry."

—D.J., *The Life You Imagine*, 2000

"Our last name came from a slave owner."

—D.J., about participating in PBS's *Finding Your Roots* with Professor Henry Louis Gates Jr., *Jeter Unfiltered*, 2014

"[Henry Louis] Gates [Jr.] . . . discovered that Jeter, on his father's side, descends from Green Jeter, an Alabama slave, born May 1844. Upon being set free after the Civil War, Green 'thrived,' became a minister, founded his own church."

—J.R. Moehringer, *ESPN The Magazine*, October 13, 2014

"When people say he's perfect, they don't understand the trials and tribulations Derek had growing up in a biracial family."

—Charles Jeter

"With me as a kid . . . all I know is my mom and my dad. It's not weird to me. . . . But you always have ignorant people, though. . . . You get looks everywhere you [go]. *You're darker than your mom; you're lighter than your dad.* People don't know what nationality you are. . . . I played baseball where it was primarily white, and then basketball was primarily black. So I had friends of all different races. You pretty much learn to deal with it."

—**D.J., to Dave Buscema,** *Game of My Life: 20 Stories of Yankees Baseball,* **2004**

"You'd go places and get stares; if you were just with one of your parents, people would give you a double-take because something just didn't seem right. . . . You'd hear some things, whispers when you walk in, laughs. It also taught you that there are people that were uneducated in terms of different races. . . . Kids would say [the N-word]; you'd hear it. It would bother you and annoy you, make you feel bad. . . . It also taught me a lot. It taught me how I didn't want to be, that I needed to learn about different people as opposed to just judging them."

—**D.J., who is proud to be from Kalamazoo despite having had to deal with the ignorance of bigots there, to Barbara Walters,** *10 Most Fascinating People of 2011,* **December 14, 2011**

"We realized that they were going to experience prejudice in life. But we taught them that you can't just be . . . an A student. You can't settle for good. You've got to be better than the best. . . . It's not to say you're not going to get what you want because you're biracial, or that there are prejudices in the world, but you have to be better than anyone else. That's life. It can be unfair sometimes."

—Dorothy Jeter

"I'M NOT RAISED TO LOOK AT SOMEONE'S COLOR. YOU LOOK AT THE PERSON."

—D.J.

"Derek was one of those kids you just never forget, and I would say that even if he wasn't playing baseball. He was the kind of student any teacher would want to have. I was just struck by how much he cared about his fellow classmates. . . . He was completely self-motivated, creative, never wasted any time. . . . He always found something to do. I remember doing his report card and thinking, 'Does he realize just how intelligent he is?'"

—**Shirley Garzelloni, Jeter's elementary school teacher at St. Augustine's Cathedral School, to Buster Olney,** *New York Times,* **April 9, 1999**

"He didn't have this 'I'm really cool' attitude. He was very genuine and humble."

—**Chris Oosterbaan, Jeter's elementary school teacher at St. Augustine's Cathedral School, to Buster Olney,** *New York Times,* **April 9, 1999**

"It was something you sort of just knew was going to happen."

—**Shirley Garzelloni, Jeter's elementary school teacher at St. Augustine's Cathedral School, about how she believed the nine-year-old boy when he emphatically told everyone he'd one day play shortstop for the Yankees**

"As a boy in Kalamazoo, I lived for game day. When the season would start, I would put my uniform on and ask my parents how I looked. I loved the whole ritual of game day: putting on my uniform, driving to the field, doing our warm-ups, hearing the crowd cheer and my name called, and taking my place at shortstop."

—**D.J.,** *Game Day,* **2001**

"His early days on the diamond in Kalamazoo were spent honing his skills in the Eastwood, Oakwood, and Westwood Little Leagues."

—**Derek Jeter biography, Turn 2, The Official Site of Derek Jeter and the Turn 2 Foundation, 2015**

"I wanted Derek to be an all-around player."

**—Charles Jeter, who played his son at second, third, and shortstop when
he coached him in Little League**

"I'd known *of* Derek for years, because everyone in Kalamazoo had heard about this
fantastic Little League ballplayer."

—Don Zomer, Jeter's varsity high school baseball coach

"I always wanted to play in Williamsport, but we were terrible when I was in Little
League. So I never got the chance."

**—D.J., in conversation with Chris Fontenelli of Toms River East,
1998 Little League world champions, moderated by Buster Olney,
New York Times Magazine, September 12, 1999**

"I remember my dad telling me . . . —my mom as well—you can't compare
yourself to the kids you're playing against in the Westwood Little League in
Kalamazoo. There are people that are working to be the same thing you want to be
all around the country . . . all over the world. . . . So I never sat down and said, 'I
think I'm good enough to play professional baseball.' It was just a matter of *what
can I do to improve?*"

—D.J., to Michael Kay, *CenterStage*, December 2003

"In terms of athletes, Dave Winfield was my guy. He was drafted in three sports,
which caught my eye. Plus, he's also the first athlete I know to start his own
foundation. I thought it was pretty cool that this professional athlete was giving
back to his community."

— D.J., PBSKids.org "It's My Life"

"It felt pretty good to know that this exciting young shortstop thought I was a role
model. I was really pleased to hear that. There were different images that people
who didn't know me had of me as a player during my career. It was important to
hear that I had affected him in the right way."

—Dave Winfield, Padres and Yankees Hall of Famer

D.J. DATA: As a boy, Derek Jeter idolized his father and Dave Winfield, but he also was drawn to a superhero on television. On February 23, 2003, Charles Jeter recalled what his young son wanted for Christmas that wasn't baseball related: "He always liked the Hulk doll. He would pose like [him]."

"I admit I was a huge Hulk fan," remembered Jeter on the same day. "I was a fan of the Lou Ferrigno Hulk, from the TV series."

"Derek Jeter: most likely to play shortstop for the New York Yankees."

—**Prescient words in Jeter's eighth-grade yearbook**

"Even my teachers told me to be more realistic."

—**D.J.**

"WHEN HE WAS 12 OR 13, I TOOK HIM TO A BASKETBALL CAMP AT THE UNIVERSITY OF MICHIGAN, AND WHEN IT WAS TIME FOR HIM TO MEET THE OTHER KIDS, I HAD TO PUSH HIM TO MAKE CONVERSATION."
—**CHARLES JETER, TO MICHAEL SILVER, *SPORTS ILLUSTRATED*, JUNE 21, 1999**

"When he was in eighth grade and was about to switch from parochial school to a public school, we sent him over to the Y to play basketball against older kids as a way of toughening him up. He went, but he took his mother with him."

—**Charles Jeter, to Michael Silver, *Sports Illustrated*, June 21, 1999**

"I almost didn't go to Kalamazoo Central. My parents thought I should go to Hackett, a Catholic high school. . . . Since my parents knew I wanted to play baseball and basketball, they thought I might have trouble doing it at a school as large as Central. I think they thought I'd be fine in baseball, but I wasn't the greatest basketball player, and that's what worried them. . . . I begged them to let me go to Central, so my mother made a deal with me. She told me that I could go there if I made the Kazoo Blues basketball team, an elite Amateur Athletic Union team that drew its players from all over western Michigan."

—**D.J., *The Life You Imagine*, 2000**

DEREK JETER, BASKETBALL PLAYER

"Derek was an outstanding athlete. Basically the thing that set him apart was not his basketball ability, but his athleticism and his ability to work hard. He always tried to be better than everyone else in drills. He wasn't a natural basketball player, but he was an athlete."

—**Walter Hall, coach of the Kazoo Blues, who gave Jeter a spot on the team, thereby allowing him to attend, with his parents' permission, Kalamazoo Central High**

"My mother's plan worked. Making that team gave me even more confidence going into high school. I was already a confident kid, but playing with the Kazoo Blues and traveling to different parts of the country enhanced my attitude and made me feel I could accomplish anything."

—**D.J., *The Life You Imagine*, 2000**

"As he reached his full of height of 6 feet 3 inches, he played AAU ball [against such] future NBA stars [as Detroit's] Chris Webber and Jalen Rose."

— **Mark Stewart, *Derek Jeter: Substance and Style*, 1999**

"Derek probably got dunked on more than anybody in the state of Michigan."

—**Greg Williams, Blues assistant coach**

"I don't know about getting dunked on. Power lay-ups, maybe."

—**D.J.**

"On paper, we didn't belong in the same gym with those guys. And Derek came off the bench and shot Oklahoma right out of the tournament."

—**Walter Hall, Blues head coach**

"IT DIDN'T MATTER IF DEREK HAD MISSED 20 SHOTS IN A ROW. IF THE GAME WAS ON THE LINE AND HE GOT THE BALL AGAIN, HE WAS PUTTING IT UP."
—DAVID HART, BLUES POINT GUARD, ON JETER'S NEARLY AUTOMATIC JUMP SHOT FROM 15 FEET OUT TO BEYOND THE 3-POINT LINE

"After that game, no matter what I was playing, I always wanted to be there with the game on the line."

—D.J., about hitting a 3-pointer as the clock expired to give the Kalamazoo Central basketball team a 1-point victory over Portage Central when he was a sophomore in high school

"He always wanted the last shot. He usually didn't make them, but he was never afraid to fail."

—Charles Jeter

"I kept safe because I made friends with the bullies."

—D.J., about going to a large high school, PBSKids.org "It's My Life"

"Derek enrolled at Kalamazoo Central High School in 1988, and immediately began making a name for himself as a student athlete. . . . In the classroom, he maintained an A-minus average. On the basketball court, he became the varsity's starting shooting guard."

—Mark Stewart, *Derek Jeter: Substance and Style,* 1999

"I played a lot of sports, so I got a chance to know a lot of people. I tried everything, including basketball and soccer. I was too skinny to play football though! I did anything that had me running around and had to do with sports."

—D.J., PBSKids.org "It's My Life"

"I played basketball in high school, and it really got me in shape for the baseball season, [including] with conditioning and lateral movement."

—D.J., who became an honorable mention all-state guard in high school,
***Tim McCarver Show*, May 9, 2000**

"I remember the cold. We weren't that good of a high school [baseball] team. We played 20 games a season. We'd get rained out or snowed out a lot."

—D.J., who kept in shape waiting for the baseball season by playing basketball, running cross country, and fielding grounders in the school gym, 2010

"On the baseball diamond, Derek was simply the best shortstop anyone at the school had ever seen."

—Mark Stewart, *Derek Jeter: Substance and Style*, 1999

"I knew that he wasn't going to be on the JV for too long."

—Norm Copeland, Jeter's junior varsity baseball coach as a freshman, after seeing Jeter's powerful arm

"You never see a kid that long and lean throwing a ball that hard."

—Courtney Jasiak, Jeter's 21-year-old coach for Brundage Roofing, an under-16 baseball team

"I used to long-toss with my dad to strengthen my arm."

—D.J., who was promoted to the varsity baseball team after two-thirds of a season by coach Marv Signeski, prompting All-Conference shortstop Craig Humphrey to willingly shift to second base to make room for the stronger-armed youngster

"He would throw the ball 91, 92 miles an hour from short to first. I had to put a better athlete at first just to handle his throws. . . . Derek hit balls normal high school players just couldn't handle."

—Don Zomer, Jeter's second varsity baseball coach at Kalamazoo Central High School

"First time I saw him, he was playing for Kalamazoo Central. He was about 15 years old and as skinny as the bat he was using. And I looked at him and said, 'Oh my God, this kid is something else. He was . . . playing on the varsity, hitting third, always the first one to practice and the last one to leave. . . . He just stuck out like a sore thumb. . . . There was him, and there was everybody else. It isn't even comparable. Just the way he went about it. . . . Just low-key, hustled his a– off, shined above everyone else."

—**Ace Adams, University of Michigan assistant baseball coach and recruiter, to Sweeny Murti,** *SportsNet New York,* **September 22, 2014**

"He was really quiet; he didn't say a word. He just went about his business."

—**Courtney Jasiak, Brundage Roofing coach**

"When Jeter was 15, he played third base for Rathco, a summer league team sponsored by a company that produces highway safety equipment, road barriers, and such. The next season, he joined the Kalamazoo Maroons. . . . The team played games almost daily, with little time for practice. . . . He would arrive early for games and take grounders."

—**Buster Olney,** *New York Times,* **March 29, 1998**

"After games, he would stand out there and take grounders as long as there was somebody there to hit balls to him. . . . He worked his rear end off."

—**Mike Hinga, Jeter's coach for three summers with the Kalamazoo Maroons, an elite traveling team**

"He was almost like a colt—long arms, long legs, very thin. You wouldn't look at that and go, 'Yeah, for sure.' But you could see there was this huge, huge upside."

—**Mike Hinga, Kalamazoo Maroons coach**

"HE WAS THE LAST ONE OFF THE FIELD EVERY NIGHT. . . . HE ALWAYS WANTED MORE: 'HOW ABOUT ONE MORE TURN IN THE BATTING CAGE? OR 25 MORE GROUND BALLS?'"
—DON ZOMER, KALAMAZOO CENTRAL HIGH'S VARSITY BASEBALL COACH, ABOUT JETER'S WORK ETHIC AND LOVE OF BASEBALL

"Derek always had the desire to be the best."

—Charles Jeter

"In the evenings, after his team had finished playing, Derek, his parents, and his sister, Sharlee, would often hop the fence of the high school field to play some more."

—Matt Christopher, *On the Field with . . . Derek Jeter*, 2000

"Some people went to the movies for fun. We went to the field. It was all part of being very close."

—Sharlee Jeter, Derek's sister

"Our family time was spent at the baseball field. We lived behind my high school, which had a baseball field and a softball field, and we'd go out there—my parents, my sister, and myself. We'd take turns hitting a baseball, and then we'd get out the softball, and we played Wiffle ball."

—D.J., *Tim McCarver Show*, May 9, 2000

"My mom and sister would be in the outfield and would flag down all the balls I would hit."

—D.J., about when his father threw him batting practice every evening

"My sister, Sharlee, used to run circles around me. It's the truth, I'm not lying to you. She's the best shortstop in the family. Now, my dad will tell you he's the best, but he couldn't hit too well. My sister could hit. . . . Sharlee was a better athlete than me—by far."

—D.J., who often praised his sister's skills in softball, volleyball, and basketball,
Tim McCarver Show

"Before high school games, [my mother would] go into the backyard and throw me batting practice [with a Wiffle ball]."

—D.J., MLB.com, May 10, 2001

"I'm going to college at some point. I'd like to become a doctor."

—D.J., revealing that he envisioned a life other than playing baseball

"I tutored in the computer lab when I was in [high] school. I didn't exactly love it, but as I got older I learned the importance of volunteering."

—D.J., about his interests *off* the ball field, PBSKids.org "It's My Life"

"He just had an easy manner, no signs of conceit, and when he was helping people, he didn't make any of them feel less important."

—Sally Padley, Jeter's British literature teacher at Kalamazoo Central High, to Buster Olney, *New York Times*, April 9, 1999

"I didn't get into too much trouble—or, I should say, I didn't get caught."

—D.J., to Barbara Walters, *10 Most Fascinating People of 2011*, December 14, 2011

"He would say, 'I'm going to play for the Yankees' and you'd say, 'Yeah, right.' It wasn't cocky. He just really believed that was what he was going to do."

—Mike Hinga, Kalamazoo Maroons coach

"He always had focus."

—Charles Jeter

D.J. DATA: Derek Jeter hoped to become a major league baseball player although there had been few major leaguers to come out of Kalamazoo, and no stars. According to *The Baseball Almanac*, the only previous Kalamazoo players were Connie Berry (debut 1948, final season 1954), John Ganzel (debut 1898, final season 1919), Mike Hart (1980), Ron Jackson (debut 1954, final season 1960), Stubby Magner (1911), Rudy Miller (1929), and Mike Squires (debut 1975, final season 1985).

"The first time that I had an opportunity to see him was in 1991 in Mount Morris, Michigan, and it was an evaluation camp. And when I walked into the park, they were hitting ground balls, and the first thing that he did was he went into the hole, fielded the ball, and did his classic jump pass/throw to first base—something that you just don't normally see a 16-year-old do. And from that point in time—during the whole camp—he had my undivided attention."

—Dick Groch, Yankees scout in Michigan, to Sweeny Murti, *SportsNet New York*, September 22, 2014

"He always stayed away. He kept his distance."

—D.J., about being unaware Dick Groch, Yankees scout, was watching him play

"I did not want him to know that I was at the ballpark. I sat in my car. I was in the bushes. I was in the woods. I didn't want him to play for me, because I wanted to see how he handled failure. And every game that he played was the same."

—Dick Groch, Yankees scout, quoted by Ronald Blum, *Associated Press*, September 25, 2014

"Even his outs were impressive."

—Don Zomer, Central High School varsity baseball coach, about Jeter batting .557 as a junior

"After my junior year, which was actually my best year, I didn't even make the All-Conference or All-District teams. I thought [race] definitely had something to do with it. Yeah, definitely, without question. We had some great [players], but I thought at least I could have made the All-District team, but it didn't happen. And [later] they said I was the best player in the country, so I thought there was a little something going into that."

—D.J., whose parents told him racism would always be part of his life, to Michael Kay, *CenterStage*, December 2003

"He'll be among the first 10 players selected in the developmental draft next June. He'll command a six-figure signing bonus, which is more than anyone from here has ever received. He's worth it, too."

—**Keith Roberts, Detroit Tigers scout,** *Kalamazoo Gazette***, August 14, 1991**

"I was surprised to hear I'd be picked so high."

—**D.J., to** *Baseball America*

"We had Derek up for his official visit in 1991 to Ann Arbor on a weekend we were playing Notre Dame. We brought him into this restaurant, the Cottage Inn, and the owner opened up the restaurant just for me, [University of Michigan head baseball coach] Bill Freehan, Mr. and Mrs. Jeter, Derek and his host, a then-current Michigan baseball player. We were the only ones in the restaurant, and his mother turned to me—and this is unbelievable, because I loved this kid and so did Bill—and said, 'Mr. Adams, do you really think Derek is good enough to play here next year at Michigan?'"

—**Ace Adams, University of Michigan assistant baseball coach**

"Mrs. Jeter, he could've started here when he was in eighth grade."

—**Ace Adams, recalling his response to Dorothy Jeter's question, to Buster Olney,** *New York Times***, April 9, 1999**

"He['ll be] hitting third and playing short; that's the end of the story on that one."

—**Bill Freehan, University of Michigan baseball coach and former Detroit Tigers catcher, to Jeter's parents**

"Derek's an outstanding young man. You can tell by the way he conducts himself. He's the type of young man you want in your program."

—**Bill Freehan, to a reporter about the youngster he considered the best high school player he had ever seen**

"He considered offers from Notre Dame; the University of Miami, Fla.; and Western Michigan University, but recently signed a letter of intent to the University of Michigan."

—*Kalamazoo Gazette*, **March 17, 1992**

"I feel more comfortable at the U of M. It's a very good academic school, and it's close to home."

—**D.J.**, *Kalamazoo Gazette*, **March 17, 1992**

"The last time the Yankees convened in Florida for the start of the baseball season without [Derek] Jeter in their major-league camp, George H.W. Bush was in the White House, Johnny Carson was the host of the *Tonight Show*, and a gallon of gas cost about a dollar."

—**Jim Baumbach, about spring 1992, *Newsday*, February 15, 2015**

"BY HIS SENIOR YEAR, IT WAS CLEAR THAT DEREK WAS MORE THAN JUST A LOCAL HERO; HE WAS AMONG THE BEST HIGH SCHOOL PLAYERS IN THE NATION. THERE WERE NOW 35 TO 40 MAJOR LEAGUE SCOUTS IN THE STANDS FOR EVERY KALAMAZOO CENTRAL GAME."

—ROBERT CRAIG, *DEREK JETER: A BIOGRAPHY*, 1999

"I was wondering why they were the only team that didn't call."

—**D.J., about being contacted by all 28 major league teams except the Yankees prior to the amateur draft**

D.J. DATA: The Yankees had selected only two shortstops as their first draft pick prior to 1992 when Jeter was eligible, Dennis Sherrill in 1974 and Rex Hudler in 1978. Neither became a starter in the major leagues.

"Portage Central's Ryan Topham and Kalamazoo Central's Derek Jeter are two of the top baseball prospects in the state, and they met Saturday afternoon for a Big Eight Conference doubleheader. . . . The rumor buzzing around the ball park was that at least 35 or 40 pro scouts were there to witness the Kalamazoo area's best ball talent. . . . They each homered in their first official at-bats in a doubleheader swept by Portage, 12–8 and 10–0. . . . Jeter ran the count to 3-and-1 before he rocketed a letter-high fastball from Chris Quinn into the trees behind the 385 marker in straight away center field. . . . Jeter's day was cut short in the first inning of the second game when he sprained his ankle sliding across first base after beating out an infield hit."

—Andy Latora, *Kalamazoo Gazette*, April 12, 1992

"I didn't think it was broken, but I was afraid to move it. When I finally did, it hurt, but it was OK."

—D.J., about spraining his ankle, which would cause him to limp for the rest of the year and limit him to only one home run in his next 50 at bats

"I worried about my future."

—D.J., who was relieved when X-rays showed a sprain rather than a break

"The injury taught him a valuable lesson. . . . He learned that everything could change in an instant."

—Matt Christopher, *On the Field with . . . Derek Jeter*, 2000

"Before injuring an ankle running over a slippery base in April, Jeter was considered a possible No. 1 choice overall [in the June 1992 amateur draft] because of his speed, arm strength, and hitting."

—Jack Curry, *New York Times*, June 2, 1992

"We set [a] solo hitter up in our one-car garage, which became my personal hitting area, and I probably used it every day of the year, whether it was warm or cold. I was so dedicated that I'd sometimes take 1,000 swings a day. I was so dedicated that I would leave school during my free sixth period in my senior year and walk home to practice my swing for 45 minutes."

—D.J., *The Life You Imagine*, 2000

"That season, he hit .508, after missing several games because of a twisted ankle. . . . He struck out just once the entire season and was 12 for 12 in stolen bases. At season's end, Derek's star status was confirmed. He was named 1992's High School Player of the Year by the American Baseball Coaches Association, and also won the Gatorade Award, given to the nation's top prep student-athlete in any sport."

—Robert Craig, *Derek Jeter: A Biography*, 1999

"I might have missed that pitch."

—**Dick Bird, umpire who called Jeter out on strikes on a 3–2 pitch, his only whiff in his senior year,** *Newsday*, **2012**

"Yeah, it was a bad call. . . . If it was close, I'm swinging at it. I've always been that way."

—D.J., *Newsday*, 2012

"Bird [says] that Jeter immediately walked back to the dugout, not even glancing back with a dirty look, like many kids would. That memory stuck with him."

—**Jim Baumbach,** *Newsday*, **September 29, 2012**

"Why would you complain about the umpire? Control what you can control."

—**Charles Jeter, to his son after he once grumbled about a bad third-strike call**

"Success is when you make your own goals. You reach them all and don't short-change yourself. Keep working hard. Don't let anyone tell you you can't do it. This applies not only to sports but to everything in life."

—**D.J., giving advice to youngsters after being selected the Baseball Player of the Year by the Michigan High School Baseball Coaches Association,** *Kalamazoo Gazette*, **March 17, 1992**

"B'nai B'rith to Honor Top Prep Scholar-Athletes"

—**Headline about Jeter and two others from Kalamazoo Central being among the students from nine local high schools who were to be honored at the Congregation of Moses Synagogue, *Kalamazoo Gazette*, May 27, 1992**

"Gliding runner w/ burst-type acceleration. Very qk. feet, very gd. lower body control. Arm strength to spare! Excellent carry and can throw from all angles + body positions."

—**Chuck McMichael, Kansas City Royals scout**

"Slender, agile body with long arms and legs. Large feet. . . . Outstanding infield instincts. Soft hands and strong, accurate arm. Bat has quickness with little long stroke. Makes contact with gap power. Will hit occasional long ball. Comes to play."

—**Tony Stieil, Atlanta Braves scout**

"Both [Kansas City and Atlanta's] scouts . . . noted [17-year-old] Jeter as a pull or straightaway hitter, a far cry from the opposite-field, inside-out swing Jeter . . . perfected through his career."

—**Nick Corasaniti, *New York Times***

"A YANKEE! A FIVE-TOOL PLAYER. WILL BE A ML STAR TIMES FIVE!!"
—DICK GROCH, YANKEES SCOUT IN HIS GLOWING REPORT TO THE ORGANIZATION IN WHICH HE ALSO RANKED JETER AS BEING EXCELLENT IN DEDICATION, EMOTIONAL MATURITY, AND AGILITY, APRIL 8, 1992

"Above average arm, quick release. Accurate throws with outstanding carry. Soft hands, good range, active feet. Very good runner. Flow on the bases. Shows power potential. Quick bat."

—**Dick Groch, Yankees scout, grading Jeter's abilities, April 8, 1992**

"Anxious hitter. Needs to learn to be more patient at the plate. Swing slightly long."

—**Dick Groch, grading Jeter's weaknesses, April 8, 1992**

"Long, lean, sinewy body. Long arms, long legs, narrow waist, thin ankles. Live, electric movements."

—**Dick Groch, giving Jeter's physical description, in his report to the organization, April 8, 1992**

"The scout, Dick Groch, just couldn't have been any higher on him. Everybody we sent in had the same feeling. We were almost to the point of not wanting to get our hopes up too much. . . . We sent the West Coast guy in, Don Lindberg, and he loved him. Jack Gillis was our national cross-checker, and he loved him. I had been in to see him. I thought this was the guy for us."

—**Bill Livesey, Yankees director of scouting, quoted by Daniel Carp, USA Today, September 4, 2014**

"You were like, 'This kid's too good to be true.' No—he was true."

—**Mitch Lukevics, Yankees director of minor league operations, quoted by Daniel Carp, USA Today, September 4, 2014**

D.J. DATA: Jeter's high school honors included:

Michigan High School Coaches Association Player of the Year 1992

Scholastic Coach Magazine's Gatorade High School Athlete of the Year 1992

USA Today High School Baseball Player of the Year 1992

Baseball America's Top National Athlete of the Year 1992

American Baseball Coaches Association High School Player of the Year 1992

"You get excited just watching him warm up."

—**Ed Santa, Colorado Rockies scout, May 1992**

"He's got the softest hands I've ever seen."

—**Hal Newhouser, Hall of Fame pitcher and Houston Astros scout who pushed his team to select Jeter as the first pick in the draft**

"My dad talks to the scouts, agents, and front-office people. . . . I let him handle all that stuff, and I play baseball."

—**D.J., to Paul Morgan,** *Kalamazoo Gazette*

"A car in the driveway of the Jeter household has a University of Michigan-Go Blue bumper sticker on it."

—**Paul Morgan,** *Kalamazoo Gazette***, May 31, 1992**

"As the famous story goes, Groch was asked in the Yankees' draft room about the possibility of Jeter not signing so he could head to play for the University of Michigan instead."

—**Anthony McCarron, New York** *Daily News*

"The only place he's going is Cooperstown."

—**Dick Groch, Yankees scout**

"It was a huge possibility."

—**D.J., about whether he seriously considered going to the University of Michigan rather than signing a major league contract after graduating from high school**

"Nobody knows this, but Jeter . . . wanted to go to Michigan with his girlfriend, and he wanted to play there.

—**Ace Adams, assistant baseball coach at the University of Michigan, quoted by Ian O'Connor,** *The Captain***, 2011**

"Sources in Houston say that the Astros have narrowed their selection [for the top pick in the amateur draft] to either Jeter or Cal-State Fullerton third baseman, Phil Nevin, *Baseball America's* College Player of the Year. Jeter was the . . . pick as top high school player."

—**Paul Morgan,** *Kalamazoo Gazette*, **May 31, 1992**

"Signability was a factor. We had narrowed it to [Phil] Nevin and Jeter. There was some interest in Mr. [Jeffrey] Hammonds, too, but it had become quite clear signability was going to be an issue there. We did have some diversity of opinion. As I recall, there was not a consensus one way or the other."

—**Dan O'Brien, Astros scouting director, quoted by Daniel Carp,**
USA Today, **September 4, 2014**

"NO ONE IS WORTH $1 MILLION DOLLARS, BUT IF ONE KID IS WORTH THAT, IT'S THIS KID."
—HAL NEWHOUSER, HALL OF FAME PITCHER AND HOUSTON SCOUT WHO TRIED TO PERSUADE THE ASTROS TO TAKE JETER RATHER THAN NEVIN

"The Yankees have the No. 6 pick. . . . The Yankees narrowed their list to 10–12 players before beginning extensive meetings Thursday in Tampa, Fla., but declined all comment on what their plans were. . . . The Yankees are reportedly interested in three players: [Pepperdine pitcher] Derek Wallace, Miami catcher Charles Johnson, and Derek Jeter, a high school shortstop from Kalamazoo, Mich. . . . 'High school players don't worry us,' [Yankees vice president of scouting and player development Brian] Sabean said. 'It's more of a commitment. You're looking at four or five years before he's called up, and that's being conservative.' Jeter hit .557 as a high school junior and .508 as a senior. He has good speed and is considered a first-rate shortstop."

—**Mark J. Czerwinski,** *Bergen Record*, **May 31, 1992**

"We had to convince Mr. Steinbrenner to go with a high school player. He wasn't really high on high school players at the time. It took too long for them, in his mind. . . . If you can say, 'This guy is going to be as good as he's capable of being,' then you're comfortable. And we knew that [Jeter] would be as good as he was capable of being."

—**Bill Livesey, Yankees director of scouting,**
quoted by Daniel Carp, *USA Today,* **September 4, 2014**

"The Yankees had some competition for Jeter. . . . The Astros held the No. 1 pick overall, and their scout who trailed Jeter, Hall of Fame pitcher Hal Newhouser, pushed for Houston to take Jeter. The Reds had a scout who lived in nearby Battle Creek, about 20 miles away, who had been a regular to see Jeter, too, and they picked fifth, one spot ahead of the Yankees."

—**Anthony McCarron, New York** *Daily News*

"The team I was actually most worried about was the Reds. They had a part-time scout in Battle Creek (Mich.). I know Cincy liked him. Boy, would things have been so different if they got him."

—**Dick Groch, Yankees scout, quoted by Daniel Carp,**
USA Today, **September 4, 2014**

"Jeter was a no-brainer for us at number 5. . . . We were sure we were going to get him. It was a done deal. He had blazing speed, he was smart, he hit rockets into the Riverfront seats when we had him in as a high school junior. Every single thing Jeter did was special."

—**Gene Bennett, Cincinnati scout**

"Just in case, Groch says, the Yankees had a scout sitting in a car near the house of Jim Pittsley, a high school pitcher from Pennsylvania who was eventually taken 17th by the Royals. . . . Pittsley appeared in 81 major-league games."

—**Anthony McCarron, New York** *Daily News,* **February 15, 2014**

"They never contacted me until the night before [the draft]."

—D.J., about the Yankees' seeming indifference toward him

"I couldn't sleep the night before. It was a big, big day. . . . I think it was the most nervous time of my life because that one day determines my whole life, where I go, what city I go to, and who I'm playing for."

—D.J.

"When you have that type of expectation with a young player, and you have the sixth pick in the draft, every pick you're holding your breath."

—Mitch Lukevics, Yankees director of minor league operations, about when the draft began, quoted by Daniel Carp, USA Today, September 4, 2014

"The Astros took Phil Nevin [with the first pick] . . . [Hal] Newhouser resigned after Houston passed on Jeter."

—Anthony McCarron, New York Daily News

"The Reds chose Chad Mottola, and the Yanks took Jeter, the first high school player chosen."

—Anthony McCarron, New York Daily News

"I couldn't believe it. Without question, it was the most disappointing thing that ever happened to me as a scout."

—Gene Bennett, Cincinnati scout, after learning that the Reds had passed on Jeter and selected Chad Mottola with their fifth pick

"A CHEER IMMEDIATELY WENT UP IN THE YANKEES DRAFT ROOM IN TAMPA, ONE LOUD ENOUGH TO ECHO TO THE BRONX. FISTS WERE PUMPED, AND BACKS WERE SLAPPED. SOMEHOW, SOME WAY, DEREK JETER HAD MADE IT UNSCATHED TO THE SIXTH PICK."

—IAN O'CONNOR, THE CAPTAIN, 2011

"I get to hear about it every year at draft time. You always hear about the Brady Six, the six quarterbacks drafted before [New England Patriots superstar] Tom Brady. Well, we are the Jeter Five. The five biggest failures in the history of the game. I guess I can laugh about it now."

—**Phil Nevin, the top draft choice in 1992, quoted by Daniel Carp,**
USA Today, **September 4, 2014**

D.J. DATA: The player the Cincinnati Reds unexpectedly drafted fifth in the 1992 draft, allowing the Yankees to select Jeter sixth, was Chad Mottola, an outfielder at the University of Central Florida. He would play in 35 games with the Reds in 1996, which was also Jeter's rookie year, and appear in 24 more games with other teams from 2000 to 2006, before his major league career ended. He hit .200 lifetime in just 125 big-league at-bats. He went 0-for-4 in his lone Yankee Stadium appearance in 2006. The New York family members he invited to that game considered Jeter their favorite player, and Mottola said, "They all ended up with Jeter jerseys."

"I didn't even know the Yankees picked sixth."

—**D.J., who believed he'd be chosen either first or fifth until a local reporter called and informed him on draft day that five teams had picked already, and he was still available**

"Though it would take another four years before anyone realized it, the most significant development during that '92 season was the decision of scouting and player development VP Bill Livesey to take a[n] 18-year-old high school shortstop from Kalamazoo, Michigan, named Derek Jeter as the Yankees' number-one pick in the June amateur draft."

—**Bill Madden,** *Steinbrenner: The Last Lion of Baseball,* **2010**

"Say this much for the Yankees. They rarely go along with the crowd. So it shouldn't be surprising that in the first round of a free-agent draft dominated by the selection of college players, they chose a high school player. Derek Jeter, a shortstop from Kalamazoo (Mich.) Central High School, was the sixth pick overall Monday, and the first high schooler selected. Twenty-one of 28 first-round picks were college players. Jeter has athletic genes. The 6-foot-3 right-handed hitter is a second cousin of former Giants defensive end Gary Jeter and Eugene Jeter, who also played in the National Football League. His father, Charles, was a good-field, no-hit shortstop at a small college in Nashville, Tenn. Jeter had the credentials. . . . His biggest concern was whether the scouts would be scared off by an ankle injury he suffered on April 11. The Yankees aren't about to invest the $1.55 million they paid pitcher Brien Taylor, last year's No. 1 pick. But they could be tempted to make Jeter an offer he can't refuse."

—**John Rowe,** *Bergen Record,* **June 2, 1992**

"The draft is like a crapshoot, so how amazing it was to be a Yankees fan being selected as the sixth pick by the Yankees in the 1992 draft. Actually, I was supposed to go fifth to Cincinnati, and if that happened, I'd have been stuck behind Barry Larkin. So I was real fortunate, not only because the Yankees drafted me, but also because Cincinnati overlooked me."

—**D.J.,** *Tim McCarver Show,* **May 9, 2000**

"Hard to believe."

—**Charles Jeter**

"It was a freak happening."

—**D.J.**

"The phone rang, and my mom answered and said the Yankees were on the phone. Oh, man, I can't even describe how I felt."

—**D.J.**

> **"MY FAVORITE [MEMORY] WAS . . . WHEN HE GOT THE PHONE CALL—JUST TO SEE HIS EYES LIGHT UP. IT WAS LIKE, WOW, I CAN'T BELIEVE THIS IS HAPPENING."**
> **—DOROTHY JETER, TO MEREDITH MARAKOVITS, YES NETWORK, 2014**

"The Yankees must now begin the process of signing the 17-year-old. . . . As the sixth pick, Jeter could probably command a contract close to $400,000. . . . The club released a statement about Jeter that simply said he was the best athlete available."

—Jack Curry, *New York Times*, June 2, 1992

"So, while Derek was playing his final summer games for the Kalamazoo Maroons (not only shortstopping but, on his 18th birthday, pitching a few innings), Dr. Jeter was facing down a trio of Yankee negotiators, one of whom, Dick Groch, was the scout who alerted the Yankees to Derek's abilities."

—Patrick Giles, *Derek Jeter: Pride of the Yankees*, 1998

"We'll make a decision as a family. It is my dream to play professionally, whether it is now or after college."

—D.J.

"Ace Adams, formerly the assistant baseball coach at the University of Michigan, said the Jeters . . . informed him daily of the progress of his contract negotiations, so that the Wolverines would be prepared to replace Jeter if he signed with the Yankees."

—Buster Olney, *New York Times*, April 9, 1999

"We gave him $700,000 plus $100,000 for college. What broke the stalemate was that he wanted equipment for the Kalamazoo high school and recreation programs. We took care of that."

—Dick Groch, Yankees scout, quoted by Daniel Carp, *USA Today*, September 4, 2014

"Education is a big thing in our family. Signing with the Yankees was no easy decision because I really wanted to go to school and play baseball at Michigan. But I couldn't say no when they were paying for college, too."

—D.J., who was told by Michigan baseball coach Bill Freehan that he'd be insane not to accept the $800,000 package

"The money was definitely a plus, but [the Yankees'] interest was what made the difference. I got the feeling they were very high on me."

—D.J.

"I'm happy with the package, and it's the most anyone has gotten in the first round."

—D.J., to Paul Morgan, *Kalamazoo Gazette*

"They were nervous as all get-out. Not nervous he would fail, just normal kid-going-to-college nervous. They knew he would be well taken care of."

—Paul Morgan, *Kalamazoo Gazette* sportswriter, about Jeter's parents

"If anybody ever saw that family together, they could understand how hard it must have been to leave them. Derek's so much the big athlete, but there's still some of the little boy in him."

—Shirley Garzelloni, Jeter's elementary school teacher at St. Augustine's Cathedral School

"I wouldn't have drafted me. I weighed 156 pounds fully dressed. I figured when I got on the scale [at the Yankees facility] in Tampa, they would just send me home."

—D.J.

"He had zero muscle on his body. None. Clothes just hung off him. I called him Gilligan in Skipper's clothes."

—Shawn Powell, the strength and conditioning coach at the Yankees facility in Tampa

"And Derek was scared to death."

—Steve Caruso, Jeter's first agent, who advised his family during
the contract negotiations

"First time I met [George Steinbrenner], I was 18 years old; it was right after I was
drafted. . . . Yeah, I was intimidated. You know, he has that presence when he
walks in a room; even if you don't know who he is, you know he's somebody. . . .
Yeah, I was scared to meet him."

—D.J., to Steve Serby, *New York Post*, July 5, 2009

"WE'RE EXPECTING BIG THINGS FROM YOU."
—GEORGE STEINBRENNER, YANKEES OWNER, WHEN HE FIRST MET HIS NUMBER
ONE DRAFT PICK, DEREK JETER

— TWO —

A Professional

"When I got to the Rookie League team in the Gulf Coast League in July, I was late. I didn't sign my contract until a month after the amateur draft, so I missed the first two weeks of the season. . . . I must have looked like a prima donna when I hopped out of the air-conditioned car of Bill Livesey, the vice president of player development and scouting, with a duffel bag over my shoulder."

—D.J., about becoming a professional with the Gulf Coast League (Tampa) Yankees in the summer of 1992 soon after turning 18, *The Life You Imagine*, 2000

"I remember him striking out five times in the doubleheader in his first pro games, in which Jeter went a combined 0-for-7 [and made a throwing error that lost a game] for Tampa. We knew he would have better days. . . . In baseball, when you're in development, you have bad days. Your No. 1 picks have bad days, and he had a bad day."

—Mitch Lukevics, Yankees director of minor league operations, quoted by Daniel Carp, *USA Today*, September 4, 2014

"IN THE BEGINNING, HE STUNK."
—RICKY LEDÉE, GCL YANKEES OUTFIELDER ON THE OVERMATCHED JETER, WHOSE FIRST HIT WAS A BLOOP SINGLE TO RIGHT ON HIS 15TH AT-BAT, TO JACK CURRY, *NEW YORK TIMES*, JUNE 18, 2007

"When I went to rookie ball . . . I couldn't get a hit for anything, and they tied this big, red Wiffle ball bat to my locker—you know a big sign saying, 'Maybe You Should Try This.' That was rude, man! Now looking back, it's funny, but when you're 18 years old, you want to go into the bathroom and cry because you don't know who these guys are, and now they're making fun of you."

—D.J., HBO's *Derek Jeter 3K*, July 2011

"We knew he had unlimited potential . . . but it's hard to say that he had much production that first year with the bat."

—Bill Livesey, Yankees director of scouting, quoted by Daniel Carp, *USA Today*, September 4, 2014

"I think the Gulf Coast League is the most difficult in baseball. I was used to some guy throwing maybe 85 mph. You have guys throwing 95, and one pitch is at your head, and the next one's on the outside corner."

—D.J.

"I was miserable. I had never been away from home except to stay at my grandmother's house. . . . I didn't know anybody. There was no one to turn to. Everything was new to me. My family was so far away. I was only there for eight weeks, but it seemed like eight months."

—D.J.

"Coming from high school where you had nothing but success and then coming to the professional level where you're completely overmatched and being homesick on top of that. So yeah, those were real tears, but I didn't show people for a reason."

—D.J., to reporters, April 2014

"You don't know if, in his room, he was fighting himself. But, on the field, you never saw that."

—Ricky Ledée, Tampa outfielder and future Yankees teammate, to Jack Curry, *New York Times*, June 18, 2007

D.J. DATA: Although outfielder Ricky Ledée wasn't regarded as highly as Derek Jeter, the Yankees hoped he would be a solid major leaguer. However, the 16th-round draft pick from Puerto Rico wouldn't reach the majors until 1998, and then he was only a part-timer for the world champions in '98 and '99, although he made some huge contributions. He'd play on seven teams, finishing his major league career with the Mets in 2007. In 1992, neither Ledée nor Jeter made *Baseball America's* Rookie League top prospect list that included future major league stars Johnny Damon, Edgar Rentería, José Vidro, and Jason Kendall.

"It seemed nothing was bothering [Jeter], that he had a positive frame of mind. I wish I knew. I would've helped him."

—**Gary Denbo, GCL Yankees manager, who was among those in the Yankees organization who continued to praise Jeter to him and his father**

"He had bat speed, he was fearless, and he was a coach's dream from the outset. He worked hard every day."

—**Gary Denbo, who over the years in the organization helped Jeter with his hitting, including developing his inside-out swing that sent inside pitches to right field**

"I shouldn't have done this. I should have gone to Michigan."

—**D.J., to Mark Newman, Yankees vice-president of baseball operations, 1992**

"You're not going to be a good player. You're going to be a *great* player."

—**Mark Newman, Yankees vice-president of baseball operations, to Jeter so he wouldn't be discouraged after batting just .202 in rookie ball**

"WHEN THEY TOLD ME AT TAMPA THAT I WAS [BEING PROMOTED TO GREENSBORO], I SHOULD HAVE BEEN HAPPY TO MOVE UP. BUT I JUST WANTED TO GO HOME."

—D.J.

"I told him to come home. He would still have time to go to school."

—Dorothy Jeter, to Meredith Marakovits, YES Network, 2014

"Hey, Derek, you've articulated it; you've said it all your life. Now you've got it in the palm of your hand."

—Charles Jeter, recalling what he said to encourage his son to stick with playing pro ball, despite a .202 average, fielding troubles, and his mother saying he could come home, to Meredith Marakovits, YES Network, 2014

"It was late in the '92 season, and I got a call from the Coordinator of Instruction, Mark Newman, and he told me they were going to send up Derek Jeter to Greensboro. They wanted him to get acclimated to where he was going to be the following year. I wanted to make sure he felt welcome, as I would anybody. I knew he was young, so I got a message to the hotel and told him I would pick him up and get him to the ballpark the first day. So I picked him up, and he hadn't eaten yet, so we went to a Burger King. And I think between ordering the food at the drive-thru and getting to the ballpark, he might have said 10 words. I mean, he was really quiet, very reserved, and yet confident."

—Trey Hillman, Greensboro (N.C.) Hornets manager in 1992, to Sweeny Murti, *SportsNet New York*, September 22, 2014

D.J. DATA: Derek Jeter had only three managers in his 20 years on the New York Yankees: Buck Showalter (1995), Joe Torre (1996–2007), and Joe Girardi (2008–2014). In his four-year minor league career, he had five managers, one three times: Gary Denbo (Tampa, 1992), Trey Hillman (Greensboro, 1992), Bill Evers (Greensboro, 1993), Jake Gibbs (Tampa, 1994), Bill Evers (Albany-Colonie, 1994), Stump Merrill (Columbus, 1994), and Bill Evers (Columbus, 1995).

"The thing that probably sticks out to me more than anything else was how quickly he developed relationships on a team with a bunch of guys. . . . Those guys kind of gravitated to him. Everybody goes (mockingly), 'Oh, first-round draft pick is coming up.' But the guys, just because of his demeanor, welcomed him with open arms."

—Trey Hillman, Greensboro manager in 1992, to Sweeny Murti,
SportsNet New York, September 22, 2014

"He was a very quiet guy, respectful to all his teammates . . . and very aware of his surroundings. I played with other No. 1 picks, and his attitude was much different than some of these guys."

—Rick Lantrip, Greensboro shortstop, about Jeter's arrival at the end of the 1992
season, to Anthony McCarron, New York *Daily News*, February 15, 2014

"It was the beginning of August, and they brought him up just to see how he was going to do. And when I saw him walk in, it wasn't pretty. We were on the field; I think he got there a little late. He comes out, and he's got ankle braces on, big old high-top Nikes; his hat is kind of tilted up. Skinny, skinny—I mean he's skinny now, imagine him 20 pounds less. Super skinny, and I'm like, 'This is our first-rounder, seriously?' You know I'm, like, hating on the guy a little bit. He goes out there and makes a play in the hole, shows a big arm on another play [and] makes a spin move behind second base, and then hit a home run to left-center. So he really shut me up."

—Jorge Posada, Greensboro catcher, to Sweeny Murti,
SportsNet New York, September 22, 2014

"He gets called up . . . playing shortstop [I'm pitching], and he made a couple of errors in that game. And I'm thinking, 'What is this?' I think he did hit a home run in that game, but I kind of joke around saying my first impressions were, 'Who is this kid they put behind me, ruining my games for me?' I kind of give him a hard time about that."

—Andy Pettitte, Greensboro pitcher, to Sweeny Murti,
SportsNet New York, September 22, 2014

"At first glance, everybody was like 'Are you kidding me? What?' He was a walking stick! His wrists were so thin I used to say he was going to break his wrist on a check swing."

—R.D. Long, Greensboro infielder, to Anthony McCarron, New York *Daily News*, February 15, 2014

"He was an awkward-looking kid . . . 6-3, 159 looks ostrich-like. He looked like Ichabod Crane."

—R.D. Long, to Jim Mendalaro, (Rochester, NY) *Democrat & Chronicle*, September 25, 2014

"Let's play catch."

—R.D. Long, recalling his words to his new Greensboro teammate that made Jeter feel welcome and began their friendship, to Jim Mendalaro, (Rochester, NY) *Democrat & Chronicle*, September 25, 2014

"I realized that that bloop ball over the infield wasn't an accident. I realized that a pitcher could beat him and still lose, and that's a real rarity in baseball."

—R.D. Long, on why his skeptical Greensboro teammates were impressed that the scrawny Jeter was able to handle the inside pitch, to Anthony McCarron, New York *Daily News*, February 15, 2014

"ALL OF A SUDDEN, JETER SHOWED UP, AND HE WAS JUST A GREAT GUY. HE WAS A DELIGHTFUL GUY. HE WAS JUST ALWAYS VERY WILLING TO SIGN AUTOGRAPHS, VISIT WITH THE KIDS. WHEN YOU'D SEE HIM, HE SEEMED TO ALWAYS BE SURROUNDED BY ADORING FANS AND WELL-WISHERS, AND HE WENT OUT OF HIS WAY TO ACCOMMODATE THEM."

—BOB GODFREY, GREENSBORO SEASON TICKET HOLDER, WXII 12 NEWS, JULY 8, 2011

"We saw foot speed, we saw arm strength, we saw good hands. He was just very raw. He had not had a lot of success being consistent with his defensive work. It was a matter of him getting his body into proper position to make the plays."

—Trey Hillman, Greensboro manager in 1992, about the shaky defense that would plague Jeter in the minor leagues even after his hitting came around

"People loved to get on him for who he was, the big publicity, the fact he was a first-round kid and biracial. I know he had to put up with the nonsense of being biracial."

—Nick Delvecchio, Greensboro first baseman, on what Jeter endured when the Hornets played on the road in South Atlantic League ballparks

"I didn't know what was bothering him, because I saw nothing but determination. . . . Derek, was always doing the right things. He was always working extra. He was always doing what he should be doing. Now, how he felt? I wasn't sure. I know he wasn't having a lot of success, but because he was approaching it like he was, I wasn't concerned."

—Mitch Lukevics, Yankees director of minor league operations, quoted by Daniel Carp, *USA Today*, September 4, 2014

"I hated last year. . . . Rookie League was terrible. I was homesick. I wasn't playing good. It was just as bad as it could be."

—D.J., at the Yankees' 1993 spring training camp in Fort Lauderdale to Jack Doles, *24 Hours News 8*—Kalamazoo, 1993

"The year after high school, I'm throwing with Don Mattingly and catching ground balls with Wade Boggs. At first, I was in awe, but then you realize that he's just another person."

—D.J., about his first Yankees spring training in 1993 to Jennifer Flake, *Kalamazoo Gazette*, December 30, 1993

"First time I saw him? Gangly. Long. Looked out of place, honestly. He came to spring training first year out of high school, and he looked like he was first year out of high school. And so that was my first impression."

—Don Mattingly, Yankees first baseman, on seeing Jeter for the first time at the Yankees' spring training camp, to Sweeny Murti, *SportsNet New York*, September 22, 2014

"I was talking to [Mike] Gallego a while ago. He asked how old I was, and he said, 'Do you have a girlfriend?'—I said *yeah*—because he has a daughter [not much younger than me]. So it's a little odd being the youngest one here, but it's fun."

—D.J., about Yankees veteran second baseman Mike Gallego, who wore Number 2, at spring training in Fort Lauderdale in 1993 to Jack Doles, *24 Hours News 8*—Kalamazoo, 1993

"Gerald Williams, one of my closest friends now, made me feel at ease the first time I went to spring training with the Yankees in 1993. He took me to dinner and advised me about how to act and what not to do. But I also remember a few players who got a thrill out of harassing me. . . . Why that was important to them, I'll never know. Maybe they were jealous or insecure, or maybe they had forgotten how it felt to be lost sometimes."

—D.J., *The Life You Imagine*, 2000

"I was only there two weeks, but I got an opportunity to see these [major league players]. And that's when I said to myself, 'It's not that they're throwing 100 miles an hour faster, or hitting 400 feet longer. They're just doing things more consistently.' And then I thought, 'Well, I can do some of those things. Not as consistently, but I'm capable of doing it.' That was the defining moment that helped turn my career around."

—D.J., *Men's Health*, April 2008

"We had a sweet apartment in Greensboro in '93. We had great music, and we blasted it from noon on. R. Kelly. H-Town. Mary J. Blige. Just the two of us. And we only stopped to watch *Days of Our Lives*. . . . And he [was] the *Jeopardy!* king!"

—R.D. Long, Greensboro infielder, to Jim Mendalaro, (Rochester, NY) *Democrat & Chronicle*, September 25, 2014

"R.D. was older than me. We were together a long time, so we were pretty close. You're living in an apartment for the first time, you're 18 years old, you have laundry to do. . . . I learned a lot of things from him. He definitely helped me a lot."

—D.J.

"[Derek] had not played a whole lot of baseball day in and day out [in high school]. That's the biggest adjustment for a high school player—developing a routine and a plan every time he steps onto the field."

—**Bill Evers, Greensboro manager in 1993, quoted by Daniel Carp,**
USA Today, **September 4, 2014**

"I was actually at shortstop two weeks into the season saying—it's a true story— 'Maybe they won't hit me another ball the rest of the year.' Sure enough, they hit the next one to me, and I missed it."

—**D.J., to Ed Bradley,** *60 Minutes,* **September 25, 2005**

"Every kind of error you can think of, I made."

—**D.J.**

"He . . . was making every play a little bit differently—the same [type of] ground ball he would play two or three different ways . . . and he made 56 errors that first full year. But when I looked at him I thought, 'I could relate to that.' Because I made 56 errors my first year! So I knew somewhat what he was going through, but he corrected it quickly. I didn't! I didn't even know they counted errors. At that time, I don't know I noticed anything other than him being a pretty good athlete. He was skinny, didn't have strength yet. But I don't know that I really noticed the mentality part yet, because he was careless at the time, and I couldn't see deep concentration yet."

—**Gene Michael, Yankees general manager, to Sweeny Murti,**
SportsNet New York, **September 22, 2014**

"GOD ALMIGHTY, THIS IS THE WORST SHORTSTOP I'VE EVER SEEN. WHERE DID YOU GUYS FIND HIM?"
—TIM CULLEN, GREENSBORO HORNETS EXECUTIVE, IN A SCOUTING REPORT ABOUT JETER FOR THE YANKEES, JULY 1993

"Tell that damn scorekeeper to quit giving Jeter all those bleepin' errors!"

—**Yankees officials to Greensboro officials, 1993**

"The poor kid earned every one."

—Ogi Overman, Greensboro scorekeeper, 1993

"I'm glad I didn't [draft] him. The way our system was? When he made all those errors the first two years in the minor leagues, he'd have been gone."

—Julian Mock, Cincinnati Reds director of scouting, who believed that if the Reds had drafted Jeter fifth in the 1992 amateur draft, he would have been sent home because of his poor defense

"I probably cried at least once about each error. Cried to my parents, cried myself to sleep. . . . But no one with the Yankees knew how much I was hurting. Only my parents. I don't like to show my emotions to anyone."

—D.J., *The Life You Imagine*, 2000

"In particular, grounders hit into the hole behind second were causing Derek trouble. Having learned to field the ball with both hands, he had developed the habit of reaching across his body with his throwing arm when fielding. This left him in a bad position to make his throws to first."

—Robert Craig, *Derek Jeter: A Biography*, 1999

"He would get to balls that a lot of shortstops don't get to, and try to make plays. At that point in time, finding your release point when you're playing shortstop and understanding who the hitter is and how fast [he is]—sometimes when you're at that age, you rush things and do things at such a fast pace that you cause yourself some errors. . . . He would just rush himself and think that Rickey Henderson was running all the time."

—Bill Evers, Greensboro manager in 1993

"If he made a couple of errors in a game, you could see it in his face. He definitely internalized it and was definitely hard on himself. [But] he also had a knack for bouncing back. He was out there early and late working on his fielding. That's all he did. His maturity level was definitely way ahead of his age."

—Robert Hinds, Greensboro second baseman

"Jeet, you have to prepare yourself. They might move you."

—R.D. Long, Jeter's roommate on Greensboro, to Jim Mendalaro,
(Rochester, NY) *Democrat & Chronicle*, September 25, 2014

"I'm telling you, this kid looked at me and said, 'I will never move from shortstop.' Looks me dead in the face and says that. I was so taken aback . . . I knew I was witnessing something seriously special. For him to be that mentally tough, to get it together after that season, was so impressive. He was like the Lion King. He was still a baby, but we had the chosen one."

—R.D. Long, Jeter's roommate on Greensboro in 1993, to Anthony McCarron,
New York *Daily News*, February 15, 2014

"People started talking about him as a center fielder. That is when you have to go back to the tools. The tools and the work ethic."

—Bill Livesey, Yankees scouting director

"No one ever, ever thought that he should be a center fielder. Everyone, to a T, thought that Derek Jeter would be a major league, championship-caliber shortstop."

—Mitch Lukevics, director of Yankees minor league operations, quoted by
Daniel Carp, *USA Today*, September 4, 2014

"The only thing keeping Greensboro Hornets shortstop Derek Jeter from the big leagues is maturity and experience. . . . Unquestionably, Jeter is the most heralded prospect ever to play in a Greensboro Hornets' uniform. There have been others—guys like Don Mattingly and Mike Pagliarulo and Greg Gagne who played here and went on to illustrious big league careers—but none came to Greensboro with such acclaim. Jeter is what baseball people call a 'can't-miss prospect.'"

—Charlie Atkinson, about the prospect who got off to a hot start with
the bat with the Hornets in 1993 despite his defensive woes,
Greensboro News & Record, May 10, 1993

"Greensboro banged out 16 hits, including three home runs, to hand Augusta a 10–9 setback before a damp crowd of 1,084 at Memorial Stadium. However, the offensive outburst would have gone for naught if not for the ninth-inning heroics of Scott Romano and Derek Jeter. Trailing 9–8, Romano led off the bottom of the ninth with a solo home run. Two outs later, Jeter singled in the winning run with a line drive off Augusta closer Mark Mesewick. Jeter's hit came on an 0–2 pitch. 'For me, 0–2 is my favorite count,' said Jeter, the New York Yankees' No. 1 draft choice last June and the only teenager on the Hornets' roster. 'It makes me concentrate more because I don't like to strike out.'"

—**Charlie Atkinson,** *Greensboro News & Record,* **May 10, 1993**

"It's nice to get off to a good start, but we've got a lot of games to go. If you're talking to me in August like this, then it'll be a good season. The way I figure, you've got to excel at every level. You just can't play here and then move up. I want to do good at every level."

—**D.J., to Charlie Atkinson,** *Greensboro News & Record,* **May 10, 1993**

"The Greensboro Hornets clinched the South Atlantic League Northern Division first-half championship Saturday night with a 9–4 victory over Capital City in a game shortened to seven innings because of rain. . . . Shortstop Derek Jeter collected three hits in, raising his average to .333, fourth best in the SAL."

—**Staff report, which highlighted the Hornets' "good hit-no field" shortstop,** *Greensboro News & Record,* **June 13, 1993**

"Derek Jeter drove in two runs with a homer and a bases-loaded walk as the Greensboro Hornets snapped a three-game losing streak with a 5–3 victory over the Asheville Tourists."

—**Staff report,** *Greensboro News & Record,* **July 20, 1993**

"This team we have here, I think we can win it all. Every person on the team believes that."

—**D.J., whose Greensboro Hornets would go 85–56 to win the Northern Division but lose in the SAL finals to the Savannah Cardinals**

"YOU KNOW, I WAS PICKED HIGH, BUT THAT'S ALL OVER WITH. I'M IN THE SAME POSITION AS EVERYONE ELSE HERE. YOU'VE GOTTA DO GOOD BEFORE YOU CAN MOVE UP. . . . I'VE GOT TO IMPROVE EVERY DAY TO GET TO THE BIG LEAGUES."

—D.J., FOX8, 1993

"It's all good for me in Greensboro, and there's an added bonus, too—because I made a new friend. He's our shortstop, maybe the only guy on the club who is skinnier than me. . . . His name is Derek Jeter, of Kalamazoo, Michigan. I had met him before, in minor league camp, but this is the first time I get to play with him, and it is some show, because the kid is a year out of high school and all limbs, and you are never sure what he will do. I see him inside-out a ball to right-center field and wind up with a triple. I see him rip doubles down the line and hit in the clutch, and play shortstop like a colt in cleats, chasing down grounders and pop flies and making jump throws from the hole. Of course, I also see him throw the ball halfway to Winston-Salem, over and over, as if he's still trying to get used to being in a six-foot-three body."

—Mariano Rivera, Greensboro starting pitcher in 1993, *The Closer*, 2014

"I KNEW—I *KNEW*—HE WAS GOING TO BE A GREAT, GREAT BALLPLAYER." —MARIANO RIVERA, GREENSBORO STARTING PITCHER IN 1993, *THE CLOSER*, 2014

"All total Jeter played 139 games for Greensboro, 11 at the conclusion of the 1992 season and the remaining 128 in 1993. During the 1993 season, he batted .295 with 56 errors, second-most by a South Atlantic League shortstop. Nevertheless, he was named the league's Most Outstanding Major League Prospect and voted by *Baseball America* as its best defensive shortstop, most exciting player and best defensive arm."

—Charlie Atkinson, *Greensboro News & Record*, September 15, 2014

"He knew he would have to work hard to fight off the label of being an unpredictable and inconsistent infielder."

—Robert Craig, *Derek Jeter: A Biography*, 1999

"He had hurt his [hand] at the end of the year and wasn't able to swing a bat. That ended up being a blessing, It was basically [35 straight days] of defensive work. We'd get that videotape of the morning session, watch it, and go out for a little more. That concentrated time to focus on just defense, I think, was real beneficial for him. We started with his feet and eventually got to his glove action. He was very raw but very gifted with great arm strength, great body control. One thing Derek has always had is great aptitude. We were able to try things, and he could pick them up and grasp them right away."

—Brian Butterfield, Yankees instructor who worked with Jeter strictly on his fielding after the 1993 season, to Seth Livingstone, *USA Today*, June 9, 2011

"His feet didn't have a purpose. His glove didn't have a purpose. [But he] didn't get down on himself."

—Brian Butterfield, Yankees instructor who ran the personal "boot camp" that Jeter would remember as "five of the most important weeks of my career"

"I'd be so excited, telling my wife and my young son [about] this kid that I had an opportunity to work with. I couldn't wait to get to wake up the next morning and watch him work and hear what he had to say and watch what he did. It really was a lot of fun. It was a great experience, a much greater experience for me than him."

—Brian Butterfield, Yankees instructor, to Katie Morrison, WEEI.com Blog Network, September 28, 2014

"Through it we saw a kid that just handled failure so well. It didn't bother him; it motivated him. Not only did he come to the instructional league, he stayed afterward. He was the first one back before spring training."

—Bill Livesey, Yankees director of scouting, quoted by Daniel Carp, *USA Today*, September 4, 2014

"At season's end, Jeter returned to his Ann Arbor apartment. He was too late to enroll in fall classes at the University of Michigan, which he has attended sporadically since he signed an $800,000 deal with the Yankees in 1992. . . . For the past two months, Jeter, a freshman, has tutored youngsters near U-M and is thinking about when he'll return to the classroom, perhaps to study business. 'I don't have to declare a major until I'm a junior . . . that gives me 10 or 15 years,' he said, chuckling. 'Eventually I'll finish. In our family, education has always come first.'"

> —D.J. to Jennifer Flake, *Kalamazoo Gazette*, December 30, 1993

"I don't think I've changed at all. About the only difference is that this year I was used to everything and I did a lot better."

> —D.J., about his personality after his improved 1993 season, to Jennifer Flake, *Kalamazoo Gazette*, December 30, 1993

"I don't like to be different. I'm not really all that outgoing."

> —D.J., stating his reaction to sudden fame, to Jennifer Flake, *Kalamazoo Gazette*, December 30, 1993

"You always want to be the best at what you do. We'll have to see what happens."

> —D.J., who hoped he'd be promoted to Double-A Albany in 1994, to Jennifer Flake, *Kalamazoo Gazette*, December 30, 1993

"The second spring, huge improvement over the first spring."

> —Don Mattingly, Yankees first baseman, evaluating Jeter, to Sweeny Murti, *SportsNet New York*, September 22, 2014

"We're winning by a run, and [the other team] has a man on third with two outs in the ninth. There's a chopper hit over the mound, Jeter rushes in and catches it on the short hop and does that Jeter thing you see today. This is the first time he pulled it off, and he gets the runner. In one year, this kid went from the worst shortstop I've ever seen to lights out. Now he's obviously going to be something."

> —R.D. Long, Jeter's roommate at Greensboro, where Jeter stayed only briefly in 1994 before being promoted to Double-A Albany, to Jim Mendalaro, (Rochester, NY) *Democrat & Chronicle*, September 25, 2014

"He goes to the Florida State League, and he shows us he can hit the ball the other way better than anybody and hits [.329]. Well, he earns the right to go to AA Albany."

—**Mitch Lukevics, Yankees director of minor league operations, quoted by Daniel Carp, USA Today, September 4, 2014**

"You could see how special of a player Derek Jeter was even then, and Mariano (Rivera). . . . man, he did pretty well for himself."

—**Jake Gibbs, Class A Tampa manager who took the T-Yankees to the FSL title in 1994, 2014**

"I have been fortunate to see a lot of youngsters who made it to the majors. I remember seeing Derek Jeter, and his manager at the time, Jake Gibbs, said that the young man was going to be a superstar."

—**Dick Vitale, college basketball commentator, Dick Vitale Blog, July 14, 2014**

"THE FIRST YEAR, HE STRUGGLES WITH HIS OFFENSE, PLAYS GOOD DEFENSE. THE SECOND YEAR, HE HAS GOOD OFFENSE, STRUGGLES WITH HIS DEFENSE. THE NEXT YEAR, HE PUT IT ALL TOGETHER, AND IT WAS A SIGHT TO BE SEEN." —BILL LIVESEY, YANKEES DIRECTOR OF SCOUTING, QUOTED BY DANIEL CARP, USA TODAY, SEPTEMBER 4, 2014

"The normally deliberate Yankees had to accelerate Jeter through the minor leagues to continue to challenge him."

—*Baseball America*, 1995

"There's always a transitional phase you have to go through whenever you move from one level to a higher level. I had to make adjustments at each. The pitchers have more control. You've got to be more patient. You really have to try to learn the strike zone and not get yourself out."

—D.J.

"There was no air-conditioning in the third-floor apartment in downtown Albany that Roger Burnett shared with Derek Jeter and Matt Luke, another Yankees prospect. In the two-bedroom apartment . . . Burnett had one bedroom, Jeter had the other, and Luke had the living-room couch or floor, which might have been more comfortable. Burnett and Jeter mostly hung out watching *SportsCenter* after playing their own games. Burnett recalls Jeter moping when a girlfriend broke up with him. 'We were homebodies,' Burnett says."

> —Anthony McCarron, New York *Daily News*, February 15, 2014

"[Jeter had a] cocky edge, but it wasn't off-putting. It used to draw you in. Just cocky enough. Sure of himself. We used to talk about his knack for getting hits. It was like nobody else I ever played with. We called them 'Jeter hits'—shooting it between second and first, just past someone's outstretched arms. . . . He was hitting everything. That was the year he figured it all out. He just shot above everybody."

> —Roger Burnett, Albany-Colonie infielder, to Anthony McCarron,
> New York *Daily News*, February 15, 2014

"The potential was there, and all of a sudden that third year all of the potential began to get turned into production. He had the tools; now the skills with the tools were beginning to produce results. And you went, 'Holy cow! Wow! What can't this guy do?'"

> —Bill Livesey, Yankees director of scouting, quoted by
> Daniel Carp, *USA Today*, September 4, 2014

"Sometimes things just click, and that helps out with your confidence. . . . Once I got rolling [on offense], I had all the confidence in the world."

> —D.J., to Michael Kay, *CenterStage*, December 2003

"That apartment, 'hotter than fire,' [Roger] Burnett says, with beat-up rented furniture and sirens wailing nearby late at night, wasn't Jeter's home for long. He played only 34 games in Albany that season, a rocket ride over three minor-league levels that left him just one step from the majors."

> —Anthony McCarron, New York *Daily News*, February 15, 2014

"[Everywhere I went], I was supposedly going to get traded. . . . I was at Double A . . . and they called me at the trade deadline. . . . They told me I was going to Triple A. I [had] thought I was getting traded to the Florida Marlins for [reliever] Bryan Harvey."

—D.J., to Michael Kay, *CenterStage*, December 2003

"To move through three levels at the age that he was just shows you how focused [he was] and how his ability became evident to a lot of people higher up."

—Bill Evers, Albany-Colonie manager in 1994 and Columbus Clippers manager in 1995, quoted by Daniel Carp, *USA Today*, September 4, 2014

"We were very conservative with the movement of our players. We hadn't had anybody do that. So we knew it was something special."

—Bill Livesey, Yankees director of scouting, on Jeter's unprecedented move from Class A Greensboro to Class AA Albany-Colonie to Class AAA Columbus in one season, quoted by Daniel Carp, *USA Today*, September 4, 2014

"Here's the guy that was called up from Double A, Derek Jeter . . . 2–1. It goes off [Pat] Combs and ricochets all the way into left field. Now Jeter's going for two; he's got the speed. And he will be in there with a stand-up double. So a nice first at-bat for Derek Jeter in Triple-A baseball. He gets a double with one down here in the first inning."

—Terry Smith, announcing Jeter's first Triple-A hit in his first at-bat with the Columbus Clippers, August 1, 1994

"Didn't faze him one bit."

—Stump Merrill, Columbus manager in 1994, about Jeter's second promotion of 1994 to the Class AAA Clippers for the final 35 games of the season

"I remember going from rookie ball to A, to Double A, then to Triple A. At every level, it seemed like the game was faster. The bigger the situation, the more the game speeds up. That's all mental. It messes people up. You think, 'I've got to do this, I've got to do that,' when in reality, all you have to do is the same thing you've always been doing."

—D.J., *Men's Health*, April 2008

"We don't like to use that word [*phenom*]. He's done everything he can do to get himself better, and hopefully he'll have a big prosperous career in the big leagues."

—**Stump Merrill, manager of the 74–68, third-place Columbus Clippers, to Clay Hall, ABC 6, Columbus, 1994**

"It's not stretching it to say Derek Jeter is on fire; the 20-year-old shortstop [is] on the fast track to New York."

—**Clay Hall, ABC 6, Columbus, 1994**

"IN MY TENURE HERE, THERE'S TWO YOUNG PLAYERS THAT REALLY STOOD OUT THE FIRST TIME I SAW THEM. THE FIRST ONE WAS DON MATTINGLY. THE SECOND ONE WAS DEREK JETER."
—KEN SCHNACKE, COLUMBUS GM, 10 TV, COLUMBUS, 2014

"I hate to say it; he almost looked like a bat boy. He was only 20 years-old, and he even looked younger than that. . . . He was great with our fans. He was great with everybody. . . . He had that effervescence that made him fun to be around."

—**Joe Santry, Columbus director of media relations, 10 TV, Columbus, 2014**

"Scouts expect Jeter's power to increase as he grows into his 6-foot-3 frame. They also expect his defense to improve with time, another part of his game that Jeter improved on in 1994. After 56 errors in 1993, Jeter cut that to 25, and people in the Yankees' system see continued improvement."

—*Baseball America*, **1995**

"I think it comes easy to work hard. I was always taught, 'Don't shortchange yourself. Keep working to get better.'"

—**D.J., on his improved fielding**

"Everything."

—Stump Merrill, Columbus manager, about what impressed him about Jeter, 1994

"Everything."

—D.J., about what he thought he needed to improve in his game, 1994

"Those were really fun times to be around and see those guys [Jeter, Posada, and Rivera] come up."

—Ken Schnacke, Columbus general manager, 10 TV, Columbus, 2014

"He's unbelievable. If he's not the full package, I haven't seen one."

—Stump Merrill, Jeter's manager at Triple-A Columbus, where he played solid defense and batted .349, giving him a combined .344 for 1994, with 50 steals in 55 attempts

"1994 would be the breakout year for Derek. It was as if a completely different player had taken the place of the raw rookie league prospect. . . . Derek's meteoric rise through the ranks of the Yankees' minor league system was practically unheard of for a minor league prospect. . . . At season's end, he was named Minor League Player of the Year by the publications *Baseball America,* the *Sporting News,* and *USA Today Baseball Weekly.*"

—Robert Craig, *Derek Jeter: A Biography,* 1999

"At every level, he flashed the skills and potential that have the Yankees thinking about making him their shortstop in 1995, even though he'll only be 20 years old on Opening Day. Those skills also made him *Baseball America's* 1994 Minor League Player of the Year."

—*Baseball America,* 1995

"One of the most exciting shortstops to come into minor league baseball in years. He excelled at three different levels in 1994, and never missed a beat in shooting from Class-A to Triple-A. We are extremely confident that Derek will be another in the long line of *Baseball America* minor league players of the year who've gone on to successful careers in the major leagues."

—Jim Callis, *Baseball America*

"That skinny kid who committed all those errors last year while playing shortstop for the Greensboro Hornets is now the reigning Minor League Baseball Player of the Year."

—**Charlie Atkinson**, *Greensboro News & Record*, September 15, 1994

"EVERY YEAR, I LOOK FOR DEREK JETER TO STUMBLE A LITTLE, AND HE DOESN'T STUMBLE. HE JUST SEEMS TO DOMINATE. DOMINATED AT ROOKIE, DOMINATED AT A, MOVED UP DOUBLE A, WE'LL TRY HIM THERE, IT'S A LITTLE QUICK MOVE, WE FORCE-FED HIM, HE DOMINATED THERE. THEN WE FORCE-FED HIM TO COLUMBUS, AND HE DOMINATED THERE. HE COULD BE ONE OF THOSE SPECIAL ONES."

—GEORGE STEINBRENNER, YANKEES OWNER

THE DEREK JETER-MICHAEL JORDAN CONNECTION

"I first met Michael [Jordan] when he was playing baseball. I was in the Arizona Fall League, and he was out there. We just crossed paths briefly. And I was shocked that he knew who I was."

—**D.J., about meeting basketball superstar Michael Jordan, who was temporarily retired from the NBA's Chicago Bulls, to Brandon Steiner, Derek Jeter Day Steiner Sports event, December 6, 2014**

"That chance meeting would have been 1994, when a 21-year-old Jeter was a rising star in the Yankees organization playing shortstop for the Chandler Diamondbacks, and Jordan, already 31 and a three-time NBA Champion, was playing right field for the Scottsdale Scorpions after playing 102 games for the White Sox' Double-A affiliate in Birmingham, Alabama. That AFL season would mark the end of Jordan's baseball career and just the beginning of Jeter's, but 'His Airness' knew even then that [Jeter] was going to be something special."

—**Lou DiPietro, YESNetwork.com, September 8, 2014**

"That's the first chance I had to meet [Derek], and he was a classy guy right then. I was a student and watching him, and he was a great teacher and educator just by watching him. Obviously you could see that he was good, and I was fascinated with the way he played."

—Michael Jordan, Scottsdale Scorpions outfielder and
temporarily retired NBA superstar

"Our relationship has grown throughout the years, and he's like an older brother I never had. We've had a lot of conversations about life and about competing, both on and off the field or court."

—D.J., quoted by Lou DiPietro, YESNetwork.com, September 8, 2014

"I think one of the things a professional strives for is perfection. You work hard each and every day, and when you do it the right way and with conviction, as Derek has done, you tend to respond under pressure. In pressure situations, usually it's who puts forth effort, and very obviously he puts forth the effort in the right way because he's always responded in the right way."

—Michael Jordan, basketball Hall of Famer, September 8, 2014

"You've got to give him credit, and give credit to all the people that taught him to do the right things. I totally admire him. Being in a city like New York where one little hiccup basically could fry him, he did it in a way where no one could criticize him, and he's done his job for 20 years. Knowing the expectations of others, he's done it the right way and made the right decisions in an era where very few people take the time to say 'what if' before they make (bad) decisions, and I think that says a lot about him."

—Michael Jordan, basketball Hall of Famer, 2014

"Starting in November 1994, Jeter began a five-day-a-week, off-season regimen designed by [the Yankees' Tampa-based strength-and-conditioning coach Shawn] Powell. He. . . put on 40 pounds of muscle, increased strength dramatically across the board, and not lost quickness."

—**Joel Sherman, *New York Post*, March 31, 1999**

"I felt as though I moved [to Tampa] originally out of necessity; I needed to work out. I've always prided myself on working hard, and I always thought when I was in the minor leagues, if it came down to a decision between myself and another player, I wanted everyone to see how hard I was working. That's why I moved here. I fell in love with this area a long, long time ago. This is home for me. I don't plan on going anywhere."

—**D.J., recalling his move in 1994 to Tampa, Florida, 2014**

"Mr. Steinbrenner went out and signed [shortstop Tony] Fernández from Toronto [before the 1995 season]. Mr. Steinbrenner actually signed him to a two-year deal. George called me and said, 'I want you to call Derek and tell him we gave [Fernández] a two-year deal, but really we need one year and [then Derek's] going to be our shortstop.' I joked, and I said, 'I don't think I have to tell him that, sir.' So he says, 'Hey! Do what I tell you to do,' as only George could. I get him on the phone, and I said, 'Derek, Mr. Steinbrenner wants me to relay this to you.' 'Gee, I appreciate that very much,' he said, 'but I know it will work out.'"

—**Bill Livesey, Yankees director of scouting, quoted by Daniel Carp, *USA Today*, September 4, 2014**

"I'm sure he used [Fernández's signing] as a motivational force, without a doubt. Knowing Derek, he's always looking ahead. It drove him to the point of getting better day in and day out."

—**Bill Evers, Columbus Clippers manager in 1995, quoted by Daniel Carp, *USA Today*, September 4, 2014**

"1995 would be the last time the Yankees would gather in Fort Lauderdale for spring training. After [Andy] Pettitte retired in 2010, and [Jorge] Posada in 2011, Jeter and [Mariano] Rivera would be the last of the Fort-Lauderdale–trained players on the team."

—**Marty Appel,** *Pinstripe Empire,* **2012**

"I remember Derek in spring training of 1995. Shy, reserved, highly touted. The word was out about this guy. . . . He had a really good chance of being the Yankees shortstop. He was in a group of four or five guys, which we all found out later . . . were those Core Four or Core Five guys. But the word was that he was not only talented, but a fine young man. He came into our camp, and he . . . looked at the floor a lot, 'Yes sir, no sir.' Did all his work, came early, and stayed late. And we even made comments, 'What a pleasure it is having this guy around!' You didn't even know he was around; he was just like one of those veteran Yankees for many years. He handled himself very well even then."

—**Gene Monahan, Yankees trainer, to Sweeny Murti,** *SportsNet New York,* **September 22, 2014**

"The third spring it was, 'Wow, this guy is getting close.' And that's what you see with the guy that made the adjustments so fast."

—**Don Mattingly, Yankees first baseman, to Sweeny Murti,** *SportsNet New York,* **September 22, 2014**

"The players are striking for the future of the game."

—**D.J., stating why he wouldn't be a replacement player in exhibition games while major leaguers were on strike during the preseason in 1995**

"When he was doing well, he wanted to do better than that because he saw what was ahead of him—an established big leaguer that the Yankees had traded for. But I don't think that stopped Derek one bit. It just motivated him."

—**Bill Evers, Columbus Clippers manager in 1995, about Jeter getting off to a fast start with the team, quoted by Daniel Carp,** *USA Today,* **September 4, 2014**

"In 1995, when Tony [Fernández, the Yankees' starting shortstop] got hurt, I thought I was getting traded again. The manager called and said, 'Are you up?' It was like 6 o'clock in the morning. 'So splash some water in your face, I'm coming to your room.' I said 'I'm done; I'm out of here.'"

—D.J., to Michael Kay, *CenterStage*, December 2003

"I said, 'Derek, do you want the good news or the bad news?' He says, 'Tell me the bad news.' I said, 'The bad news is, you're not going to be wearing a Columbus Clippers uniform again.' And he looked at me like, 'Am I going back to Albany?' 'And the good part, Derek, is that you're going to the big leagues.'"

—Bill Evers, Columbus Clippers manager in 1995, quoted by Daniel Carp, *USA Today*, September 4, 2014

"I said, 'Not funny to joke like that.'"

—D.J., about being in a Norfolk, Virginia, hotel room when his manager, Bill Evers, told him he had been called up by the Yankees

"He is one of the most special players I've ever had the honor of managing in my over 2,500 minor league games. In my 20 years of managing, he's one of my favorite guys."

—Bill Evers, Jeter's manager at Greensboro, Albany, and Columbus, quoted by Daniel Carp, *USA Today*, September 4, 2014

"The Derek Jeter era of Yankees baseball is imminent as injuries and a lengthy offensive slump have forced the Yankees to consider calling up their top prospect."

—Bob Hertzel, *Bergen Record*, May 29, 1995

"Derek Jeter, not yet 21 years old, and hitting .354 at Columbus. Offense does not figure to be a problem. . . . However, there remains a question about his defense. He made five errors in the first nine games at Columbus before settling in and playing solid defense in recent games. His problems mostly are throwing errors."

—Bob Hertzel, forecasting Jeter would be brought up when the Yankees visited Seattle, *Bergen Record*, May 29, 1995

"Dad, I'm out of here."

—D.J., upon hearing in late May 1995 that he was called up by
the Yankees and asked to join them in Seattle

"You ask any minor leaguer, and they will tell you they are ready. It is the Yankees' job
to decide if I'm ready. I think I'm ready, and now I have to go out and play."

—D.J.

"They didn't give him that number by accident."

—Johnny Damon, future Yankees teammate, about how the Yankees,
looking toward the future, assigned Jeter, who wore number 70
in the 1995 New York Yankee Yearbook, the number 2, the only single-digit
number besides 6 that the team hadn't retired

"When you project a single-digit at Yankees Stadium, you'd better be right."

—Buck Showalter, Yankees manager

"I wanted 13. My dad was 13, so I always used 13 in the minor leagues. Jim Leyritz
had it, and he wasn't giving it up. . . . Everyone always says, 'Did they give [you] 2
for a certain reason?' I think honestly it was because it was the smallest jersey."

—D.J., to Michael Kay, *CenterStage*, December 2003

"Of all the promising young athletes to emerge from developmental programs,
including high school and college competition, only a handful have made it to
the big time. Jeter is the first Kalamazoo product in the majors since Mike Squires
retired in 1985. . . . It's almost a one-in-a-million shot for a young man or woman
making it to the top in professional sports."

—Jack Moss, *Kalamazoo Gazette*

"The Yankees decided their present offensive problems are significant enough for them to speed up the future. . . . [Yankees manager Buck] Showalter said Jeter will be an everyday player while he is a Yankee, but he did much to defuse any possible controversy that he would hold the position if he does well and [Tony] Fernández returns [from a ribcage strain]."

—**Joel Sherman**, *New York Post*, May 30, 1995

CLASSIC MOMENT:
MAY 28, 1995, KINGDOME, SEATTLE

"Tony Fernández had been hurt. And I saw Tony Fernández on the elevator. 'I know he's hurt, but if I trip him a little, maybe he'll be out longer.'"

—**Charles Jeter, joking about his son having his first opportunity to play shortstop for the Yankees, to Meredith Marakovits, YES Network, 2014**

"Going out there to Seattle was great. Going down and sitting in the stadium; I will never forget sitting there among [the] people. To see my son, major league player, first year, first time on a major league field . . . I will never forget that. It plays in my mind all the time."

—**Charles Jeter, about seeing his son's major league debut in the Kingdome, to Meredith Marakovits, YES Network, 2014**

"It's just as important. Somebody had to be there for her, too."

—**D.J., explaining that his mother wasn't at his first major league game because she was at Sharlee's softball game in Michigan**

"At the age of 20, Derek had become the American League's youngest active player, and the second youngest ever to debut as a Yankee. . . . His reportedly inconsistent defense was flawless that night."

—Robert Craig, *Derek Jeter: A Biography*, 1999

"I was 0-for-5."

—D.J., stating his primary memory of his major league debut, which the Yankees would lose 8–7 in 12 innings despite Seattle starter Rafael Carmona allowing seven runs and 10 hits, quoted by Erik Boland, *Newsday*, 2014

"He had a 0-for-5 debut on Monday, but handled it all with a veteran's poker face."

—Tom Friend, *New York Times*, May 31, 1995

"Veteran? I've got to get a hit first."

—D.J.

"After the game, my dad was in town, and we tried to get something to eat, and everything was closed. We ended up walking into a McDonald's. . . . I treated."

—D.J.

D.J. DATA: Jeter became the first Yankees first-round pick to play for the parent club since Thurman Munson was drafted in 1968 and played for the Yankees from 1969 until his death during the 1979 season.

"Whatever advice Charles gave to Derek [after his first game] proved helpful the next night."

—Robert Craig, *Derek Jeter: A Biography*, 1999

"Here's the kid Derek Jeter hunting for his first major league hit, and [he] sends a . . . base hit into left. Now put that ball back in the Yankees dugout. Derek Jeter after going 0-for-6 finally has his first major league hit right by [third baseman] Mike Blowers. [They're] throwing the ball over to the Yankees dugout. I'm sure that will be the first of a lot of hits for that brilliant young infielder, Derek Jeter."

—Dave Niehaus, Seattle broadcaster, about Jeter's first base hit coming in his second major league game off Seattle right-hander Sterling Hitchcock, KIRO-TV 7, May 30, 1995

"And something to add to the trophy case. That's a ball you want to keep."

—Ron Fairly, Seattle broadcaster, KIRO-TV 7, May 30, 1995

"YOU'RE VERY NERVOUS WHEN YOU COME UP. IT'S SORT OF A WEIGHT OFF YOUR SHOULDERS ONCE YOU GET THAT FIRST ONE. A LOT OF TIMES, THE FIRST OF ANYTHING IS THE MOST DIFFICULT."
—D.J., QUOTED BY ERIK BOLAND, *NEWSDAY*, 2014

"His dad was sitting right behind us at the time, so that was a thrill, too."

—Brian Butterfield, Yankees first base coach who greeted Jeter after his first hit, to Mark Herrmann, *Newsday*, March 29, 2014

"I got to first, and there was Tino [Martinez playing there for Seattle]. I had never met Tino before, and he looked at me and said, 'Congratulations, that's just the first of many.'"

—D.J., HBO's *Derek Jeter 3K*, July 2011

"The Yankees lost to the Mariners, 7–3, [but] Derek Jeter collected the first two hits of his major league career, scored the two runs that tied this game in the seventh inning, and . . . in the eighth, Jeter made a diving stab to turn a potential extra-base hit into a single. [Pitcher Mélido] Pérez thanked him."

—Tom Friend, *New York Times*, May 31, 1995

"Am I really here?"

—D.J., before his first game in Yankee Stadium, June 2, 1995

"TO PLAY IN YANKEE STADIUM FOR THE FIRST TIME—EVERYTHING JUST SEEMED SO MUCH BIGGER; IT'S LARGER THAN LIFE."
—D.J., TO MICHAEL KAY, *CENTERSTAGE*, DECEMBER 2003

"Initially, you're in awe, and rightfully so with everything that's around here, all the history. But work-related, this is your home."

—D.J.

"About 10 minutes before the game started, [Sharlee, Derek's Kalamazoo friend Josh Ewbank, and I] wanted to see Derek. We had to bribe the ushers to get down to the edge of the field. Just before the ballgame, Derek came out of the dugout to play catch with Don Mattingly! We're standing there alongside the field watching him get ready. Derek sees us, waves to us, turns to Mattingly and says 'Just a minute.' He comes over, greets us—gives his sister a big kiss—and with Mattingly waiting for him, says 'God, it's nice to have you here. Talk to you later. Now I have to play ball.' Fantastic. Fantastic young man."

—Don Zomer, Kalamazoo Central High baseball coach
at Jeter's Yankee Stadium debut

"At shortstop, Derek Jeter, number 2."

—Bob Sheppard, Yankees public address announcer

"He got a hit—that was so exciting!"

—Don Zomer, Kalamazoo Central High varsity baseball coach
at Jeter's Yankee Stadium debut

"The first thing we noticed was how his teammates gravitated toward him and liked everything about him. He has a great personality and magnetism."

—Brian Butterfield, Yankees coach in 1995, to Mark Herrmann,
Newsday, March 29, 2014

"I just remember what a positive, upbeat kid he was, always smiling, yet working very hard. He's one of the finest kids I've ever been around."

—**Brian Butterfield, Yankees coach**

"The thing that impressed me most is the way he carried himself. He has a lot of intangibles other people don't come to the big leagues with."

—**Buck Showalter, Yankees manager in 1995**

"There are some who have that 'deer in the headlights' kind of look; some of them just not sure; you can tell by their body language. One thing that struck me about Derek early on, he had a presence about him that gave you the impression he felt like he belonged here. That he wasn't intimidated, that he was ready to seize the opportunity to get his career started with the Yankees."

—**Willie Randolph, Yankees coach, to Mark Herrmann,** *Newsday*, **March 29, 2014**

"He was real sincere. He had alert eyes. He took in what was going on around him and made adjustments. He wanted to fit in. You could see his skill set was going to allow him to be pretty good."

—**Buck Showalter, Yankees manager**

"He was . . . pretty hard on himself. He'd take ground balls and batting practice, and if things didn't go just right, he'd get a little frustrated, as most guys do."

—**Buck Showalter, Yankees manager in 1995, to Mike Tulumello,**
Derek Jeter: A Yankee for the New Millennium, **2000**

"I've nothing to lead me to believe he couldn't play in the major leagues. I like what I'm seeing of the mental and emotional side. We're just letting him play. This early in his career, I want nothing but the game to challenge him."

—**Buck Showalter, Yankees manager**

"I learned a lot from listening and watching. . . . I watched how [Don Mattingly] went about his business, how he dealt with the media, [how] he dealt with his teammates."

—D.J., a future Yankees captain about watching his predecessor, to Brandon Steiner, Steiner Sports event

"You could argue that the four best players to debut [in the majors] in 1995 were all Yankees—Jeter, Rivera, Pettitte, and Posada."

—Joel Sherman, *New York Post*, September 9, 2013

"It was a dream come true. It's tough to put into words and explain how I felt. The only thing that hurt a little was I was sent down before we went to play in Detroit. A lot of my friends and family were going to come see me."

—D.J., about the first of his two major league stints in 1995

"Derek gets the same news I do. Back to the bushes. The date is June 11. The two of us have known nothing but advancement. Going in reverse is not what we have in mind."

—Mariano Rivera, Yankees pitcher, *The Closer*, 2014

"We both cried. . . . He got lit up, and they sent us both down I think for punishment on the same day. So we went back to the hotel, and we were crying and saying that we were going to be back, and we had to keep working hard."

—D.J., to Brandon Steiner, Derek Jeter Day Steiner Sports event, December 6, 2014

"In the best interest of him and the Yankees, we knew he needed to play down below and finish off some things."

—Buck Showalter, Yankees manager in 1995

"He's a talented youngster who should only get better. I think he has some things to learn, but he should do that because I think he has a good aptitude, and I think he has the proper attitude."

—Gene Michael, Yankees general manager, to Clay Hall, ABC 6, Columbus

"I hope so. I wouldn't say they penciled me in. I mean you never know what's going to happen, but hopefully I get another opportunity to go up there and maybe stay this time."

—D.J., on whether he thinks he is the Yankees shortstop of the future, to Clay Hall, ABC 6, Columbus, 1995

"Clearly Derek Jeter has few peers in the minors. Someday soon, they might say the same thing in the big leagues."

—Clay Hall, ABC 6, Columbus, 1995

D.J. DATA: Jeter's minor league honors included:

» South Atlantic League All-Star playing for Class A Greensboro 1993

» Most Outstanding Major League prospect (chosen by SAL managers) 1993

» MVP of Florida State League playing for Class A Tampa 1994

» Minor League Player of the Year playing for Class A Tampa, Class AA Albany, Class AAA Columbus 1994

» International League All-Star playing for Columbus 1995

"The second time around, I saw everything, because I *didn't* play."

—D.J., about his September recall by the Yankees after batting .317 at Columbus

"Everyone says you have to have patience. That's easier said than done, but it's out of my control. I can only control how I progress. My job is to be ready if I'm called on."

—D.J.

"I wanted Derek Jeter and a few other young kids we had, such as Andy Fox and Mariano Rivera . . . on the roster at the end of the season because I wanted them exposed to the wild-card chase. I was not expecting him to contribute on the field. . . . But I thought it was pretty obvious that Derek was going to get a chance to be a player in the major leagues, and every little thing you can expose him to is a positive. What was impressive was how he was in a soak-it-in mode as opposed to a wild mode. He was very curious and was asking a lot of questions."

—Buck Showalter, Yankees manager in 1995, to Mike Tulumello, *Derek Jeter: A Yankee for the New Millennium*, 2000

"We were on the bench, and we weren't playing. Roberto Alomar is playing [for Toronto], and he makes a hell of a . . . play in the hole and threw, and we jumped up and were like 'Ohhhhhhh!' like we were fans and everybody in the dugout looked at us like, 'What the hell are you doing?' Buck Showalter and Mike Stanley and all the other guys were looking at us, and I was like, 'Oh boy.'"

—Jorge Posada, Yankees catcher, to Sweeny Murti, NewYork.cbslocal.com, September 23, 2014

"We sat on the bench together. . . . 'Don't worry,' I told him. 'You'll own this town someday. First of all, you're good-looking. You can play. And you're not afraid. But the most important thing I want to tell you is don't make mistakes. Do the right things. Make the right decisions and live right. I wish I had to do it all over again. I wish somebody told me what I'm telling you now. You're going to be great in this town. They're gonna love you in this town. But don't allow this town to eat you up.'"

—Darryl Strawberry, Yankees outfielder, *Straw: Finding My Way*, 2009

"I love him, man. . . . Straw's like a big brother. [He told me] what to expect in New York. He came up like I did. He took me under his wing."

—D.J.

"I remember coming [into Milwaukee in] '95. It was my first time, and I really hadn't played in September, and Bernie [Williams] missed a flight from Puerto Rico. Imagine that."

—D.J., on getting a rare late-season start, quoted by Adam McCalvy, MLB.com, May 9, 2014

"[Bernie] Williams had traveled home to be with his wife and newborn baby. He was supposed to make it to Milwaukee in time for a series opener against the Brewers, with the Yankees leading the Angels by a half-game with five to play in the race for the AL Wild Card. Manager Buck Showalter shuffled his starting lineup, creating an opening for the rookie Jeter to make his 14th Major League start. His second-inning double off Milwaukee's Scott Karl gave the Yankees a lead in what would become a 5–4 victory. Jeter watched most of it from the bench. When Williams arrived, Jeter was removed from the game in the third inning. Still, it was widely considered his first big hit."

—Adam McCalvy, MLB.com, May 9, 2014

"It was [my first big hit], because we didn't clinch the Wild Card until the last day of the season that year. I wasn't supposed to play. I think I was just up so I could sort of watch and soak in the environment. It was a big hit for us at the time."

—D.J., about what he considered a defining moment in his career, quoted by Adam McCalvy, MLB.com, May 9, 2014

"Buck took out Derek when Bernie [Williams] showed up [after missing his flight from Puerto Rico], and I was thinking, 'Leave him in the game.' . . . When I saw Jeter run and watched how the ball jumped off his bat, I was like, 'Wow, this kid's got some talent.'"

—David Cone, Yankees pitcher

"We're dealing with a very valuable commodity. . . . We want to make sure we handle him correctly."

—Buck Showalter, Yankees manager

"He didn't even play, and it seemed like he was disappointed. I remember when I was leaving the bench, everybody was kind of stunned. He just stayed there. Some young kids would just get up and go, get out of the way. He was just sitting there, just kind of staring out at the field."

—Willie Randolph, Yankees coach, on how Jeter, a nonroster player, was very upset that Seattle beat the Yankees in the clinching Game 5 of the 1995 ALCS, to Mark Herrmann, *Newsday*, March 29, 2014

"I learned a lot by just watching how players like Mattingly and David Cone dealt with that loss. It made me hate losing even more."

—D.J., *The Life You Imagine*, 2000

WINNING AND LOSING

"Can't stand it. It makes me sick."

—D.J., on losing

"I think there's something wrong with me. I like to win in everything I do, regardless of what it is. You want to race down the street; I want to beat you. If we're playing checkers, I want to win. You beat me; it's going to bother me. I just enjoy competition."

—D.J.

"I'm very, very competitive. If my grandmother asks to race me down the street, I'm going to try to beat her. And I'll probably enjoy it!"

—D.J.

"If I play Mom at something, I want to beat her pretty bad. But afterwards, she's still going to be my mom. That's part of the fun of it all. But when I compete, I always want to win."

—D.J., PBSKids.org "It's My Life"

"If you're going to play at all, you're out to win. Baseball, board games, playing *Jeopardy!* I hate to lose."

—D.J.

"There's no use playing if you aren't trying to take it all."

—D.J., *Game Day*, 2001

"I THINK HOW YOU PLAY THE GAME IS IMPORTANT, BUT FOR ME IT'S ABOUT IF YOU WIN OR LOSE. IN MY MIND, IF YOU DON'T WIN, IT'S A FAILURE."
—D.J., TO BARBARA WALTERS, *10 MOST FASCINATING PEOPLE OF 2011*, DECEMBER 14, 2011

"It's simple if you look at it as: Try to win. That's the bottom line. If you win, everybody benefits. It's not like, 'I won; I lost.' It's, 'We won; we lost.' That's the only way I've thought about it."

—D.J.

"The message was you have to be a good sport. Win graciously, and you have to lose with a little class."

—D.J., about the lesson he was taught as a boy by his father after he refused to shake hands with the winning team in Little League because he was mad about losing and disappointed in his teammates

"What I saw then, in 1993 [at Greensboro], is the same thing I see [in 2003]: a man with an insatiable desire to be the best and to win."

—Mariano Rivera, Yankees reliever, *The Closer*, 2014

"Derek never had enough of winning."

—Joe Torre, Yankees manager from 1996 to 2007

"You forget about it whether it was 15–2 or 3–2. It's still a loss. It doesn't matter what the score was if we win tomorrow."

—D.J.

"It's never over. You don't want to be in the position to be down four runs in the ninth inning, but it's not over until the last out."

—D.J.

"I've never seen Derek not look like he was going to win whatever battle he was going to be involved in."

—Mike Borzello, Yankees bullpen coach

"Never take a victory home with you. Cherish the triumph for a few moments, but remember that there's another game tomorrow that you need to win to get to the postseason. Don't dwell on the losses. If you overthink a game you lost, you will drive yourself crazy. You have to learn to shrug off the errors and mistakes and learn from them."

—D.J., *Game Day*, 2001

"I don't see why people look at things negatively if they haven't happened yet. Sure, when things are over, sometimes negative things happen, but I don't see why, going into it, you would think like that, because otherwise you're already defeated."

—D.J.

"I wasn't dreaming about parades as a kid, but now I do. Every year."

—D.J.

"When you're playing tight games, anything can happen. If you get a cheap hit or run hard or make a double play or steal a base, you can change the whole direction of the game. That's why it's so important to focus on the little things because it's the little things that turn a game around."

—D.J., *Game Day*, 2001

"During the regular season, I really concentrate on getting to the moment where every at bat and play matters, where every game is on the line."

—D.J., expressing the philosophy of a winner

"Derek's not the greatest player in the league. Even in his best years. But he knows how to win. He knows how to get the hit in the big spot. He knows what it takes. He knows how to run the bases. . . . And it doesn't matter to him what the consequences of failure might be."

—Mike Mussina, Yankees pitcher

"I've never understood it [that] it feels better that *we've made it to the World Series and lost*. . . . What did you accomplish? You lost."

—D.J., to Brandon Steiner, Steiner Sports event

"[George] Steinbrenner believed that a season without a World Series title was a failure, and Jeter adopted the mantra as his own. It was consistent with his internal wiring. Jeter, like Steinbrenner, has never understood the concept of a moral victory. The object of the game is to win, and unless you win the World Series, you've failed to reach your goal."

—Tyler Kepner, introduction, *Derek Jeter: From the Pages of the New York Times*, 2011

"When you win, it's fun; when you lose, it's magnified."

—D.J., to Ed Bradley, *60 Minutes*, September 25, 2005

"If I don't win, I'm not fun to be around."

—D.J., to Brandon Steiner, Steiner Sports event

"He's a winner."

—Clayton Kershaw, Los Angeles Dodgers pitcher, 2014's NL Cy Young
and MVP winner, to Matthew Stucko, YES Network, 2014

"If you look at the past winners—you've got people like Roberto Kelly; last year
Don Sparks . . . good players. So it's a great honor."

—D.J., about being selected Clipper of the Year for 1995, to Scott Good,
10 TV, Columbus *Kids News Network*, 1995

"If that's your dream to play baseball, go out and work hard. It doesn't really have
to be baseball. It could be anything you want to be. It doesn't really have to be a
professional sport. If you want to be a doctor . . . you've got to study and stay up
late and do good in school. Whatever you want to be—don't let anyone tell you
that you can't be it. You can do whatever you want."

—D.J., giving advice to a young reporter to tell other kids who want to be
ballplayers, to Scott Good, 10 TV, Columbus *Kids News Network*, 1995

"We made a plan that winter that he was going to be our shortstop."

—Gene Michael, Yankees general manager to Sweeny Murti,
SportsNet New York, September 22, 2014

THREE

A Major League Star

"The hype that has followed Jeter throughout a marvelous minor league career will finally be transferred to the Bronx on a full-time basis."

—Jack Curry, after the Yankees organization announces, on December 12, 1995, that Jeter will be the team's starting shortstop in 1996, *New York Times*

"We may suffer some growing pains going into this thing, but our plan is to make Derek our starter."

—Joe Torre, Yankees manager beginning in 1996

"I'M GOING TO BE READY TO EARN THE JOB. IT'S AN OPPORTUNITY I'VE BEEN WAITING FOR MY WHOLE LIFE."

—D.J.

"I was impressed with Jeter before I really knew him. When I got the job, they told me he was going to be the shortstop. At that point, though, all the kid was to me was a name. So when I talked to the media, I just basically said, yeah, he's going to be the shortstop. Then I saw how he answered the same questions. Somebody would say, 'Sounds like you're the shortstop.' And Derek would say, 'I'm going to get the opportunity to be the shortstop. I'm going to get the opportunity to win the job.' And I remember thinking, 'Wait a second, this kid is answering those questions better than I did.' From the start, there was never a sense of entitlement."

—Joe Torre, Yankees manager, February 17, 2014

"EVERYONE FEARS REJECTION."

—D.J.

"In the spring of 1996, the Yankees—somewhat uneasy with the unproven Jeter manning shortstop on a team that considered itself serious postseason contenders—discussed trading for veteran shortstop Félix Fermín of the Mariners. The deal would have sent Mariano Rivera to Seattle. A trade to send one future Hall of Famer packing and another back to the minors? Imagine that seismic shift."

—Sweeny Murti, *SportsNet New York*, September 22, 2014

"[Jeter] got off to kind of a rough start, basically because he was probably nervous, a young kid. And we knew we had a good team; he comes into spring training, and we [thought], 'This is going to be our shortstop, really?'"

—Paul O'Neill, Yankees outfielder, to Sweeny Murti, *SportsNet New York*, September 22, 2014

"I had a terrible spring training."

—D.J.

"He didn't have a very good spring, but he never seemed to panic. I look at players' reactions when bad things happen to them. Having a bad spring didn't seem to change him. I did have a sense early on that there was something special about him."

—Joe Torre, Yankees manager, to Ted Berg, *USA Today*, September 26, 2014

"He's not ready to play."

—Clyde King, Yankees special advisor, recommending near the end of spring training that Jeter be given more seasoning, March 1996

"It's too late. We're already committed to him."

—Joe Torre, Yankees manager, March 1996

"[Clyde] King said something about Jeter needing to improve on his footwork. Because of that, there was this unfair question most of the spring as to whether Jeter was going to win the job. There was no question in [Joe] Torre's mind, of course, and that's all that mattered."

—Don Zimmer, Yankees bench coach, *Zim: A Baseball Life*, 2001

"You get to the point in a kid's career, and it's obvious that keeping him in the minors will no longer do him any good."

—Joe Torre, Yankees manager

"I've never hid the fact that Jeter was one of my pet projects early on and one of my real favorites. . . . Jeter is about the most coachable player you could ever want."

—Don Zimmer, Yankees bench coach, *Zim: A Baseball Life*, 2001

"He was proud to get number 2 because all the other single digits (except 6, which belongs to manager Joe Torre) were worn by Yankee legends and have been retired. Jeter can match the names of those legends to their retired numbers, a remarkable feat for a big league rookie in this day and age."

—Gerry Callahan, *Sports Illustrated*, May 6, 1996

"WE WENT FROM 'WE COULDN'T WIN WITH JETER,' TO 'WE COULDN'T WIN WITHOUT HIM.'"
—GENE MICHAEL, YANKEES VICE-PRESIDENT OF SCOUTING AND FORMER MANAGER AND GENERAL MANAGER

"As soon as I saw Jeter in spring training, I said to myself, 'I don't even know how one guy can have so much ability.' I knew right away he had a chance to be a superstar."

—Mariano Duncan, a long-time shortstop who was given the Yankees' second base job in 1996 when Tony Fernández was injured

"I picked [up things] from a lot of guys. . . . Guys like [David Cone]—you saw the way Coney dealt with the media, in terms of being responsible and available . . . Tim Raines, how he enjoyed every day. He had a smile every single day. . . . Gerald Williams, he was always so positive. . . . Tino [Martinez], he played hard and was intense. I took pieces from everyone."

— D.J., quoted by Joe Torre and Tom Verducci, *The Yankee Years*, 2009

HAVE FUN; STAY POSITIVE

"You can't go around trying to perform and be positive when you're even thinking of negative stuff. I'm positive by nature. I know that most people are negative, but I don't want to hear it."

—D.J., April 4, 2009

"[My mother's] the most optimistic person I think I've met. She's always positive; she always says you can do anything you put your mind to as long as you work hard. I think I get a lot of those traits from her."

—D.J., May 11, 2008

"[Tim] Raines showed me how to have a good time and still be serious when it mattered."

—D.J., *The Life You Imagine*, 2000

"Derek Jeter enjoys playing baseball. He's like a kid at a family picnic. To him, this isn't a job. He's never had a job in his life. He's just playing baseball."

—Dick Groch, Yankees scout

"During the off-season, I go to the movies almost every day. You hear about women buying shoes? I buy DVDs. I definitely have a problem."

— D.J., to Nicole Blades, *Women's Health*, March 5, 2008

"I like to dance and sing when there's no one around, but, if I'm out, I'm really shy about it. So it takes a lot to get me going, but I enjoy being around music."

— D.J., who fancied himself as a big fan of hip-hop and R&B

"I hosted *Saturday Night Live* [in 2001]. . . . I had a great time doing it, but I was scared to death."

— D.J., PBSKids.org's "It's My Life"

"YOU GOTTA HAVE FUN. REGARDLESS OF HOW YOU LOOK AT IT, WE'RE PLAYING A GAME. IT'S A BUSINESS. IT'S OUR JOB, BUT I DON'T THINK YOU CAN DO WELL UNLESS YOU'RE HAVING FUN."

—D.J.

"At one point, he told me, 'Don't put your head down, no matter what happens.' I appreciated it from him."

— José Reyes, New York Mets shortstop, about Jeter sharing his positive approach with his crosstown rival, 2005

"Keep your head up, keep doing what you're doing, and it'll get better."

— D.J., in a phone call to New York Giants' quarterback Eli Manning because the rookie was struggling, 2004

"The money. The celebrity status. The pressure. Not many players really enjoy the game anymore, but he does. You have to credit his parents. Derek's all business out there, but he knows when to have fun. I just hope he still enjoys it when he's making a lot of money, and some people are saying he's not worth all that money."

—Joe Torre, Yankees manager

"It still is a game for me. Obviously, there are more demands off the field, but I'm on the field, it's still as fun as it's always been. It may change when the game ends, but on the field it's always fun."

—D.J., PBSKids.org's "It's My Life"

"I've never had a problem with criticism, I understand criticism. I don't have to like it. I don't have to like answering questions about it. I try to stay positive; that's just how I deal with it. . . . [To be] able to play this long here in New York is to try to stay positive."

—D.J., 2011

"I'm optimistic by nature. Even when things are going poorly, you've got to find something positive. You have to. Because if you get caught up in being negative all the time, you'll never get out of any kind of funk."

—D.J., to Tyler Kepner, *New York Times*, May 13, 2007

"I'm not perfect. I have made errors that have caused us to lose games. I have dropped balls, struck out with men on base, been caught stealing to end a rally. The best players fail at times. But I look at all the balls I catch, not the ones I miss, and I savor the game-winning hits and try not to worry about the strikeouts. The second after we lose a game, I tell myself to forget it. I'll just get them next time."

—D.J., *Game Day*, 2001

"George Steinbrenner's advisers wanted Jeter in place. But all involved were hoping for a reliable glove and a .240 batting average.

—Ian O'Connor, New York *Daily News*, October 20, 1996

"I was saying to myself, 'I know Derek's not going to be satisfied with no .240.'"

—Charles Jeter

"Being a middle infielder, I know defense comes first. But I want to hit, too. I'm not going to be happy if I hit .240."

—D.J.

"Derek Jeter lined a double to end an 0-for-11 spring and followed it up with a beautiful bunt single. His defensive footwork was more Ali than off-key when he conceived two exquisite, charging plays on slow rollers. For the first time this exhibition season, Jeter was a work of art yesterday against the White Sox, not a shaky work in progress."

—Joel Sherman, *New York Post*, March 7, 1996

"JETER WALKING ON BOSS' TIGHTROPE"

—Article title, *New York Post*, March 7, 1996

"It is never too early to ponder how long a rope Jeter has—and whether it has a noose at the end of it."

—Joel Sherman, *New York Post*, March 7, 1996

"What [the Yankees] got instead [of a .240 hitter] was baseball's version of a natural-born killer."

—Ian O'Connor, New York *Daily News*, October 20, 1996

"Now, no one knew he was going to turn out to be the player he turned out to be—one of the best shortstops ever, a Hall of Famer."

—Willie Randolph, Yankees coach, to Sweeny Murti, *SportsNet New York*, September 22, 2014

CLASSIC MOMENT:
APRIL 2, 1996, JACOBS FIELD, CLEVELAND

"The manager and shortstop were in this together, joined at the hip as they faced their greatest baseball challenge. Jeter was batting ninth in [Joe] Torre's order, and he represented the Yankees' sixth different Opening Day shortstop in six years."

—Ian O'Connor, *The Captain*, 2011

"Oh, he got around on that one. That's gone. Holy Cow! He creamed it. His first big league home run."

—Phil Rizzuto, Yankees Hall of Famer and broadcaster made his signature call when Jeter homered on Opening Day against Cleveland's Dennis Martinez

"When he hit that home run, I went, 'Wow, this could be some kind of player.'"

—Clyde King, Yankees special advisor

"It was a lucky moment. I don't hit homers. I wouldn't expect too many more."

—D.J., exhibiting a soon-to-be-familiar humility about personal accomplishments and even telling reporters that David Cone was the individual most responsible for the team victory

"Jeter not only gave Yankees fans reason to recall Tom Tresh, the last rookie to start at short for the Yankees, in 1962, but he also became the first Yankees rookie to hit an opening-day home run since Jerry Kenney in 1969. He also made an immediate impression with the glove to help preserve David Cone's 7–1 victory over Cleveland. . . . In the second inning, Jeter ranged far to his right to make a backhanded snare of a Sandy Alomar [Jr.] grounder in the hole for the out. . . . Then in the seventh, Jeter contributed the pivotal defensive play of the game. Cone was nursing a two-run lead in the seventh when Alomar hit a two-out double. Omar Vizquel then flicked a Cone pitch in the air toward no man's land in shallow center. . . . But Yankees' panic turned to glee as Jeter ranged out to make an over-the-shoulder running one-handed catch."

—Claire Smith, *New York Times*, April 3, 1996

"It was hit kind of high, so I thought I had a pretty good chance to get it."

**—D.J., about robbing Cleveland's Gold Glove shortstop
Omar Vizquel of a run-scoring hit**

"Who would have guessed that the best defensive shortstop in the house would be Jeter, whose fielding skills have been questioned, and not [Omar] Vizquel and his magic glove?"

—Joel Sherman, *New York Post*, April 3, 1996

"Don't get me wrong, I enjoyed the home run, but playing defense comes first."

—D.J.

"I think that play he made on Opening Day—a play only Ozzie Smith makes with regularity—opened some eyes, as did the homer."

—Joe Torre, Yankees manager

"All of us thought, if he could just hold his own defensively that would be enough. And really, from the Opening Day in Cleveland, it was sort of like, 'Wow!'"

—David Cone, Yankees pitcher

"She's just as important as I am. My parents equally divide it. She's the best player, too, so they wanted to see her. Why would they want to only see me?"

**—D.J., telling reporters that only his mother was at Opening Day in Yankee
Stadium because his father was back home watching Sharlee play
her softball opener at Kalamazoo Central High**

"[Derek's] major league game is important. But, to our daughter, her game is just as important."

—Charles Jeter

"In my mind, that was almost the beginning because I was there on Opening Day."

—D.J., HBO's *Derek Jeter 3K*, July 2011

"Jeter looked even smoother with three hits and three runs scored to spark a 5–1 victory over the American League champions the next night."

—Jack Curry, *New York Times*, April 7, 1996

"In spring of 1996, the three players under the biggest microscope were Jeter, who at 21 was trying to win the shortstop job; Tino Martinez, who was being asked to replace Don Mattingly at first; and [Joe] Girardi, who was brought in to replace fan favorite Mike Stanley at catcher. . . . Jeter hit .314 and was named Rookie of the Year, Martinez hit 25 homers and led with team in RBIs with 117, and Girardi took charge of the pitching while hitting a career-high .294."

—Don Zimmer, Yankees bench coach, *Zim: A Baseball Life*, 2001

"WHEN WE CAME UP, WE WERE THINKING ABOUT KEEPING OUR JOBS. MY JOB WAS TO KEEP MY JOB. WE DIDN'T THINK 10 OR 15 YEARS INTO THE FUTURE. IF YOU RECALL, IF WE DIDN'T DO OUR JOB, OUR OWNER WOULD GET RID OF US."
—D.J., 2014

"Jeter was a star from . . . Opening Day [1996]. He changed the entire talent level of the team as a middle infielder who can do it all."

—Joel Sherman, *New York Post*

"What he saw in 1996, even with Mattingly gone, was an entire team of players that carried the same kind of ethic Jeter had learned from his parents. He saw a team build on hard work and the prioritizing of team success over individual goals. The kid fit right in."

—Tom Verducci, *The Yankee Years*, Joe Torre and Tom Verducci, 2009

I AM A NEW YORK YANKEE!

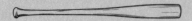

"I have the greatest job in the world. Only one person can have it. You have shortstops on other teams—I'm not knocking other teams—but there's only one shortstop on the Yankees."

—D.J.

"To put on the pinstripes, it's just a different feel."

—D.J., to Michael Kay, *CenterStage*, December 2003

"I was born in New Jersey so I was a big Yankees fan, and it's something I always told people I was going to do, but they laughed at me and said *you'll never play in New York*. It's really a dream come true for me."

—D.J., after playing briefly on the Yankees in 1995, to Scott Good, 10 TV, Columbus *Kids News Network*, 1995

"He's going to be able to play in the toughest venue in all of athletics, and that's Yankee Stadium. And this guy, he was going to capture this entire city. He was going to capture New York."

—Dick Groch, Yankees scout

"I love New York. In New York, you can do whatever you want whenever you want. That can be good, and that can be bad. But it's where I want to live."

—D.J., on becoming the rare Yankees player who chose to find an apartment in New York City rather than live in the suburbs

"I think the difference between New York and other cities is that the change can be so dramatic because the media attention here is so much more. But I love New York."

—D.J.

"You have to enjoy playing in this type of microscope. Just because you enjoy it doesn't mean you're going to go out there and be successful."

—D.J.

"I want to thank the good Lord for making me a Yankee."

—Joe DiMaggio, Yankees Hall of Famer's inspiring words on the sign that Jeter always touched as he walked from the clubhouse down the tunnel to the dugout and that later became one of his few mementos from the old Yankee Stadium

"MY HEROES, MY DREAMS, AND MY FUTURE LIE IN YANKEE STADIUM, AND THEY CAN'T TAKE THAT FROM ME."

—D.J.

"My office is at Yankee Stadium."

—D.J.

"Yankee Stadium is my favorite stadium; I'm not going to lie to you. There's a certain feel you get in Yankee Stadium."

—D.J.

"You always hear players say, 'I'd never play in New York.' I don't know why you'd say that—unless you're afraid to fail."

—D.J.

"I'm very fortunate to be doing exactly what I want to do for the team I've always wanted to play for, playing the position I've always wanted to play. You talk about living a dream or someone living a dream—if I went back 30 years ago and someone told me, 'Sit down and write out what your dream would be to do,' I'd be sitting right here."

—D.J., to Seth Mnookin, *GQ*, April 2011

"God, I hope I wear this jersey forever."

—D.J.

"When I retire, I want to be remembered as a Yankee."

—D.J.

"One of the best things about being a Yankee is that you have guys like Whitey Ford, Phil Rizzuto, Ron Guidry, and Reggie Jackson wandering around the locker room offering you advice."

—D.J.

"HE DOESN'T NEED ANY ADVICE FROM ME. HE'S JUST GOT TO KEEP DOING WHAT HE'S DOING."
—YOGI BERRA, YANKEES HALL OF FAMER

"The way he handles himself is something you don't see in rookies. He plays like he belongs in the major leagues. Every time he's in a pressure situation, he comes through. I like him so much because even after a bad game, he comes to the park with the right attitude. It's like he's been playing in the majors for five years."

—Mariano Duncan, Yankees second baseman

"He's like kid dynamite; he's got so much going for him. He's a tough kid, both physically and mentally. That will enable him to do a lot of things."

—Joe Torre, Yankees manager

"Should I swing at the first pitch?"

—D.J., asking his familiar, friendly question to kids in the stands while in the on-deck circle

"To me, it doesn't seem that I am going out of my way to be friendly; that's just the way I am."

—D.J., on why he often speaks to fans at the ballpark

"I try to sign [autographs] for as many kids as possible. Kids come first, and I'll always sign for a kid before an adult. It's funny, because I was never big into autographs as a kid. The only player who I ever wanted an autograph from was Dave Winfield."

—D.J., whose mother climbed over a barrier on her teenage son's behalf to get Winfield's signature

"We were in Chicago, it was the eighth inning, and we were down by a run. Derek was on second base with two outs. And he ran. He was caught stealing. They got him out when he shouldn't have been running at all. And I was ready to explode. . . . I turned to [bench coach Don Zimmer] and said, 'I'm not going to say anything to the kid tonight. I'll get him tomorrow.' So the inning's over, and he goes to his position without coming into the dugout. . . . So we get through the inning, and he comes off the field. Does he go hide somewhere? Does he sit down at the other end of the dugout? No. He comes right to us—just comes in, scoots between Zim and me and forces us to make room for him. He's there to take his lumps and get it out of the way. I looked at him, slapped him on the back of his head, and said, 'Get outta here.' He knew. He didn't need to be scolded. I was pretty sure before that we had something special in him. But what he did that night just reinforced it. I thought that was extraordinary."

—Joe Torre, Yankees manager, to Marty Noble, *Derek Jeter: A Yankee for the New Millennium*, 2000

"The thing that sets Derek apart is that he's not afraid to fail."

—Charlie Hayes, Yankees third baseman

"You play every day. You're going to fail more than you're going to succeed. You've got to stay tough when you do fail, or you'll be in tough shape."

—D.J., 1996

"I'M NOT AFRAID TO MAKE MISTAKES. AS LONG AS I LEARN FROM THEM."
—D.J.

"Derek always listens, and when he hears something, he processes it and then uses it. I never hesitate to go to him and tell him something I think he needs. We have an understanding. . . . There are still times he seems like he gets caught by surprise in the field. He could be more selective when he's hitting. But all that's just experience."

—**Willie Randolph, Yankees coach, quoted by Luke Cyphers, New York** *Daily News,* **September 29, 1998**

"[Jeter] coolly slapped Joe Hudson's next pitch between shortstop and third to score two runs, break a 5–5 tie in the seventh inning, and help the Yankees to a 7–5 victory [over Boston] at Yankee Stadium last night. Once Jeter rounded first base, he . . . was celebrating the first four-hit game of his career. Jeter's first three singles did not figure in the scoring, but his final single off Hudson was crucial."

—**Jack Curry,** *New York Times,* **July 3, 1996**

"He's taken on a lot of responsibility. As long as he keeps working hard, I'm not sure what his limit is."

—**Joe Torre, Yankees manager**

"I'm having fun. . . . I don't think about the pressure of the situation."

—**D.J.**

"Jeter says he can't recall ever being nervous during his first season in the majors. 'But I do have butterflies, especially while I'm waiting for the game to start,' he admits. There is a difference between being nervous and having butterflies, he explains. The pregame fluttering is a youngster's let's-play-ball excitement. Once on the field, Jeter is the coolest man in pinstripes. The over-the-hill shoulder catch, the backpedaling grab, the diving snag, the off-balance throw, the clutch hit—the rookie made them all look effortless. Jeter is never frightened of the moment in the spotlight."

—**Kelly Whiteside,** *Sports Illustrated Presents: The Champs! 1996 New York Yankees: A Special Collector's Edition,* **November 13, 1996**

"When Derek Jeter was a rookie . . . the veteran players [like David Cone, Darryl Strawberry, and Tim Raines] scrutinized him. They were waiting for Jeter to do something that was immature, something that would require them to scold Jeter. It was all part of the clubhouse culture and was a way for the older players to teach some lessons. Eventually, every young player needed to be reprimanded, even playfully, for something. So the veterans waited. They waited for Jeter to wear a garish outfit on the team plane, speak at the wrong time during a team meeting, or miss a sign during a game."

—Jack Curry, YES Network, February 12, 2014

"We were waiting for him to make a mistake, like a cop with a radar gun. He never did. Derek handled himself as well as anyone could."

—David Cone, quoted by Jack Curry, YES Network, February 12, 2014

"Every once in a while, I'd catch him messing around at shortstop before a game, doing fancy stuff. You know, throwing the ball behind his back, things like that. I'd stop that because that's just creating bad habits. But that was it. That was the extent of any kind of stuff."

—Joe Torre, Yankees manager, *The Yankee Years*, Joe Torre and Tom Verducci, 2009

"You are 21 years old and starting at shortstop for the Yankees. You are already being mentioned as a Rookie of the Year candidate, and you have been the most impressive player on the field when it has not been drenched. You are creeping toward the stardom that has been forecast since 1992. You could behave like a star, or you could continue behaving like your modest self. Derek Jeter behaves like himself, and that is refreshing. Very refreshing."

—Jack Curry, *New York Times*, April 7, 1996

"I tell Derek that the important thing is to be in front of the locker after every game, good or bad, win or lose. You've got to take the questions head on."

—Dwight Gooden, Yankees pitcher

FOR 20 YEARS: HANDLING THE MEDIA

"I don't agree with people who, when they're playing well, walk around with their chests puffed out and wait for reporters at their locker, but who hide in the training room as things go bad."

—D.J., to Michael Silver, *Sports Illustrated*, June 21, 1999

"Probably the media. You're under the microscope all of the time, so you've got to keep a level head."

—D.J., in response to a question about the toughest thing he had to handle in New York in his rookie season, ESPNEWS, November 1, 1996

"Even the city's media elite behaves around him the same way his young fans do. . . . If Jeter has insisted dealing with the media is his biggest challenge, it must be added his treatment by them has been remarkably kind."

—Patrick Giles, *Derek Jeter: Pride of the Yankees*, 1998

"FOR THE MOST PART, REPORTERS IN NEW YORK HAVE BEEN VERY FAIR TO ME. THE GOSSIP PAGES—WELL, THAT'S ANOTHER STORY."

—D.J., *THE LIFE YOU IMAGINE*, 2000

"Jeter is friendly and outgoing, and the only time he ducks a question is when he is asked to praise himself."

—Gerry Callahan, about the Yankees' rookie star, *Sports Illustrated*, May 6, 1996

"What impressed me about Jeter was his seemingly instinctive knowledge about how to handle that maelstrom and walk away clean every time. If the Yankees were in a losing streak or caught up in some controversy, he would be sure to make himself available to the media before and especially after games. Jeter would stand at his locker and patiently answer every question until they ran out. Then he would look at the reporters around him and say, 'All set?' before walking away. . . . Conversely, if the Yankees were playing well, it was often hard to find Jeter. He would let his teammates dwell in the spotlight and spend time at his locker only for brief stretches. He was adept at making sure others had their chance before he appeared."

—**Peter Abraham,** *Boston Globe*, **September 26, 2014**

"[Don Mattingly] told him, 'If you want to stay out of trouble with the media and you don't want them at your locker every day, just bore them to death.' Donnie was kind of joking, but Derek might've taken it literally."

—**David Cone, Yankees pitcher**

"From the beginning, he mastered the art of avoiding controversy in remarks to the media."

—**Marty Appel,** *Pinstripe Empire*, **2012**

"A lot of times, when you say things, people will try to turn it into [something else]. Sometimes someone asks you a question, and if you don't comment or dispute what they say, they'll take it as though you agree. I've always been very aware of what I'm saying, but I'm also aware of what you're saying. I always want to make sure that my point is clear."

—**D.J., to Seth Mnookin,** *GQ*, **April 2011**

"I understand they have a job to do. . . . I think you learn you can't generalize everybody. You learn how some people work. . . . You're not going to trick me into saying anything, saying something stupid or just agreeing with what you're saying. There are a lot of people that try to trick you that way."

—**D.J., to Tom Verducci,** *Sports Illustrated*, **November 25, 2009**

"Reporters sometimes complain that Jeter is boring, and in some ways, his answers are; he does not ruminate or speak anecdotally. But if you ask a direct question, he usually gives a direct answer. And because Jeter is so reliably available, reporters know they can always get the voice of the Yankees' captain into their stories—no small thing, especially on deadline. . . . There is also this: Jeter will never allow himself to be burned by a reporter. In my eight years as the Yankees' beat writer for the *Times*, he never once asked to talk off the record. He puts his name behind everything he says."

—Tyler Kepner, introduction, *Derek Jeter: From the Pages of the New York Times*, 2011

"Derek Jeter is the star we knew so well—and not at all. He hid in plain sight. He talked often and said little. He was private even while being public. This has made Jeter both frustrating and admirable for a journalist. He never let you in: frustrating. He never let you in: admirable. . . . I have interviewed Jeter on hundreds, probably thousands, of occasions over the past two decades. . . . I wanted to know more about him and never felt I truly got in. He was warmly cold—receptive to the questions, guarded in his answers. In the end, I knew what everyone knew. He loved two items above all else: his family and being the Yankees' shortstop. Everything else you merely glimpsed or saw through others. It allowed him to maintain a pristine image, shun scandal, rise above an age when so much is spilled into the public trough for dissection and ridicule. Fans loved him for what they thought they knew."

—Joel Sherman, *New York Post*, February 12, 2014

"IF YOU KNOCK ON HIS DOOR, HE'LL TALK TO YOU FOR FOUR OR FIVE HOURS THROUGH THE SCREEN, BUT YOU'LL NEVER GET INVITED IN."
—MICHAEL KAY, YANKEES BROADCASTER

"Whatever his reservations, Jeter has never seemed comfortable sharing his thoughts publicly, and as a result tries to be as bland as possible. He offers no insights on the events of individual ballgames, or his own at-bats, never mind substantial thoughts on the various issues that forever surround the Yankees. What annoys reporters is that he has plenty more to offer, because they have seen him be funny and personable enough to host *Saturday Night Live*. . . . And reporters see what a presence Jeter is around the ballclub, laughing with teammates, forever needling someone about something. . . . But with the press, he's duller than Bud Selig. . . . Many resent him because he keeps them at arm's length, refusing to reveal anything of himself."

—**John Harper,** *A Tale of Two Cities*, **Tony Massarotti and John Harper, 2005**

"Derek Jeter was a winner, one of the great clutch performers in baseball history, and he played the game with genuine, indisputable enthusiasm that was always apparent. . . . He did whatever it took to win a game—from putting down a sacrifice bunt to hitting a home run—and he did it all because that was *the right thing to do*. But naturally, the New York media wanted more. They wanted him to be quotable and entertaining off the field, too. At least that's how we Bostonians saw it."

—**Tony Massarotti,** *A Tale of Two Cities*, **Tony Massarotti and John Harper, 2005**

"I'm not controversial. Especially here in New York, they want you to say something controversial, and my job has been to limit distractions for my team—that's my job, not to cause them."

—**D.J.**

"It was like there was a glass case around him. He was like in a museum, and there's a glass case and someone is saying 'Keep your distance.'"

—**Gay Talese, prize-winning author and sports writer about interviewing Jeter, 2012**

"Well, one, they ask me the same questions over and over, so I'm going to give you the same answers. But, two, *I don't like to talk about negative things*. Because in my mind I have to get rid of it, and I don't want to sit and dwell on it and talk about it. Because then you start thinking about it, and then it poisons your mind. That's how I deal with it. If there's another way to deal with it—in New York—someone needs to tell me."

—D.J.

"Derek Jeter prided himself, for 20 years, on saying as little as possible."

—Mike Lupica, New York *Daily News*, October 2, 2014

"When Jeter talks about a controversial subject, his words are as carefully crafted and intently dissected as though he were the Fed chairman talking about the economy."

—T.J. Quinn, New York *Daily News*, September 3, 2006

"JETER HAS DODGED MORE QUESTIONS THAN INSIDE FASTBALLS. DOESN'T MATTER HOW PERFECTLY CRAFTED IT IS, THE 38-YEAR-OLD NEW YORK YANKEES SHORTSTOP WILL FIND THE EXIT RAMP OUT OF ANY QUESTION."
—RICK REILLY, ESPN.COM, SEPTEMBER 20, 2012

"His earnest approach [when speaking to reporters], unaffected by his rise to superstar status, made him the most admirable of ballplayers. His brief, simplistic answers, on the other hand, made him a maddening subject. He had . . . mastered the art of answering questions without revealing anything about himself."

— Tony Massarotti and John Harper, *A Tale of Two Cities*, 2005

"Jeter has kept reporters at such arm's length that . . . not even the beat writers feel like they know him. He almost never acknowledges reporters by name, yet Jeter knows more than he likes to admit, and apparently reads them all."

—Tony Massarotti and John Harper, *A Tale of Two Cities*, 2005

"I always take criticism [from the media] as a challenge. It's the way I've always looked at it. When somebody criticizes you, you have to realize it's their opinion. That doesn't mean it's true. They're entitled to their opinion. You may not like it. I may not like a lot of people's opinions, but they're entitled to their opinions. So I take it as a challenge."

—D.J., to Tom Verducci, *Sports Illustrated*, November 25, 2009

"There's so much negativity [in the media]. I don't want to hear about it, I don't want to read about it, and I don't want to talk about it."

—D.J., 2014

"Despite years of politely fending off reporters' questions or offering responses that veered toward the bland, Derek Jeter is joining the news media. On Wednesday, just three days after playing his final baseball game, Jeter announced that he would publish the *Players' Tribune*, a website that gives athletes a forum to express their thoughts and feelings. According to a news release, athletes will be able to share first-person accounts, videos, podcasts, photographs, and polls on the site. Jeter said he would be closely involved. Jeter, who was careful in his conversations with reporters and repeatedly used the phrase 'I don't know' when asked this year about his impending Yankees retirement, said in a letter posted on the website Wednesday, 'I do think fans deserve more than "no comments" or "I don't knows."'"

—David Waldstein, *New York Times*, October 1, 2014

"I realize I've been guarded. I learned early on in New York, the toughest media environment in sports, that just because a reporter asks you a question doesn't mean you have to answer. I attribute much of my success in New York to my ability to understand and avoid unnecessary distractions. I do think fans deserve more than 'no comments' or 'I don't knows.' Those simple answers have always stemmed from a genuine concern that any statement, any opinion, or detail, might be distorted. I have a unique perspective. Many of you saw me after that final home game, when the enormity of the moment hit me. I'm not a robot. Neither are the other athletes who at times might seem unapproachable. We all have emotions. We just need to be sure our thoughts will come across the way we intend."

—D.J., in a letter about the reasons he was creating the *Players' Tribune* website, September 30, 2014

"[Paul] Sorrento took that big cut, but popped the ball up, and there was Jeter, the take-charge rookie, calling off everyone and squeezing it in his glove."

—Cecilia Tan, about Jeter recording the final out in Dwight Gooden's no-hitter against the White Sox on May 28, 1996, *The 50 Greatest Yankee Games*, 2005

"In the seventh inning, I told myself, 'If he still has a no-hitter, I want to catch the final out.' You're forever linked with it; you're on all the highlights. It seemed like the ball didn't want to come down. I had to backpedal, and afterwards, the guys were telling me they thought I was going to miss it. But if you saw Doc, you saw him throw his hands up. He knew I was going to get it."

—D.J.

"NO POSITION PLAYER HAS MADE SUCH A VITAL CONTRIBUTION IN HIS FIRST YEAR IN THE BRONX SINCE JOE DIMAGGIO."
—KEITH OLBERMANN, *FOX SPORTS*, 1996

"Only a few guys come along who have that tiger in them. Derek's got a real tiger down inside of him that he holds onto. When you look at the kid, take a real good look, and say he's going to be real good for a long, long time."

—Darryl Strawberry, Yankees outfielder

"One time in 1996, he was getting ready to go up to the plate, and as he walked past me in the dugout, he stopped, took my hat off, and rubbed the top of my head. Then he went up and got a base hit. From that day on, he's been rubbing my head before every at bat. Sometimes he'll rub my stomach, too."

—Don Zimmer, Yankees bench coach, *Zim: A Baseball Life*, 2001

"SHORTSLOP"

—Back page headline after Jeter's error led to the White Sox scoring five runs in the 10th inning to beat the Yankees, *New York Post*, August 8, 1996

"Straining his rib cage muscle Aug. 31 against the Red Sox [caused him to miss] five games. But his return Sept. 7 at Fenway Park was widely seen as a catalyst for the Yankees, whose lead over Boston had shrunk to 1½ games. Afterward, manager Joe Torre said, '[Jeter] gave us a lift that day. The tension seemed to go out of the dugout and we picked up momentum.' The 3–1 victory that day was the first of eight straight Yankee wins, essentially ending the AL East race."

—**Peter May,** *Boston Globe,* **October 8, 2003**

"[In September] Jeter had a 17-game hitting streak, the best by a Yankee rookie since that DiMaggio fellow had an 18-gamer in 1936—a World Championship year for the Bronx Bombers."

—**Don Bostrom,** *Morning Call,* **October 20, 1996**

"When the games mean more, it's a lot easier to play."

—**D.J., after his third hit and third RBI won a crucial game over Boston 12–11 in 10 innings**

"I watched him blossom into a major league shortstop. He has exceptional talent. He has real tools. He does a lot of things real well. He's a quiet kid, but he'll be a veteran one day and step into the spotlight."

—**Wade Boggs, Yankees third baseman**

"His best asset is his head."

—**Jimmy Key, Yankees pitcher**

"Near the end of his rookie year in 1996, the Yankees were in Detroit and Jeter's dad drove in from Kalamazoo. Over pizza in a hotel room, Derek proposed starting a foundation, much like his idol, Dave Winfield, had. 'It was his idea,' says Charles Jeter, a substance abuse counselor. 'He asked me to be involved. I said, "Yes, if you're serious."'"

—**Mike Dodd, about the creation of the family-run Turn 2 Foundation in which Jeter would be chairman, Charles the vice-chairman, Sharlee the president, and Dorothy the treasurer,** *USA Today,* **April 13, 2010**

THE TURN 2 FOUNDATION: GIVING BACK

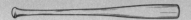

"If you have a little, you give a little back. If you have a lot, you give a lot back."

—Dorothy Jeter, to her son when he was growing up

"I started the Turn 2 Foundation for kids who are at risk of substance abuse because Dave [Winfield] had started his own non-profit years ago. I was really inspired by what he did."

—D.J., *Game Day*, 2001

"I always wanted to start a foundation once I made it to the major leagues. Even though I hadn't finished one season in the majors, it turned out to be the perfect time to begin a dialogue with my dad. . . . I was making $130,000, not the $10 million I'll earn in 2000, but my baseball dreams were unfolding as I hoped they would, and I wanted to share what I had with other people, especially kids."

—D.J., *The Life You Imagine*, 2000

"It's one thing to say something when you're young. It's another thing to follow through with it. I was happy and proud he hadn't forgotten."

—Charles Jeter, about his son telling him as a kid that if he ever made it to the majors he would start a foundation

"The foundation was created with the goal of motivating young people to 'turn to' healthy lifestyles and 'turn away' from drugs and alcohol. Turn 2 has since awarded more than $16 million in grants to youth programs in West Michigan, New York City, and the Tampa–St. Petersburg area."

—Derek Jeter biography, Turn 2, The Official Site of Derek Jeter and the Turn 2 Foundation, 2015

"I don't care if I'm playing and living somewhere else. Michigan is where I grew up, and it's where I had my first foundation event. It's where I'll continue to keep the foundation going."

—D.J., 2010

"[Turn 2] maintains a satellite office on the Western Michigan University campus and has awarded more than $3.5 million in grants in the area since its 1996 inception. . . . It remains a family affair—Sharlee, 30, recently took over as president as her parents slide into a reduced role."

—Mike Dodd, *USA Today*, April 13, 2010

"I WANTED TO ESTABLISH PROGRAMS THAT WOULD HAVE A LASTING IMPACT, AND WE'RE DOING THAT."

—D.J.

"It's a problem that faces everyone, regardless of race or where you were brought up. . . . It affects everybody. You don't have to be from a bad home or a bad neighborhood."

—D.J., explaining his decision to initiate a rehab program
as part of the foundation, 1997

"If you have dreams and aspirations to be successful, drugs and alcohol are only going to alter those dreams. Try to stay away from them and find something more productive to do with your time. The same people who are doing drugs and drinking as teens are, a lot of the time, the ones who end up doing nothing with their lives. So if you want to be a productive person, stay away from them. Try something more fun, like baseball!"

—D.J., PBSKids.org "It's My Life"

"Kids are learning to eat better, to draw more out of exercise, to play sports, and taught to behave and to socialize more easily. Significant inroads are being made with needy children . . . inroads impossible without the diligence and generosity of [Derek] Jeter, his family, and their foundations."

—Paul Attner, about Jeter being selected the *Sporting News*'s 2002 No. 1 Good Guy in Sports, *Sporting News*, July 22, 2002

"A LOT OF PEOPLE GIVE BACK. I JUST WANT TO BE MORE INVOLVED ON A PERSONAL LEVEL. I THINK IT'S FUN WHEN YOU GET AN OPPORTUNITY TO MEET KIDS AND MAKE A DIFFERENCE THE WAY THE FOUNDATION DOES. IT MAKES YOU FEEL GOOD."
—D.J., 2005

"The Turn 2 Foundation . . . does a lot for young people in Kalamazoo and New York. He's always there to lend a helping hand for a good cause. There are always a lot of people who will lend a helping hand, but Jeter looks for the opportunity."

—Jack Moss, former sports editor of the *Kalamazoo Gazette*, to David Drew, MLive Media Group, February 12, 2014

"[Derek] sneaks into town, does some good things, then quietly leaves."

—Greg Ayers, president of Discover Kalamazoo conventions and visitors bureau, 2010

"There is a mutual respect between Derek and the kids, and they are learning a lot from each other."

—Dennis Walcott, New York Urban League president and future Chancellor of New York City Schools

"It's fun for me to see the smiles on their faces and to see them enjoy themselves. I think everyone is a kid at heart, especially when it comes to holiday seasons. I always enjoy getting the opportunity to come back here talking to the kids, meeting the kids' families, and see kids who have gone through our program come back and help out."

—D.J., about surprising 200 Kalamazoo kids by appearing at his foundation's annual Turn 2 Holiday Express in December 2013

"Jeter's Leaders is a leadership development program created to empower, recognize, and enhance the skills of high school students who: promote healthy lifestyles, free of alcohol and substance abuse, achieve academically, are committed to improving their community through social change activities, serve as role models to younger students, and to deliver positive messages to their peers."

—**Jeter's Leaders Mission, Turn 2, The Official Site of Derek Jeter and the Turn 2 Foundation, 2015**

"For me, when I was a kid, volunteering was the last thing I was thinking about. When I see kids doing it now, it amazes me. It's very impressive; it gives them something productive to do as opposed to getting in trouble. For them to take time out at such a young age is remarkable. I think all kids should take a little time out to volunteer."

—**D.J.**

"There's leadership programs, after-school programs, scholarship programs—all kinds of programs. It's interesting to see them lead, because it is usually a time when kids are selfish and thinking about what they need to do. I was that way. Most kids that age are."

—**D.J., 2010**

"I like hearing the responses from families, hearing about how these kids grow up, graduate, go on to college. That's probably the most satisfying part. A lot of them will come back and help the foundation, so it's good to see them grow up."

—**D.J., to Tom Verducci, *Sports Illustrated*, November 25, 2009**

"The ultimate goal was just to help out a few people. . . . Year after year, we're getting a lot of support. It keeps getting bigger and better."

—**D.J.**

"I don't think I've ever seen a young kid play with such confidence. Mickey Mantle had the ability as a rookie, but not the poise. Jeter has them both."

—Phil Rizzuto, Yankees Hall of Fame shortstop and broadcaster about why he thought Jeter could become the greatest Yankees shortstop ever

"I LIKE WHAT I SEE OF THIS KID, JETER. HE REMINDS ME OF PHIL RIZZUTO. AND I THINK HE'S JUST AS VALUABLE TO THIS YANKEES TEAM AS RIZZUTO WAS TO US, I REALLY DO."

—JOE DIMAGGIO, YANKEES HALL OF FAMER, 1997

"He hit . . . 350 after the All-Star break. When the lights got hotter, Jeter got better. The pressure of New York, of a pennant race, wasn't a deterrent, but a source of positive juice."

—Ian O'Connor, New York *Daily News*, October 20, 1996

D.J. DATA: As a rookie, Derek Jeter hit .314 in 1996 and became the first Yankee shortstop to bat over .300 since Gil McDougald in 1956. His 78 RBIs were the most by a Yankees shortstop since Frankie Crosetti drove in 78 runs in 1936.

"You don't hit .300 with 600 at-bats unless you've adjusted to all the adjustments other people have made on you."

—Joe Torre, Yankees manager

"People have always doubted me. First, it was I couldn't play shortstop. Then, I was from a small town. In the minor leagues, people said I couldn't hit, I couldn't field, then I couldn't hit at a major league level. There's probably still some who doubt me."

—D.J.

AN UNWAVERING CONFIDENCE

"I am confident in my abilities."

—D.J.

"Jeter's success stems from confidence."

—Jack Curry, YESNetwork.com, April 13, 2012

"Either if Jeter is going good or bad, he sets the tone in the Yankees' clubhouse. His fearless confidence is combined with an ability to shake off yesterday in favor of today. It is a business-like approach that works when there are 162 regular work days."

—Andrew Marchand, ESPNNewYork.com, April 10, 2012

"I really don't like people who talk about themselves a lot. It's all right to have confidence, but without the cockiness. I don't talk too much about myself."

—D.J.

"I'm most comfortable on the field. It's something I've done my whole life."

—D.J.

"When he gets on the field, he's extremely confident. It's not something he's going to talk about, but I know it's there."

—Charles Jeter

"It all seemed to come so naturally to Jeter. He was blessed with a confidence that you can't fake, a confidence . . . that explained why no game or moment was ever too big for Jeter, as we saw throughout his career."

—John Harper, New York *Daily News*, February 12, 2014

"It can be very difficult at times [to remain confident]. But I always tend to look at past performances where I was successful. I try to think about those. If you're 0-for-20, 0-for-30, in my mind the chances of you getting a hit really increases. So if I'm 0-for-20, I think I'm a better hitter when I go to the plate. I guess you try to trick yourself. . . . I never try to get too high or too low and just play every game and treat every game like it's the same."

—D.J., Derek Jeter Day Steiner Sports event, December 6, 2014

"DEREK JUST BELIEVES HE'S THE BEST PLAYER ON THE FIELD, AND IT DOESN'T MATTER THAT A LOT OF THE TIME, HE'S NOT THE MOST TALENTED. HE KNOWS HE'S GOING TO BEAT YOU ANYWAY."
—JOHN FLAHERTY, YANKEES CATCHER AND BROADCASTER

"He's absolutely sure of himself all the time, but not in a way that can be counterproductive. He's not arrogant; he's confident. He's sure he's going to do well."

—Joe Torre, Yankees manager

"Derek has more inner arrogance than anybody I've ever met."

—Charles Jeter

"That attitude and that arrogance come from the inside. I think you have to have it to make it this far. You have to feel like you're the best player on the field, the player that thousands of people will stare at all game."

—D.J., *The Life You Imagine*, 2000

"Yeah, I'm confident. I don't like cocky people. Confidence is how you feel. Cockiness is how you act. I'm always confident. There are times when you struggle, like I could be 0 for 100, but if a big game is on the line, I expect to do well."

—D.J., to Diane K. Shah, *Playboy*, June 2004

"He always believed he'd get a hit the next time up."

—**Paul O'Neill, Yankees outfielder**

"Most of the Yankees—most players—would fight to maintain their wavering morale at one time or another, but Jeter's confidence was resolute and steady, like a flag waving over the team in the worst of times."

—**Buster Olney, *The Last Night of the Yankee Dynasty*, 2004**

"Jeter knows that he won't come close to getting a hit in every at bat. But Jeter plays the game as if he can. Until Jeter makes an out, he believes he is going to get a hit. And, if he makes an out, he thinks he's going to collect a hit in the next at bat. Paul O'Neill has said that Jeter was as confident as any teammate he ever had. Of all the players I have ever covered, Jeter is as indomitable as any of them. Jeter believes he is going to succeed. There's no fear, no doubt, and no anxiety permeating Jeter's world. Long ago, Jeter told me that he refuses to be afraid to fail because, if he was, that would prevent him from succeeding. Prepare, prepare, prepare, and then have fun playing the game. That's Jeter's simple approach."

—**Jack Curry, YESNetwork.com, April 13, 2012**

"As the Yankees clinched the American league East last night, the kid at shortstop has been the difference in their season. . . . When the games mean more, some young players find it harder to play. But this rookie hasn't. . . . Jeter doesn't scare."

—**Dave Anderson, following the Yankees' 19–2 win over Milwaukee in which Jeter's two-run double contributed to a 10-run second inning, *New York Times*, September 26, 1996**

D.J. DATA: On September 28, 1996, at Fenway Park, Derek Jeter, Jorge Posada, Andy Pettitte, and Mariano Rivera—who would eventually be called the Core Four because of their many years as Yankees teammates—played in the same game for the first time. Jeter started at shortstop and went 0-for-4, Posada struck out pinch hitting for Paul O'Neill, Pettitte started and pitched two innings, and Rivera pitched an inning of relief in the Yankees' 4–2 victory over the Red Sox, beating Roger Clemens. They all first played in the majors in 1995. Pettitte came up in April 1995, Rivera followed 24 days later, Jeter came 6 days after that, and Posada debuted in September 1995.

"I returned to Yankee Stadium for the first game of three against the second-place Baltimore Orioles that would more or less settle the pennant race. . . . Most of all, I reveled in Derek Jeter, who seems a character out of a storybook. A hero of the 90s. A shortstop, just 21, handsome, unflappable, graceful. And this year, he's emerged as a star, almost supernaturally composed in the pennant race frying pan. . . . I can recognize his walk from behind, the way I used to be able to do with Maris, Mantle, Munson, and Mattingly."

—Bruce Weber, *New York Times*, September 29, 1996

"After the first playoff game against Texas, after [Jeter] had left six runners on [in a 6–2 loss], all the writers were asking me, 'Are you going to talk to him?' I didn't see any reason to. He just hadn't gotten a big hit. So what? He didn't seem to act any differently."

—Joe Torre, Yankees manager, *Chasing the Dream*, 1997

"Everyone in the media said I was a rookie who couldn't handle the playoffs. Sometimes you get hits, and sometimes you don't. If I go 0-for-the-World Series, I'm still going to tell you I wanted to be out there."

—D.J.

"Derek Jeter, who started or finished as many big rallies for us as anyone, opened the 12th inning [of the 4–4 game with Texas] with a single. Tim Raines walked. Then I asked Charlie Hayes to bunt. He made the right play by bunting it to [Dean] Palmer. The third baseman fielded the ball cleanly but threw it wildly to first base. The ball may have been slippery because of the light rain that was falling. Jeter came running home with the winning run."

—Joe Torre, Yankees manager, on Jeter's third hit of the game and the rally that prevented the Rangers from going up 2–0 in the 1996 ALDS and lead to a New York victory in 5 games, *Chasing the Dream*, 1997

"So was born his reputation as a clutch postseason player."

—Tom Verducci, *The Yankee Years*, Joe Torre and Tom Verducci, 2009

CLASSIC MOMENT:
OCTOBER 9, 1996, YANKEE STADIUM, NEW YORK

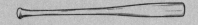

"For the fourth straight game, we rallied to victory after trailing as late as the seventh inning. Mr. Rally himself, Jeter, tied the game with one out in the eighth inning with one of the most unforgettable and controversial home runs of all time."

—Joe Torre, Yankees manager, about the most famous play in the Yankees' 11-inning Game 1 victory over Baltimore in the ALCS, *Chasing the Dream*, 1997

"It's a judgment call. Sometimes you're gonna get it right; sometimes you're gonna call it wrong. I don't think that won the game for us."

—D.J., on his fly ball that was ruled a home run by umpire Rich Garcia in the eighth inning of an eventual Yankees' victory in Game 1 of the ALCS, although a 12-year-old, hooky-playing Yankees fan, Jeffrey Maier, interfered with the ball by sticking his glove over the right-field fence before outfielder Tony Tarasco could leap for it

"Attaboy."

—D.J., what he tells reporters he would say to Jeffrey Maier

"Do I feel bad? We won the game. Why should I feel bad?"

—D.J.

"I don't blame the kid for reaching out to catch Jeter's fly ball. I would have done the same thing at that age. What bothered me was that the media turned him into a hero."

—Joe Torre, Yankees manager, *Chasing the Dream*, 1997

"Even to this day, almost 20 years after the fact, this glove still continues to elicit smiles from Yankees fans and curses from Orioles fans. It's an innocuous enough little black leather Mizuno glove, but it still inspires big emotions and commanded a big-time auction price."

—Chris Ivy, director of sports auctions at Heritage after the glove Jeffrey Maier wore to interfere with Jeter's long fly in 1996 was sold at auction by its second owner for $22,705, February 22, 2015

"The Orioles, however, got even. They won the second game 5–3 behind lefthander David Wells, and when the series moved to Camden Yards for Game 3, [Baltimore's] Mike Mussina . . . had a four-hitter and a 2–1 lead with two outs, and nobody on base in the eighth inning. Just seven pitches later, the Yankees were ahead 5–2. . . . The Yankees' rally began with a double by Jeter, the . . . troublemaking kid, who hit .417 in the series."

—Tom Verducci, *Sports Illustrated Presents: The Champs! 1996 New York Yankees: A Special Collector's Edition*, November 13, 1996

"I haven't played a full year yet, so putting me there with Cal Ripken is ridiculous. It's like he's the teacher, and everyone else is the student."

—D.J., on being compared to Baltimore's future Hall of Famer
during the regular season and ALCS

"Thanks for paving the way."

—D.J., respectfully to the Orioles' Cal Ripken Jr., the first of the tall,
slugging shortstops in the American League

"At 7:20 p.m. on October 13, 1996, Cal Ripken, who was born one month and one day before my debut in the major leagues, hit a ground ball to Jeter. Derek threw the baseball in the dirt to first base to Tino Martinez, who made a great play to catch it for the final out of a 6–4 victory. Thirty-six years and 4,272 games since I put on a major league uniform for the first time, my dream had come true. Joseph Paul Torre finally was going to the World Series."

—Joe Torre, Yankees manager, *Chasing a Dream,* 1997

"JETER THREW OUT RIPKEN ON A GROUNDER TO END GAME 5 AND SECURE THE YANKEES' FIRST LEAGUE TITLE IN 15 YEARS—THEIR LONGEST DROUGHT SINCE WINNING THE FIRST OF THEIR 34 PENNANTS IN 1921."
—TOM VERDUCCI, *SPORTS ILLUSTRATED PRESENTS: THE CHAMPS! 1996 NEW YORK YANKEES: A SPECIAL COLLECTOR'S EDITION,* NOVEMBER 13, 1996

"You always want to lean on experienced players in the postseason. But Derek doesn't see the postseason as something different."

—Joe Torre, Yankees manager, after Jeter helped lead the Yankees over Texas
in the ALDS and Baltimore in the 1996 ALCS

"I'm not sure people understand how good the two of them can be."

—Joe Girardi, Yankees catcher on Jeter and center fielder Bernie Williams,
the two stars of the ALCS victory over Baltimore, October 18, 1996

"When he runs out to his position for Game 1, when he stops at short while Bernie Williams keeps going to the outfield, it will be the first time Derek Jeter has ever attended a Series game in person."

—Mike Lupica, New York Daily News, October 20, 1996

"This is what you've always thought about. From the time you start playing ball, you think about the World Series. And if you've ever been inside Yankee Stadium, you think about playing here."

—D.J.

"You don't just accidentally show up in the World Series."

—D.J.

"I'm going to savor every minute of this World Series. Who knows? I might never get back here. I've talked with guys like Cecil Fielder and Tim Raines, and they thought they might never make it."

—D.J., to Don Bostrom, Morning Call, October 20, 1996

"This cat will literally be on the couch, we'll be talking, and he'll just fall asleep. He's facing [Atlanta's star pitcher Greg Maddux in Game 2 of the World Series] tomorrow, and he just falls asleep."

—R.D. Long, Jeter's minor league teammate and friend,
on Jeter remaining calm even in the postseason

"IT JUST BLEW ME AWAY HOW RELAXED DEREK WAS."
—JOE GIRARDI, YANKEES CATCHER

"HE WAS A ROOKIE, AND SIX MONTHS LATER, HE WAS MAKING PLAYS IN THE WORLD SERIES, AND IN BETWEEN, IT SEEMED HE PLAYED A PART IN EVERY BIG RALLY WE HAD."
—JOE TORRE, YANKEES MANAGER, AS TOLD TO MARTY NOBLE, *DEREK JETER: A YANKEE FOR THE NEW MILLENNIUM*, 2000

"Everybody wrote us off. We read in the papers that it was over [after losing Game 2 4–0 to Greg Maddux]. We picked up the Atlanta papers, and they said the Braves were going to dominate us."

—D.J., at the conclusion of the 1996 World Series

"As had happened so often in the season, especially October, a rally began with the unflappable kid, Jeter. He plays every game, including the World Series, like it's Saturday morning on the sandlots of Marine Park."

—Joe Torre, Yankees manager, about Game 4 of the 1996 World Series, when the Yankees rallied from 6–0 down to the Braves to win 8–6 in 10 innings, *Chasing the Dream*, 1997

"Before the decisive Game 6 of the World Series [against Atlanta], a relaxed Jeter went through his usual routine: He put on his headphones, listened to Mariah Carey, pulled on his number 2 uniform, and slipped on his hightop cleats, which are stitched with the message TURN 2 on the heels. . . . Jeter was laughing and smiling during the national anthem. Pressure? What pressure? For Jeter, it seemed, the game was no different from playing nine for some American Legion team back home in Kalamazoo."

—Kelly Whiteside, *Sports Illustrated Presents: The Champs! 1996 New York Yankees: A Special Collector's Edition*, November 13, 1996

"[With one run in and Joe Girardi on third], we kept the rally going. [Braves manager Bobby] Cox thought I would squeeze on the first pitch to Jeter—he called a pitch-out—but Derek was swinging too hot a bat for me to give up an out. Jeter knocked the next pitch into center field for a single, to drive in Girardi. Then Jeter stole second base and, after Boggsy flied out, scored on a single by Bernie Williams. We had a 3–0 lead on [Greg] Maddux."

—**Joe Torre, Yankees manager, on the Yankees scoring all their runs in the third inning off an otherwise impenetrable Greg Maddux in what would be a 3–1 victory to give them a six-game World Series championship over Atlanta,** *Chasing the Dream,* **1997**

"He wants the ball hit to him in the last inning of the last game, with the whole World Series at stake."

—**Charlie Hayes, Yankees third baseman who squeezed a foul pop-up to end Game 6 with Jeter looking on to give his team a World Series victory over Atlanta, October, 1996**

"I'M JUST SO HAPPY. IT'S JUST MAGIC. JUST MAGIC."
—D.J., DURING THE LOCKER-ROOM CELEBRATION OF THE YANKEES' FIRST WORLD SERIES TITLE SINCE 1978

"I told Derek Jeter, who was in his rookie year, about how I'd accomplished so much during my career but would give it all back in a heartbeat just to be *in* a World Series, just to be part of a team in the World Series. It wasn't to win a title. . . . It took me 39 years and 4,272 games to make it to the World Series in 1996. And we won."

—**Joe Torre, Yankees manager expressing what it meant to him personally to beat Atlanta in six games in the 1996 World Series,** *Tim McCarver Show*

"With his baggy jeans, high-top sneakers, snazzy sunglasses, and hip-hop strut, Jeter always looked as if he belonged on a college campus whenever he sauntered into the clubhouse. But Jeter's poise emerged, and he played a significant role in the postseason with a .361 average."

—**Jack Curry,** *New York Times,* **January 3, 1997**

"This year has been a fantasy. A dream come true. It's been an absolutely perfect year."

—D.J., following the world champion Yankees' ticker tape parade to
City Hall that attracted three million people

"Jeter will undoubtedly win the Rookie of the Year award, and he would win any awards for poise under pressure."

—Jack Curry, *Gold Collectors Series Magazine New York
1996 American League Champions Tribute*, 1996

"It began with a fifth-inning solo homer off Dennis Martinez, followed by a spectacular over-the-head, run-saving grab of Omar Vizquel's blooper into shallow left-center field. From that attention-grabbing afternoon, on a blustery, snow-delayed Opening Day in Cleveland, Derek Jeter embarked on his personal journey to star status as the Yankees' shortstop. It was a dream he began cultivating as a kid, and yesterday it culminated in his winning AL Rookie of the Year by a unanimous vote."

—Bill Madden, New York *Daily News*, November 5, 1996

D.J. DATA: In 1996, Derek Jeter became the seventh New York Yankee to be selected the American League Rookie of the Year, following Gil McDougald, 1951; Bob Grim, 1954; Tony Kubek, 1957; Tom Tresh, 1962; Stan Bahnsen, 1968; and Dave Righetti, 1981.

**"I WANTED TO MAKE THE TEAM, PLAY WELL, AND WIN A WORLD CHAMPIONSHIP. TO DO ALL THREE AND WIN THIS AWARD, TOO . . . WELL, I'M STILL DREAMING."
—D.J., UPON BEING UNANIMOUSLY SELECTED THE AMERICAN LEAGUE ROOKIE OF THE YEAR, NOVEMBER 4, 1996**

"I had rough periods all season. In spring training, I thought they were going to send me out when the season started. [Mr. Torre] told me I was the shortstop, and he was behind me every time I had a problem or didn't play well."

"Derek Jeter is a remarkable story."

"I felt that if I just did what I had done in the minor leagues, I'd be successful."

"Jeter had a season filled with one-way approval from fans, teammates, and media. And he earned it with precocious play on the field and humility off it. He demonstrated an intelligence that convinced he could be a Yankees captain someday and—for his sake—smart enough to not let 1996 overwhelm his life and career."

"This isn't going to go to my head. I can't go home if my head is too big. My parents wouldn't let me in the house."

"We won the World Series."

"I first met [Rachel Robinson] at the Baseball Writers dinner in 1996 in New York, and I had the opportunity to talk to her. She sat right next to me that day, the day I received my Rookie of the Year award. Throughout the years, she's been to the Turn 2 Foundation dinner . . . and we've honored her, and her daughter, Sharon, as well. It's great because she's a wonderful person."

"I just want to say that one of the main rewards of winning this award is the opportunity to sit up here next to a woman like Mrs. Robinson."

—D.J., to the audience at the Baseball Writers' dinner when he received his Rookie of the Year award

A DEBT TO JACKIE ROBINSON

"[Because I was] an African-American, [Jackie Robinson] was one of the first players I learned about. Obviously, I wouldn't be here today if it wasn't for his legacy."

—D.J., MLB.com, 2008

"I would choose Jackie Robinson, Lou Gehrig, and Martin Luther King. I think that would be a good group—some interesting stories."

—D.J., on the three people he'd choose for a golf foursome, to Jeff Rude, Golfweek.com, February 6, 2012

"JACKIE ROBINSON WAS THE ONE PERSON I WOULD HAVE LOVED THE OPPORTUNITY TO SIT DOWN AND TALK TO."

—D.J.

"Unfortunately, I never got the opportunity to meet him, but [I got] to meet his wife [Rachel]; she had just as much a role as he did, maybe even bigger. There were times when he felt he couldn't deal with it, and she was the one who made him feel like he could again."

—D.J., *Inside Sports*, August 1997

"[I'm grateful for] the relationship that I've built with [Jackie Robinson's] daughter and wife throughout the years. Getting to know them and how special they are just goes to show how special he had to be."

—D.J., MLB.com, 2008

"Their foundation has done so many good things for the community. For me personally, it's given me the opportunity to know Mrs. Robinson throughout the years. I think everything they stand for is just great, and I'm honored to be associated with them."

—D.J., about being a strong supporter of the Jackie Robinson Foundation, MLB.com, 2008

"I don't think anyone would relate to it. Being the first, I'm sure he went through things that people couldn't even imagine. So, no, I can't imagine what he went through. It says even more about him as a person. I don't know how I could have handled it. . . . You'd like to think you'd deal with it in the same way he did, but you don't know. Who knows if anyone is strong enough to do that. . . . You're talking about adversity while you're playing, and then you're dealing with things away from the field that no one else has to deal with. I think how strong he was mentally is probably the one thing that sticks out most."

—D.J., MLB.com, 2008

"Anything that draws attention to what Jackie was able to do is a positive thing. Anytime you can draw attention to what he stood for, what he did, and what he went through in a positive light—I think it should be celebrated every year."

—D.J., approving of Major League Baseball celebrating Jackie Robinson Day every year, MLB.com, 2008

SHARLEE JETER'S TRIBUTE TO HER BROTHER

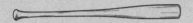

"I am not a big fan of Derek's because of his many successes in baseball, but because of his personality and the role he plays as my big brother. He tells me right from wrong, he recognizes my successes, and, best of all, he is honest with me. Derek supports me in everything I do and takes time from a busy schedule to talk to me about things that may not even be very important. I believe that the bond between a brother and sister is very important. Sometimes, people take God's gift of having a sibling for granted. You don't know how much you're missing until it's gone. I've gone through almost four years in high school, and I can count on two hands how many times I've had a chance to sit face to face with Derek and tell him what's been going on in school and sports. I've had to accept the fact that Derek will never see me play high school softball, something that my teammates may take for granted. There are days when I wish I had a brother to argue with because I've had a bad day. There are all the things I have not had for almost five years. But one thing I have had is someone who loves me for me, someone who made me realize that hard work does pay off, and someone who has made me extremely proud. Derek, thank you for being my big brother, and thank you for giving me my identity. To you, I am Sharlee, not Derek Jeter's sister. You have helped mold me into the person I am today, and now it is my turn to make you proud, and I promise I will. I love you. And, remember, you are my hero, not because of your baseball ability, but because of your support and love and making me proud to say that you are my brother."

—**Sharlee Jeter, whose brother Derek treasured her speech on Derek Jeter Day at Kalamazoo Central High, 1996**

"Every time I see Charlie Hayes catch that last ball [to end the World Series], I get chills. We were like a family for the whole year. When I watch that videotape, it's like we scaled the mountain together. [But] you can't go into this year talking about last year."

—D.J., quoted by Jack Curry, *New York Times*, January 3, 1997

"Jinx? What Jinx?"

—Title of a cover article on Jeter prior to his sophomore season,
Yankees Magazine, Vol. 18, Issue 6, 1997

"[Derek] came to spring training the same guy this year as he was last. A lot of guys who have big rookie years come to spring training, and their attitudes are different. Not this kid. I like this kid a lot."

—Mariano Duncan, Yankees infielder, 1997

"He'll now have a lot of forces pushing him in different directions: his agents, the media, and, of course, all the women. Keeping up his work habits will be the key. I'll notice right away this spring if he's changing. If he stops working, he'll have a problem."

—Joe Torre, Yankees manager, *Chasing the Dream*, 1997

"While shortstop Derek Jeter's playing this season for little more than baseball's basic wage, he's making out like a bandit off the field. Everyone wants the young Yankee as a product endorser. The 1996 Rookie of the Year will grace the pages of Pepsi's upcoming catalog, along with established sports stars like Shaquille O'Neal, Andre Agassi, and Deion Sanders. Jeter is being touted as the representative of 'Generation Next.' A promotional tie-in offers one fan the chance to throw out the first pitch of game two in this year's World Series, coached by Jeter himself. (The deal stands whether or not the Yankees are there.)"

—*New York Post*, April 6, 1997

"It's a great honor. Being on a baseball card, I guess, was one of my dreams when I was growing up. Every kid dreams about it, and I was the same. It was just kind of weird when I first looked at [my portrait by renowned artist Peter Max]. But it looks great. I think it takes a lot to make a picture of me look good, so I really think Peter did a great job."

—D.J., about being one of 10 baseball superstars chosen to be featured in the *Peter Max Serigraphs* set for the Topps Gallery collection, quoted by Charles De Biase Jr., *Staten Island Advance*, April 24, 1997

"Derek Jeter knows there are some theories predicting that he might sputter on the field and turn surlier off it after a superb rookie year with the Yankees. To Jeter, there is no evidence to support these beliefs."

—Jack Curry, *New York Times*, January 31, 1997

"In 1997, he battled, bizarrely, low expectations. A sophomore slump was predicted for him, and, even though he finished the season well, with a .291 average and 70 runs batted in, worries about his long-term performance as a Yankee were heard. For someone as dedicated to always improving as he is, this dust storm of speculation couldn't have been easy to tolerate, or ignore."

—Patrick Giles, *Derek Jeter: Pride of the Yankees*, 1998

"I'VE MADE A LOT OF MISTAKES. . . . PART OF THE PROBLEM IS THAT I'M TRYING TO PROVE LAST YEAR WASN'T A FLUKE."
—D.J., GIVING HIMSELF SOME BAD MARKS FOR 1997, WHEN HIS AVERAGE DROPPED FROM .314 TO .291, STILL IMPRESSIVE BUT HIS LOWEST AVERAGE UNTIL 2010

"I thought there was a glaring deficiency in that he strikes out a lot. But then you recognize that Derek does strike out, but, when he shouldn't strike out, he doesn't. When he needs to put the ball in play, he puts the ball in play."

—Joe Torre, Yankees manager, commenting how the aggressive Jeter's strikeouts went up to 125 in 1997, but he seemed to make better contact overall

"He seemed to have perfect instincts for the game. His trademark movements—raising his right arm for a brief 'time!' before each pitch (that began in his second season), his quarterback-like rifle throws to first while airborne in short left field, his line drives to the opposite field, and his unselfish approach all contributed to what was going to be a Hall of Fame career."

—Marty Appel, *Pinstripe Empire,* 2012

A REAL KNACK FOR HITTING

"Now if you want to be considered one of the top shortstops, or compete with the other shortstops out there, you have to hit."

—**D.J., about how shortstop was no longer strictly a defensive position because of Baltimore's Cal Ripken and then Seattle's Alex Rodriguez, Boston's Nomar Garciaparra, Oakland's Miguel Tejada, and himself entering the majors in the mid-1990s**

"If you're going to win games, you're going to have to come up with the big hits. That's the bottom line."

—**D.J.**

"We know Derek Jeter by heart. . . . The between-pitches bat tucked up in his armpit. The fingertip helmet-twiddle. The left front foot wide open, out of the box until the last moment, and the copy-at-a-crossing right hand ritually lifted astern until the foot swings shut. The look of expectation, a little night-light gleam, under the helmet."

—**Roger Angell,** *New Yorker,* **September 8, 2014**

"I'm an aggressive hitter. I don't really change when I'm batting leadoff."

—**D.J.**

"Nothing different hitting first or second, except the fact that you hit about two minutes earlier. Really, no difference—zero. I change absolutely nothing no matter where I am in the lineup."

—D.J.

"I'll hit wherever [they] want me to, as long as it's not 10th."

—D.J.

"Attend a Little League game or an American Legion game or a high-school baseball game anywhere in our area. Look at the kids who come to the plate one after the other, and see how alike they all look: right arm up, absently asking for time from the umpire, then both hands on the bat, the right elbow cocked up near the ear, the bat waving like a wand high above their heads—the unmistakable stance of a Derek Jeter at-bat. Ask the kids on the team how many of them asked for No. 2."

—Mike Vaccaro, about what Jeter described as a non-textbook stance with his right knee bent and his left foot raised a little as he torqued his body prior to leaning forward and swinging, *New York Post*, February 12, 2014

"His approach to hitting—like his attitude toward the game—had hardly changed from the days he played Little League: See the ball, hit the ball. If a pitch was thrown within the strike zone, he probably was going to swing, and if the ball was outside the strike zone, Jeter, always aggressive, might swing anyway. Experience taught him to anticipate where a pitcher might try to throw next, and the tilt of his body in the batter's box sometimes betrayed his thoughts. But Jeter concerned himself much less than other good hitters with the identity of the pitch or even the pitcher, or how the ball-strike count might affect his options."

—Buster Olney, *The Last Night of the Yankee Dynasty*, 2004

"AS FAR AS WHAT PITCHERS DO, I REALLY DON'T CARE. ALL I WANT TO KNOW IS WHAT THEY'VE GOT. I DON'T GET INTO ALL THAT STUFF. IT MAKES YOU THINK TOO MUCH. I DON'T WANT TO THINK."
—D.J., ABOUT WHY HE WAS UNINTERESTED IN HEARING HOW OPPOSING PITCHERS PLANNED TO PITCH TO HIM, JUNE 15, 2007

"Jeter never wanted to complicate matters. Over the years, I would try to get him to talk about hitting, his approach at the plate, etc., and he'd look at me as if I were speaking a foreign language."

—John Harper, New York *Daily News*, April 13, 2012

"He progressed as a hitter. He was understanding his swing and what he needed to do on certain pitches. He made adjustments quicker than any young person I've seen. He just understood what pitchers were trying to do, and then he wouldn't try to overcompensate. If they were trying to get him out away, he would go ahead and hit the ball to right field."

—Bill Evers, Jeter's manager at Greensboro in 1993,
Albany in 1994, and Columbus in 1995

"I DON'T THINK THERE IS A RIGHT-HANDED HITTER IN BASEBALL TODAY WHO IS MORE ADEPT AT GOING TO RIGHT FIELD WITH TWO STRIKES, REGARDLESS IF THE PITCH IS INSIDE OR OUTSIDE."
—TIM MCCARVER, *TIM MCCARVER SHOW*, MAY 9, 2000

"At times, I try to pull it, and it just goes that way. . . . I can't explain it."

—D.J., *Tim McCarver Show*, May 9, 2000

"Derek always had that beautiful inside-out swing. . . . If you ask pitchers, they'll tell you he's difficult to pitch to. He drives the ball so well to right-center, and he can battle off that inside pitch. That's what makes him so effective with two strikes. He's almost always able to put the ball in play. You'll rarely see him hit a pop fly for an out; the ball usually goes back in the stands, and that's because he keeps his hands back so well."

—Nomar Garciaparra, Red Sox shortstop, to Tony Massarotti,
Derek Jeter: A Yankee for the New Millennium, 2000

"Derek has always been a tough guy to get with two strikes because his swing covers so much ground through the hitting zone. . . . His bat gets into the hitting zone quickly and stays there, so even if the ball gets deep on him or he's fooled, he's still able to get the good part of the bat on the ball and go to the opposite field. If you look from overhead, he hits balls that are two or three ball-widths inside of the plate. Not many people can get into position to get the barrel of the bat on those pitches and drive them, especially with two strikes."

—**Gary Denbo, Jeter's manager in the Gulf Coast League and his long-time hitting instructor**

"Jeter does not delve too deeply into hitting theory and, with a few exceptions— notably Roy Halladay and the longtime reliever Mike Timlin—rarely admits that a pitcher is generally hard to hit. As always, he would rather give simple answers that say a lot. When he hits the ball the opposite way, Jeter will say, it is usually a fastball. When he turns on a pitch and pulls it, it is usually a breaking ball or a changeup. It takes Hall of Fame–level pitch recognition, reflexes, and confidence to wait on every pitch the way Jeter does, but when he speaks about hitting, he makes it seem easy."

—**Tyler Kepner, introduction,** *Derek Jeter: From the Pages of the New York Times*, **2011**

"It sounds like trouble."

—**D.J., describing a good fastball to documentarian Jonathan Hock,** *Fastball*, **2015**

"It could have been Randy Johnson on the mound or a recent call-up from Class AAA, and Jeter might have looked great or terrible [in his first at-bat]. It didn't matter: The opposing pitcher never had anything, or at least nothing insurmountable. Even if the pitcher got him out the first time, Jeter was certain he would get the pitcher the next time."

—**Buster Olney,** *The Last Night of the Yankee Dynasty*, **2004**

"It didn't matter if the guy was on his way to a no-hitter. He stunk. Nobody was ever more respectful than Jeet, but in the game, he refused to give the guy any credit. Ever."

—Russell Martin, former Yankees catcher on how Jeter always insisted to his teammates that the opposing pitcher had nothing that day, quoted by David Waldstein, *New York Times*, March 1, 2015

"Jeter watched videotape constantly, before and during games, but he was less interested in his swing than the pitch location. And he cared more about timing the pitches than about the particular strengths of the pitcher."

—Buster Olney, *The Last Night of the Yankee Dynasty*, 2004

"I've got to step up to the plate and see the ways in which I can advance a runner."

—D.J., *Game Day*, 2001

"Derek would always do the little things [at the plate]. He'd move the runner over and make you work really hard on the mound. He had that inside-out swing, and he'd hit a little flare over the second baseman and frustrate the crap out of you. He wouldn't necessarily hit it hard, but he had a knack for getting the bat on the ball."

—Dave Mlicki, Detroit pitcher

"Offensively, you never know, but he possesses a lot of power. You don't always know where it is, but he has opposite field power; he has center field power. That part of the game could develop, and he could be a real great home run hitter."

—Cal Ripken Jr., Orioles' former shortstop and current third baseman, quoted by John Delcos, *Derek Jeter: A Yankee for the New Millennium*, 2000

"It still astounds me—Derek's brilliance as a hitter has always felt fresh and surprising, for some reason—and here it comes one more time. The pitch is low and inside, and Derek, pulling back his upper body and tucking in his chin as if avoiding an arriving No. 4 train, now jerks his left elbow and shoulder sharply upward while slashing powerfully down at and through the ball, with his hands almost grazing his belt. His right knee drops and twists, and the swing, opening now, carries his body into a golf-like lift and turn that sweetly frees him while he watches the diminishing dot of the ball headed toward the right corner. What! You can't hit like that—nobody can! Do it again, Derek."

—Roger Angell, *New Yorker*, September 8, 2014

"TO WATCH JETER IS TO SEE MICHELANGELO WITH A BAT."
—JOSHUA PRAGER, *NEW YORK TIMES*, AUGUST 18, 2012

"The popular Yankees shortstop has hit an endorsement grand slam, signing four major deals, including two national contracts for roughly $1.5 million a year, since helping lead the Bronx Bombers to the World Championship last year. . . . Jeter has emerged as one of the best-liked major leaguers and one of the most popular among corporations looking for clean-as-a-whistle athletes to push their products."

—Richard Wilner, *New York Post*, June 25, 1997

"After the Yankees won the World Series in 1996, his popularity exploded. I was lucky enough to meet Jeter in 1997 during a Pepsi promotion at Toys R Us KidsWorld in Elizabeth. It seemed like thousands of fans, young and old, were corralled like cattle. Jeter went from person to person, graciously taking a picture with each fan. The moment is a blur, but I do remember him putting his arm around my back—and then my legs shaking and going numb about five minutes afterward. I was not able to speak a word to him."

—Jennifer Amato, managing editor with Greater Media Newspapers, *Suburban*, October 9, 2014

"Bottom of the fifth, Derek Jeter comes to the plate, and like clockwork, every 15-year-old girl in the house screams like a banshee for the 'dreamiest Yankee.' They scream even louder when Derek takes an 0–2 fastball and deposits the sucker in the first row of seats in left, just barely clearing the fence. Derek laughs as he trots back to the dugout, swearing that the only reason that ball got out was that every fan down the left-field line must have inhaled at the same time. It's now 7–6."

—David Wells, Yankees pitcher on Jeter's go-ahead homer that followed
Tim Raines's homer and preceded Paul O'Neill's homer—
back-to-back-to-back—in an 8–6 victory in Game 1 of the 1997 ALDS

"I got spoiled my first year. The year we won it all. But when we lost in the [1997] playoffs . . . that was the worst feeling. I thought we had a team that was much better than the one that beat us. Other people might think something else, but that's just how I feel. So it was very disappointing to me."

—D.J., about Cleveland winning the ALDS in five games to prevent the Yankees
from going to the World Series in 1997 for the only time
between 1996 and 2001, *Steppin' Out* magazine, 1998

FOUR

A Champion

"Chuck can hit, steal bases, turn a double play—everything you could want in a second baseman. As a shortstop, whenever you can work with a guy like that every day, it's exciting. I'm looking forward to it."

—D.J., about All-Star Chuck Knoblauch, who was acquired from Minnesota in the off-season for three top prospects to play second base for the Yankees in 1998

"Knoblauch and Jeter could redefine middle-infield excellence as they play together in the years to come, starting this year for a Yankees team that looks so good 'it's sickening,' said Andy Pettitte."

—Buster Olney, *New York Times*, March 29, 1998

"We all think we have a shot at winning another championship."

—D.J., looking forward to 1998, when the Yankees would capture the first of three consecutive world titles

"Sitting there in the sunshine, hair flowing, tan skin glowing, smiling constantly, Mariah Carey obviously knows absolutely nothing about the game of baseball . . . but nobody cares. Every time Derek steps into the batter's box, Mariah cheers, Derek smiles, and the rest of us sigh. Of *course* we're jealous. . . . It's a testament to Derek's character that we don't just instantly hate the poor guy for having it all. I mean, really, he's young, rich, handsome, talented, up-close-and-personal with Mariah Carey. . . . I've had teammates who would have been strung up for less."

—**David Wells, Yankees pitcher, about the privacy-obsessed Jeter having his high-profile girlfriend, singer Mariah Carey, at spring training in 1998, *Perfect I'm Not*, 2003**

"[Mariah]'s larger than life. (I was very young at the time.) You can't even compare in terms of how well someone's known, between me and her. Two famous people can have a relationship, but it's tough obviously because of all the media attention. . . . If two people get along, it doesn't have to make a difference."

—**D.J., about dating Mariah Carey, to Michael Kay, *CenterStage*, December 2003**

"Jeter caught Mariah Carey's eye in 1997, and by '98, she made a trip to spring training that drew plenty of media attention. The couple split in late 1998, with publicists citing 'media pressure.'"

—**Thomas McKenna, about Derek Jeter ultimately blaming unrelenting media scrutiny for causing Carey and him to stop dating, *Huffington Post*, October 4, 2014**

"On May 17, 1998, David Wells pitched . . . the 15th perfect game in MLB history, blanking the Minnesota Twins . . . 4–0. . . . Wells' perfect game featured two men who were or would eventually become part of the 3,000 hit club; Derek Jeter was the Yankees starting shortstop, of course, and Paul Molitor, who had reached the milestone in 1996, was Minnesota's DH that day."

—**Lou DiPietro, about Wells's gem, in which Jeter, who went 1-for-3 with a walk and stolen base on offense, had only one putout and one assist on defense, YESNetwork.com, May 5, 2013**

"I feel just like a little kid. I always used to watch the game with my father."

—D.J., about being added as a reserve to his first All-Star Game, July 2, 1998

"I'm in the clubhouse, I'm not saying anything, I'm just looking around, I'm in awe."

—D.J., about being at his first All-Star Game

"Jeter replaced starting shortstop Alex Rodriguez in the bottom of the fifth inning. In Jeter's only at-bat of the night, Roberto Alomar scored on a passed ball before Ugueth Urbina fanned Jeter swinging for the second out of the sixth inning. The American League prevailed, 13–8."

—Newsday

"It doesn't feel different being here [at the All-Star Game]. I feel like I'm on an All-Star team every day."

—D.J.

"WE DIDN'T HAVE A GUY THAT STARTED IN THE ALL-STAR GAME, BUT I'VE NEVER BEEN AROUND A GROUP OF GUYS THAT WANTED TO WIN EVERY SINGLE DAY LIKE THAT TEAM IN '98."
—D.J., ABOUT THE DOMINANT YANKEES, TO STEVE SERBY, *NEW YORK POST*, MAY 6, 2004

"The Yankees have 25 heroes."

—D.J.

"We rely on everyone."

—D.J.

"A season this spectacular must have been a deliverance for Derek. All year, his private life heated airwaves and sold newspapers, but nobody could stop him on the ball field. He has always had the gift of responding well to his surroundings, and he was surrounded by a team not of solo champions, but an ensemble that played together better than any other in the history of baseball."

—**Patrick Giles,** *Derek Jeter: Pride of the Yankees,* **1998**

"Derek was the centerpiece of the entire team. We took on his persona, which was to show up and win the game no matter what happened the day before. We never changed who we were, no matter how many games in a row we won, and a lot of that was Derek's personality. He was more of a leader than anyone knew. We had a relentless nature where nobody gave away an at-bat no matter what the score was, and that's who Derek was."

—**David Cone, Yankees pitcher**

"He doesn't push himself on people, or claim a leadership role. It just sort of happens."

—**David Cone, Yankees pitcher**

"Torre was in the habit of resting his regulars in September. He removed two of his outfielders in the sixth inning of a game in Baltimore, and a blooper subsequently fell between Jeter and the subs, to the chagrin of Wells, the pitcher. The left-hander turned to the dugout in frustration and spread his hands, as if to say, Are we trying? Jeter saw the uncharitable gesture and began yelling at Wells, telling him in so many words that no one on this team does that stuff. Wells, 11 years older, later backed down and apologized. It was remarkable, some teammates felt, that someone that young could naturally take charge in that situation."

—**Buster Olney,** *New York Times,* **January 20, 2000**

"That was baloney."

"Derek's so much more colorful inside the locker room than he is out on the field, and over the course of the year, our team needed that."

"It was [for] a hefty price, but the [Knoblauch] trade paid immediate dividends for the Yankees. Knoblauch—the team's first bona fide leadoff hitter since Rickey Henderson—hit 40 points below his career average in Minnesota, but he stole 31 bases and scored 117 runs. More important, he allowed everyone else to find their proper niche below him in the order. Most notable in this regard was Jeter, who hit .324 and scored 127 runs from the number-two hole and finished third in the American League Most Valuable Player voting."

"I still need to cut down on my strikeouts."

"Me ending the streak—it just happened to be against the Yankees. I didn't tell anybody. It seemed like [Jeter] was the first one to be aware, like he always seemed to be. He stood up on the top step of the dugout, and everyone joined him and applauded. The look on his face when I didn't take the field was pretty cool."

"A few years after the advent of the Three Tenors, the Three Shortstops made their first big splash. Just as Pavarotti, Domingo, and Carreras had done much to popularize opera with the masses, the equally dynamic trio of New York's Derek Jeter, Boston's Nomar Garciaparra, and Seattle's Alex Rodriguez would rekindle America's interest in baseball in the post-strike years. . . . Most significant, because there are three of them rather than just one groundbreaker—as was the case with Cal Ripken Jr.—they have had the enormous effect of forever redefining the shortstop position. (Ozzie Smith changed the position also, but only defensively.) It's not just that they are tall for shortstops—Rodriguez and Jeter are six-feet-three and Garciaparra is six feet—but they are all both excellent fielders and excellent power hitters."

—**Tim McCarver,** *The Perfect Season,* **1999**

"Jeter has an inside-out swing that enables him to go the other way on the inside pitch, but rarely does he hit any ball over the fence the opposite way. Yet, oddly enough, he jolted one ball out to right at Yankee Stadium early in the season that probably outdistanced anything Rodriguez and Garciaparra hit that way all year. Knowing that I don't concede that a tightly-wrapped ball is the reason for so many homers in the majors, Joe Torre told me that Jeter's mammoth opposite-field drive into the upper deck in right was proof that the little white rat was wrapped tighter than a pro wrestler's corset."

—**Tim McCarver,** *The Perfect Season,* **1999**

"Perhaps their power gives Rodriguez and Garciaparra a slight edge over Jeter with the bat, but I rate him the superior fielder. They don't come in on the ball as well as Jeter, nor do they have his range."

—**Tim McCarver,** *The Perfect Season,* **1999**

"They all go to their left so well. Derek probably goes to the right the best."

—**Ozzie Smith, future Hall of Fame Padres and Cardinals shortstop**

A BETTER SHORTSTOP THAN EXPECTED

"If I hadn't worked on my defense religiously in the Instructional League in 1993 and the years since then, there's no guarantee I would have made it to the Yankees as a shortstop. I turned myself into an above-average defensive player."

—D.J., *The Life You Imagine*, 2000

"I had him when he was a baby, when he was a rookie. We worked mostly on his throwing. He made a lot of throwing errors in the minor leagues, but that was mostly (about) trying to find his release point."

—**Willie Randolph, Yankees coach**

"When he came up to the big leagues in 1995, I was playing first, and he was playing short a little bit, and I noticed every play was bang-bang. Every play he made, whether it was a routine play or a tough ball, it was a banger. I had to get out there and get to every ball as if the runner was going to beat it. I don't know if he remembers or not, but I said something to him about guys like Alan Trammell, those guys who catch it and throw it at the same time. They have their feet lined up as they catch the ball. And you know what, I watched him the next day fielding grounders, and he had it. He made the adjustment. He was getting his feet in position and was throwing as he got it, and I loved it. I was like, this kid is going to be good."

—**Don Mattingly, Yankees first baseman**

"Even in my best years, I couldn't carry Jeter's glove."

—**Phil Rizzuto, Hall of Fame Yankees shortstop and broadcaster, to Dan Schlossberg,** *Derek Jeter: A Yankee for the New Millennium*, 2000

"I've never seen anybody throw a guy out like he does, going into the hole, deep on the outfield grass, jumping up in the air like a football quarterback, firing, and getting fast runners at first base."

—Phil Rizzuto, Yankees Hall of Fame shortstop and broadcaster, to Dan Schlossberg, *Derek Jeter: A Yankee for the New Millennium*, 2000

"It was a move I did in the minors, but just in practice, just messing around. I kept working on it and having fun with it until it got to a point where I realized I could pull it off. I didn't try it in a game for quite a while. . . . I like to think that I was an okay athlete growing up, and I think playing other sports helped me to learn different moves, to be able to integrate jumping in my defense maybe more than other guys would."

—D.J., *Jeter Unfiltered*, 2014

"[Willie] Randolph calls it the Y.A. Tittle play, in honor of the former Giants quarterback, and most of the time, Randolph and [Luis] Sojo believe Jeter will be better off just planting his right foot, setting his body and throwing, rather than going airborne."

—Buster Olney, *New York Times*, March 12, 2000

"Jeter goes into the hole better than anyone in the league, including [Omar] Vizquel. Watch how he plants his foot and throws out batters with a strong, accurate arm. [Nomar] Garciaparra and [Alex] Rodriguez make this play, too, but not with the consistency of Jeter. Even better is how Jeter goes to his left. If you're in the park on this play, you might hear teammates of the batter yell from the dugout for grounders to stay down because they know shortstops usually need the ball to come up to make a clean play. But Jeter is the rare shortstop who will stay down with the ball, pick it up, and throw across his body to make the play. It's an extraordinary talent."

—Tim McCarver, *The Perfect Season*, 1999

"He's got a great arm. I'd say to him, 'C'mon, you've got to use your arm.'"

—**Luis Sojo, Yankees infielder, who along with Torre and Zimmer preferred Jeter on balls hit into the hole to plant his right foot rather than jump in the air to make the long throw to first**

"Although more experienced players and coaches cautioned against these virtuoso leaps and midair plays, Jeter only improved doing them. They never appeared show-offy, full of the flash that other players sometimes add to gain applause or media approval."

—**Patrick Giles, *Derek Jeter: Pride of the Yankees*, 1998**

"Jeter preferred leaping over runners as he turned double plays, stomping on the bag and jumping toward first base. Yankees indielder, [Luis] Sojo told him: Sure, you can do that now when you're young. What happens when you can't jump so high? 'You can get into a lot of trouble doing that,' Sojo said. So Sojo explained to Jeter that the safest place to hide from the runner in turning a double play is behind the base; no runner slides hard across second base, which serves as breastwork for the middle infielder turning a double play. Stay behind the base as you prepare to take the throw, Sojo showed Jeter, then hit the back corner of the bag with your right foot and push away, toward the outfield. This is what Jeter does now, for the most part."

—**Buster Olney, *New York Times*, August 12, 1998**

"Most definitely [having played basketball helped me at shortstop]. Defensively in basketball, you have the lateral movement, you're always on your toes. It's the same thing when you're playing baseball. When you're playing shortstop, you should be moving on every play."

—**D.J., *Tim McCarver Show*, May 9, 2000**

"[There's] one thing that I haven't seen in baseball in all my years. This guy is so tall, but he charges the ball with two hands and throws the guy out. Two hands—you don't know how hard that is, and he does it so easy."

—**Luis Sojo, Yankees infielder**

"Being a taller shortstop, it's real difficult to get down low and throw in one motion, so that's something I really had to work on, especially in the minor leagues."

—D.J., on charging the ball and throwing to first, *Tim McCarver Show*, May 9, 2000

"WHAT KIND OF SHORTSTOP IS DEREK JETER? WELL, A VERY EFFECTIVE ONE, TO BE SURE. I THINK HE'S A SLEEKER AND LEANER MODEL OF A CAL RIPKEN. HE'S OUT OF THE CAL RIPKEN MOLD IN THAT HE'S TALL AND RANGY, HAS A GREAT ARM, [AND] COVERS A LOT OF GROUND."

—OZZIE SMITH, FUTURE HALL OF FAME PADRES AND CARDINALS SHORTSTOP

"He's able to go into the hole and make the strong throw, he's able to charge the ball and make a play with the bare hand, and he's able to turn the double play."

—Ozzie Smith, future Hall of Fame Padres and Cardinals shortstop, quoted by John Delcos, *Derek Jeter: A Yankee for the New Millennium*, 2000

"Defensively, I appreciate a lot of the things he does. . . . I know how difficult certain plays are and how easy he makes it look. I think he's more blessed with range and a physical sense than I am. He can move. He has quickness. He's smooth and agile. He's also a good student of the game."

—Cal Ripken Jr., former Orioles shortstop and current third baseman, quoted by John Delcos, *Derek Jeter: A Yankee for the New Millennium*, 2000

"Out here in Arizona at a camp . . . Buck Showalter and I . . . were talking about Derek Jeter and how he makes this underhand flip . . . because shortstops nowadays use this. It's a basic thing, it's a very good weapon, and it's a very good tool. He makes that play and gives the ball to the second baseman on the double play as well as anyone, and he does it with ease and grace. It's not a real easy thing to master, and he's done it."

—Cal Ripken Jr., Orioles third baseman, quoted by John Delcos, *Derek Jeter: A Yankee for the New Millennium*, 2000

"I saw [Jeter's] boot camp [in 1993 with Brian Butterfield]. They were working on humpbackers, shallow fly balls. Watching this first-round pick diving for balls over his head, you're just hoping he got up every time, or Butter would lose his job."

—Buck Showalter, Baltimore manager, about an important part of Jeter's fielding arsenal

"MY MIND IS NEVER AT REST. . . . SINCE I'M THE SHORTSTOP, I HAVE TO KEEP UP MY END ON THE DEFENSIVE SIDE. . . . MY MENTAL FOCUS HAS TO BE FLEXIBLE ENOUGH THAT I CAN WATCH EVERYTHING THAT IS HAPPENING AROUND MY TEAMMATES AND ME AS WELL."

—D.J., *GAME DAY*, 2001

"There were times he'd play more up the middle than you'd want him. You'd move him, but then he'd keep creeping, and you'd move him back. Then he'd make that play in the hole, the one with the jump throw, and there was nobody who could make a play like that. You knew his limitations as a shortstop, but when you looked at the whole package, it worked."

—Joe Torre, *The Yankee Years*, Joe Torre and Tom Verducci, 2009

"He is the best player I've ever seen play [shortstop]. He's a complete player."

—Miguel Cairo, Yankees second baseman, 2005

"I think D.J. would win a Gold Glove out there [if he becomes a center fielder]. . . . In center field, you need a quick half-step, and you have to be in full stride with your first stride. That's what Jeter has. . . . As long as I've been in baseball, going on 42 years, D.J. has as good a baseball instinct as anyone I've ever seen. If he moved to center field, it would be an absolute breeze."

—Bobby Murcer, former Yankees center fielder, speaking hypothetically about how Jeter would adapt if he was moved to center field, to Murray Chass, *New York Times*, 2006

"I liked his smarts [in the field]. For instance . . . he seemed keenly aware that his second baseman Chuck Knoblauch was having throwing problems, so Jeter always made sure to get the ball to him on double plays quickly enough for him to have time to make an easy pivot and throw to first."

—Tim McCarver, *The Perfect Season*, 1999

"In his third season with the team, the shortstop seemed to be getting stronger, faster, surer, game after game."

—Patrick Giles, *Derek Jeter: Pride of the Yankees*, 1998

"HE'D BEEN SUMMONED BY THE BASEBALL GODS: TO CARRY THE TORCH, TO HELP SAVE THE TEAM AND THE STADIUM AND MAYBE EVEN THE GAME OF BASEBALL ITSELF."
—PETER RICHMOND, *GQ*, SEPTEMBER 1998

"The biggest star to hit New York since the Beatles."

—*Sports Cards*, in its cover story on Jeter, September 1998

"On August 29, in an 11–6 victory over the Mariners that resulted in the Yankees' clinching a postseason spot the earliest in their history, Jeter made a leaping catch, scored four runs, and had three hits, including his 17th homer, to set the team record for shortstops."

—Tim McCarver, *The Perfect Season*, 1999

"The magic number is zero. . . . Derek Jeter and Paul O'Neill each homered twice . . . as the Yankees clinched the AL East for the seventh time and the second time in three years with a 7–5 edging of the Red Sox last night at Fenway Park . . . the earliest date the Yanks have clinched the East since divisional play began in 1969. . . . The Yanks had mustered just two hits against Tim Wakefield through three innings, but both of them were mammoth home runs by the emerging MVP candidate. Solo blasts in the first and third were the [Yankees' and] career-best 18th and 19th homers for Jeter, and the second time in his career he went deep twice in one game. The other such game came Aug. 20, 1997, at Anaheim."

—Peter Botte, New York *Daily News*, September 10, 1998

"When I think of home runs, that puts me in a slump."

—D.J., about how he had trouble getting hits of any kind at the end of the season because he tried futilely to hit his 20th homer, *Tim McCarver Show*, May 9, 2000

"I could never get him out of a game. . . . We'd clinched, and I wanted to give him a couple of days off. I think he was trying to get to 20 home runs for the season. And what happened was, he stunk. Later, he came to me and said, 'Next time I'm gonna do what you ask me to do.' To me, that [encapsulated] exactly who the kid was. He was trying to do something of a personal nature, only that wasn't where he thrived. He has always thrived on being part of a team and showing the way and never being about stats. It was just about the winning. That's when he performed at his best."

—Joe Torre, Yankees manager, February 17, 2014

"You're going to lose, especially at this level when you play so many games. In 1998, we had one of the best teams ever, and we still lost 50 games."

—D.J., whose Yankees would sweep Texas to advance to the ALCS to play Cleveland, the team that eliminated them in the 1997 playoffs, PBSKids.org's "It's My Life"

"If he played a year when he didn't go to the playoffs, he'd probably go home and cry."

—**Chili Davis, Yankees outfielder**

"Jeter hit a two-run triple in Game 6 [of the ALCS against Cleveland] that proved decisive in ensuring a victory. . . . Indians outfielder Manny Ramirez literally climbed the back wall to catch it, but it landed below him, making him scramble for it as Jeter sped to third and two runs ran home, putting the Yankees ahead again. When Bernie Williams's third hit of the game sent Jeter in, fans in the stands were already lining up for World Series tickets."

—**Patrick Giles, on the late rally that gave the Yankees a 9–5 victory and the 1998 American League pennant,** *Derek Jeter: Pride of the Yankees,* **1998**

"I'm used to this [now]. . . . In '96, everything was new to me."

—**D.J., to reporters during the ALCS victory celebration**

"[It's] like a Broadway play; it's center stage. The World Series should be played in New York."

—**D.J., prior to Game 1 of the 1998 World Series, which the Yankees would sweep from the San Diego Padres**

"Derek Jeter had come to the league at the perfect time in 1996, and by this World Series, his future Hall of Fame status was on the big screen for all to see. Derek had the best instincts of anyone and played the game with perfection."

—**Paul O'Neill,** *Me and My Dad,* **2003**

"I DON'T SEE HOW YOU CAN SAY WE AREN'T THE GREATEST TEAM EVER. WE ARE UNSELFISH, AND WE DON'T CARE WHO THE HERO IS."
—D.J., CELEBRATING A WORLD SERIES VICTORY IN 1998, QUOTED BY GEORGE A. KING III, *NEW YORK POST*

"I don't think there's a person in the world who's been more spoiled than I've been.

—D.J., at the ceremony following his second Yankees World Series victory parade in three years

"Derek Jeter was the MVP of the AL [in 1998]. Yet only Mike Sullivan, out of the Cleveland chapter of the Baseball Writers' Association of America by way of the *Columbus Dispatch*, and myself voted that way. Twenty-one of the writers cast first-place ballots for the very talented [Texas Rangers outfielder Juan] Gonzalez, and five went to Red Sox shortstop Nomar Garciaparra. . . . How could the MVP of a team that set an AL record of 114 regular-season victories not be the league MVP?"

—George King, *New York Post*, November 19, 1998

"No one in the Yankee family knows Jeter's swing like [his first minor league manager Gary] Denbo. Starting in early January [1999], the two began a seven-week program into spring training. The focus has been on balance and turning on inside fastballs. This past off-season, they worked on pulling the ball with greater backspin."

—Joel Sherman, *New York Post*, March 31, 1999

"We've only scratched the surface of his ability. It might be strange to say that with all the success he has had, but I think he is still learning how to hit. I think he has a higher ceiling than Nomar Garciaparra and Alex Rodriguez."

—Gary Denbo, Jeter's GCL Yankees manager, about working on Jeter's hitting prior to the 1999 season

"The Yankees thought they had a slam-dunk arbitration case against Derek Jeter. Instead the world champs—and the foundation of baseball itself—were slammed by the arbitration upset decision."

—Peter Botte, about Jeter receiving a $5 million one-year salary for 1999, rather than Yankees GM Brian Cashman's proposed $3.2 million, New York *Daily News*, February 17, 1999

"I wouldn't really say it was ugly, but no one wants to sit there and listen to a team tell you how bad you are."

—D.J., about the arbitration process

"I would say he is happy for Derek Jeter and disappointed in me."

—Brian Cashman, Yankees GM, about owner George Steinbrenner's response to losing the arbitration decision, 1999

"The lesson is arbitration is not like a judicial system. Those men who are making the decision are swept away by a lot of things. This is the first time I can remember—and it's perfectly proper—where the popularity of a player played a great part."

—George Steinbrenner, Yankees owner, 1999

"If the Yanks make only one off-the-field move this season, let it be this: They should lock Jeter up for life. For it would be sacrilege to see him in another uniform. Sometimes the Yankee brain trust is slapped upside its collective head with a no-brainer. . . . It's not just his stats, which happen to be as gaudy as any shortstop's, or the two World Series rings he's earned in his three years with the Yankees. It's the way he does everything with dignity and class—not because he's a phony, but because that's how he was raised. He's the first to sign up for charity events, the last to say no to almost any request. We'd bet our second-born that for as long as Jeter plays, he will never think it cool to flip one-fingered salutes or use obscenities while the cameras are rolling. His parents taught him better."

—Lisa Olson, New York *Daily News*, February 24, 1999

"Even if the arbitration had gone against him, Derek would still be thrilled to be a Yankee. It means so much to him."

—Bernie Williams, Yankees outfielder, 1999

"If I leave New York, it's because they get rid of me."

—D.J.

"I thought of that one. I thought he might hit me."

—D.J., about Chuck Knoblauch and Jeter donning catcher's gear to face new Yankees acquisition Roger Clemens for the first time at live batting practice, their way of welcoming the former Boston ace who had the reputation of headhunting against New York and other teams, to reporters, February 26, 1999

"I knew something like that would happen eventually. For those two to step in with full gear like that did break the ice a little bit."

—Roger Clemens, Yankees pitcher, to reporters, February 26, 1999

"The Yankees defeated the Mets, 4–3, before a sellout crowd of 56,175 at the Stadium in their first meeting this year. The Yankees grabbed a 5–2 lead in the regular-season intercity series that began in 1997. Some participants view the series as an artificial mid-season distraction, but to [Derek] Jeter [who lives in Manhattan], it is real. . . . He came to bat with the Yankees trailing 2–1 in the fifth. With [Scott] Brosius on second . . . Jeter hammered a fastball from Rick Reed well beyond the wall in left center. The homer put the Yankees ahead 3–2 and added another page to an already remarkable season. Jeter has reached base in all 52 games this season and has hit more than half as many homers (10) as he did all last year. . . . The ball landed an estimated 418 feet from home plate, a subdued [Yankee Stadium] crowd came to life. The fans offered Jeter a thunderous standing ovation until he hopped out of the dugout for a brief curtain call, the first of his four-year career."

—Thomas Hill, New York *Daily News,* June 5, 1999

"I've learned to turn on the ball a little more. I used to inside-out a lot of balls to rightfield, but now I drive them, using more of my top hand."

—D.J., to Michael Silver, *Sports Illustrated,* June 21, 1999

"He's just phenomenal. He gets big hits, home runs. He's the key to our lineup. He's virtually carried us the first third of the season."

—David Cone, Yankees pitcher, after Jeter's three-run homer supported his 6–2 victory over Texas, June 15, 1999

"There's no reason to believe he can't be in the upper echelon of all-time great Yankees players."

—David Cone, Yankees pitcher

"HE HAS A CHANCE TO BE A HALL OF FAME PLAYER. HE'S GOT THAT MUCH TIME IN HIS CAREER, AND THAT MUCH TALENT."
—PAUL O'NEILL, YANKEES OUTFIELDER

"We have found a treasure."

—Don Zimmer, Yankees bench coach

"I can't remember any middle infielder doing what he's done, offensively and defensively, over these three months. He's just very, very special."

—Don Zimmer, Yankees bench coach

"Jeter's consistency is reminiscent of the great DiMaggio. In 1999, he set a team record by reaching base in each of the first 53 games of the season."

—Tom Robinson, *Derek Jeter: Captain On and Off the Field*, 2006

D.J. DATA: In August 1999, Jeter became the first Yankee to collect 50 hits in a month since Joe DiMaggio's 53 in July of 1941, during his 56-game hitting streak.

"Jeter is his era's DiMaggio. Admired. Diffident. By all outward appearances, charmed."

—Michael Sokolove, *New York Times Magazine*, June 23, 2011

"To see my name in the same sentence as Joe DiMaggio blows my mind."

—**D.J., 1999**

"It's unfair to them. . . . I've played three full years. It's flattering, but you've got to play longer than that to be mentioned with those guys."

—**D.J., about being compared to charismatic Hall of Famers who played baseball (Reggie Jackson), football (Joe Namath), and basketball (Walt Frazier) in New York, 1999**

"I've told him, 'I'll trade my past for your future.'"

—**Reggie Jackson, Yankees Hall of Famer**

"JETER IS A SIX-TOOL PLAYER. I'VE NEVER EATEN WITH HIM, SO I CAN'T TELL YOU IF HE HAS GOOD TABLE MANNERS, BUT I WOULD IMAGINE HE HAS THOSE TOO."

—JOHNNY OATES, RANGERS MANAGER, 1999

"His image was perfect for the game, especially as steroid allegations stirred around other stars. And he, along with Torre, Williams, Martinez, Rivera, Pettitte, and Cone, began to confound traditional Yankees haters. These were hard guys to root against. It was a most unusual development for the franchise and frustrating for those who had spent a lifetime finding the Yankees arrogant."

—**Marty Appel, *Pinstripe Empire*, 2012**

THE FANS' FAVORITE

"At times, it's tough for him to understand why people chase him down for his autograph. Fans ask him to sign his name on everything from his baseball card to, one time, a man's forehead."

—**Jennifer Flake, about Jeter as a minor leaguer heading for stardom,** *Kalamazoo Gazette*, **December 30, 1993**

"Derek Jeter was the King of Gotham City and our childhoods. He majestically guarded the walls of our bedrooms and left our teachers rolling their eyes as we managed to make every school project about the Yankees shortstop. We proudly donned his frayed number '2' jerseys in our backyard Wiffle ball battles, and we reenacted his patented backhanded-running-spinning-jumping-across-the-body-throw on our Little League fields."

—**Ben Remaly, guest columnist, NJ.com, September 28, 2014**

"New York Yankees fans are among the most enthusiastic fans in baseball. Derek Jeter is an iconic baseball player. Put those two together, and you get a special connection."

—**Saed Hindash, NJ Advance Media for NJ.com, September 23, 2014**

"It's safe to say that on most days, the Yankees shortstop receives more fan mail than any player in the major leagues."

—**Robert Craig,** *Derek Jeter: A Biography*, **1999**

"Culturally, he appeals to such a wide range of people. Everywhere you go, there are Derek Jeter fans. He makes us into sort of a traveling show in every town we go to."

—**David Cone, Yankees pitcher**

"I believe that part of the reason for all the fuss is because people don't know what nationality I am. I mean, I think they know now, but before people didn't know if I was Spanish, white, black, Indian, [Italian, Jewish]. . . . So I think I can relate to a lot of people. That definitely helps."

—D.J., explaining his immense popularity, *Steppin' Out* magazine, 1998

"I think, as a product of interracial parents, he has tremendous crossover appeal . . . cross-cultural appeal . . . transracial appeal. He is cool and classic at the same time. I don't think you can make yourself be that. I don't think you can decide to be that and work toward being that. It's just the kind of way he is. He's hip and traditional simultaneously, and that's something that is very difficult to accomplish."

—Bob Costas, broadcaster, as told to John Delcos, *Derek Jeter: A Yankee for the New Millennium*, 2000

"To understand how far the fans have come in accepting African-American players since the late forties and early fifties, consider that back then only African-Americans laid claim to Roy Campanella, although he was half Italian. Now the Yankees' handsome and vastly talented shortstop Derek Jeter, whose father is African American and mother is white, is probably the game's most popular player among all fans and is surely the number one heartthrob of female fans of all races. And as the Yankees' . . . leader, he is a unifying force among all his teammates."

—Ralph Kiner, *Baseball Forever*, 2004

"He just enjoys himself. . . . And he even realizes he's more than a ballplayer now, that people are interested in more about you than just your ability."

—Joe Torre, Yankees manager

"He's a natural. Young. Handsome. He can play his ass off, playing shortstop for the Yankees. What more do you want? The fact that he's here in the greatest sports town—greatest city in the world—makes it that much better."

—Spike Lee, movie director and renowned New York sports fan

"We go out to dinner or go out for a drink or something, and wherever we go, we walk into an establishment, and it's like everybody stops eating or drinking or whatever they're doing, and it's like they all swarm over to him, and then I'm standing over in this little corner alone. Then someone will come up to me and say, 'You know Derek Jeter?'"

—Chili Davis, Yankees outfielder, to Steve Serby, *New York Post*, June 3, 1999

"GOING OUT WITH DEREK IS LIKE GOING OUT WITH ELVIS."
—DAVID CONE, YANKEES PITCHER, ABOUT JETER'S ROCK-STAR STATUS

"We're walking down the sidewalk [in New York City], and a guy walks past us, and you could see him recognize Derek. . . . And the guy just grabbed Jeter by the arms, and he's like 'oh my God! . . . oh my God!' He was just happy shaking Jeet like 'Holy Cow!' Jeets wasn't feeling it; he went into a daze. . . . It scared the daylights out of me, too. After that, he was out of control. It's the only time I ever saw him in the twilight zone. He was wandering the street kind of out of it. Being a superstar isn't always as great as you think it is."

—R.D. Long, minor league teammate

"I don't go anywhere by myself, period. You never know when you're going to run into someone who's been drinking and is acting foolish. You like to know that someone is always watching your back."

—D.J., to Diane K. Shah, *Playboy*, June 2004

"WALKING AROUND SOMETIMES, I WOULD LOVE TO JUST BE ABLE TO WATCH PEOPLE, SEE HOW THEY ACT. SOMETIMES, I WOULD LOVE TO BE INVISIBLE."
—D.J.

"My best vacation is somewhere I could hide, somewhere warm and not a lot of people around."

—D.J.

"Not only did Derek Jeter's 3,000th hit propel him into rarefied baseball territory, it helped bump him up to America's most popular sports star as well, says PRNewswire.com. According to the poll, Jeter jumped to the No. 1 spot for the first time in his career."

—Ryan Tepperman, NESN.com, June 14, 2011

"I wanted to use the whole name, but my wife said, 'No, Jeter is a last name!'"

—Erik Peppen, soldier stationed at an army base in Hawaii, who named his fifth child Derek in 2011 soon after Jeter got his 3,000th hit, quoted by Gary Buiso, *New York Post*, September 7, 2014

"De-rek Je-ter!"

—New York fans' familiar chant at Yankee Stadium to the team's most popular player

"The fans are the ones that made this fun; it's been an extremely fun 20 seasons, and when you're out there playing as hard as you can and trying to be your best, you're doing it for the fans."

—D.J., 2014

"Yankees fans in particular pay attention; it means something to them, and they push you. They're tough, but I think they've helped shape who I am, and I don't know if I can truly thank them enough."

—D.J., 2014

"The '99 Yankees lead the Eastern Division from June 9 on, finishing four games ahead of the Red Sox. . . . Four Yankees—Derek Jeter, Tino Martinez, Paul O'Neill, and Bernie Williams—drove in 100 or more runs, and Jeter had a career season, batting .349 with 24 homers and 102 RBI."

—**Bill Madden**, *Steinbrenner: The Last Lion of Baseball*, **2010**

"I don't know how they can say you had a career season until your career is over."

—**D.J.**

"We just want to win. That's the bottom line. I think a lot of times, people may become content with one championship or a little bit of success, but we don't really reflect on what we've done in the past. We focus on the present."

—**D.J.**

"When a New York Yankee walks into a room, people will say, 'Wow, you're a member of the New York Yankees!' They don't say, 'Wow, what's it like to play with Derek Jeter? What about Bernie Williams and Roger Clemens?' This is fitting because, I am proud to point out, on the Yankees, the team is always more important than the individual players, and the statistic that matters most to my 25 players is the number of world championships we've won."

—**Joe Torre, Yankees manager, foreword to** *Raising a Team Player*, **Harry Sheehy, 2002**

"I think that group that Derek learned to play with—O'Neill and Tino and those guys—the motivation was all the same. They knew they weren't the greatest players in the league, but they knew if they did their job as a group, they could win."

—**Mike Mussina, Yankees pitcher**

"He expected a lot of himself. He was intense and expected perfection."

—**D.J., about Paul O'Neill, who like Jeter and George Steinbrenner—who dubbed him "The Warrior"—expected the Yankees to win every game, 2014**

"Every time Tino Martinez struggled and wasn't hitting as many home runs as he'd like, he talked to my dad and would hit a home run. One night before a game, I called home, and I said, 'Tino, you need to talk to my dad.' So he got on the phone, and sure enough, he hit a home run. I don't know what my problem is: I talk to my dad every day, but Tino's hitting all the homers."

—D.J., *Tim McCarver Show*, May 9, 2000

"HE'S LEGIT. HE'S VERSATILE. YOU CAN SEE HIM ON THE COVER OF *GQ*, THEN THE NEXT WEEK, HE'S ON THE COVER OF *SPORTS ILLUSTRATED*. HE'S FOCUSED. HE WORKS HARD. I'M PROUD OF HIM. I'M GLAD WE'RE WORKING TOGETHER."
—MICHAEL JORDAN, NBA STAR AND NIKE CLIENT, ABOUT WHY HE ASKED JETER TO BECOME THE FIRST JORDAN BRAND–ENDORSED BASEBALL PLAYER TO SIGN WITH HIM, 1999

D.J. DATA: In a 1999 *Sports Business Daily* poll of marketing and media executives on the most marketable baseball players, Derek Jeter finished fourth behind Ken Griffey Jr., Mark McGwire, and Sammy Sosa, sluggers who had challenged Roger Maris's single-season home run record in 1998. Jeter would finish first in the next three polls in 2003, 2005, and 2010.

"He's doing as well as probably any other player in baseball, and we've turned down a lot of things."

—Casey Close, Jeter's agent, who negotiated his deals with Nike, Coach leather goods, Florsheim shoes, Fleet Bank, and Skippy peanut butter, to Michael Silver, *Sports Illustrated*, June 21, 1999

"Before the 1999 All-Star Game, at Fenway Park, the Players of the Century were introduced, and Ted Williams was rolled out in a wheelchair, and all the current and former players surrounded him and mingled. It was something special and extremely emotional. To be there with all those great players at the same time—I got the chills. I was a little bit afraid to try to even speak to anyone."

—D.J., *Tim McCarver Show*, May 9, 2000

"I HAD THE OPPORTUNITY TO MEET HANK AARON. HE ACTUALLY APPROACHED ME. HE SAID THAT HE WANTED TO MEET ME! AND I WAS SPEECHLESS. I SAID, 'YOU'RE HANK AARON; YOU WANT TO MEET ME?' I SAID, 'I GREW UP WATCHING VIDEOS OF YOU, AND YOU'RE A BIG IDOL OF MINE.' I WAS OVERWHELMED TO SAY THE LEAST. . . . I WAS JUST LIKE ANY KID MEETING HIS HERO."

—D.J., *TIM MCCARVER SHOW*, MAY 9, 2000

"You want to let someone like Derek Jeter know you appreciate the way he plays. He does things the right way, and I like him. I watch him all the time."

—**Hank Aaron, Braves Hall of Famer and major league career home run leader, 1999**

"I got booed at the '99 All-Star Game, but I expected it because it was played in Boston. Garciaparra [of the Red Sox] played shortstop for us for the first three innings, and then [AL manager] Joe Torre let him take the field in the fourth inning. He thought if I went out there when Nomar was coming out, the cheers would outweigh the boos, and, you know, they did for a minute. But once he got in the dugout, the boos picked up a little bit. They wanted to see Nomar instead of me, so I thought I'd give them a little taste of Nomar by imitating his routine when I came to the plate. The fans appreciated it, but it didn't work. I struck out, so I did something wrong."

—D.J., *Tim McCarver Show*, May 9, 2000

"He tapped his feet back and forth, just like I do, and he couldn't keep a straight face. I thought it was hilarious. It was great. People thought he was making fun of me, but I looked at it as a sign of respect. It was all genuine and good natured."

—**Nomar Garciaparra, as told to Tony Massarotti,** *Derek Jeter: A Yankee for the Millennium,* **2000**

"In an improbable setting, David Cone performed an improbable feat yesterday. He pitched the Yankees' second perfect game in little more than a year, and he did it playing in front of Don Larsen, who pitched a perfect World Series game for the Yankees in 1956. Larsen was at Yankee Stadium to help celebrate Yogi Berra Day, and after Larsen threw the ceremonial first pitch to Berra, Cone took command of the mound and retired all 27 Montreal batters he faced as the Yankees clubbed the Expos, 6–0. . . . The Yankees had scored five runs in the second inning against Javier Vázquez with two monstrous two-run home runs, by Ricky Ledée well up the third tier in right field and by Derek Jeter deep into the Yankees' bullpen in left-center field."

—**Murray Chass,** *New York Times,* **July 19, 1999**

"We're surprised, too. While deciding to once and for all—or at least until next summer—break down the American League's do-it-all shortstops' tools and determine who was the best, we were concerned that the answer might be too obvious: the Mariners' Alex Rodriguez. He was our instinctive choice over the Yankees' Derek Jeter and the Red Sox' Nomar Garciaparra. . . . At this year's All-Star Game in Boston, we consulted 50 major league all-stars, general managers, assistant general managers, and scouts (as well as guest expert Ozzie Smith) and had them rank the three players in 18 categories. . . . And lo and behold, Jeter won out—by a considerable margin."

—**Alan Schwarz,** *Baseball America,* **August 9, 1999**

"Real punches were being thrown somewhere around the pitching mound, Cro-Magnon stuff, but on the fringes Rodriguez and Jeter waltzed away from the fray. . . . Jeter's apparent nonchalance and irreverence struck teammate Chad Curtis as heretical. Curtis immediately yapped off in front of the press: Why was that man laughing? . . . Anyone doltish enough to equate [Jeter's] smile that night with an absence of competitive fire . . . hasn't got a clue."

—Peter Richmond, about Chad Curtis yelling at Jeter in front of reporters for talking to an opponent, Rodriguez, during a skirmish between the Yankees and Mariners on August 6, 1999, *GQ*, April 2000

"It's a situation where, hey, [Chad Curtis] didn't know what we were talking about. Unless you know what's going on, then you shouldn't approach someone in that manner. . . . He apologized, but I didn't do anything wrong, so there's no reason to clear anything up."

—D.J.

"He'll be doing a lot of things that will make you go back to the record book."

—Joe Torre, Yankees manager, after Jeter got three hits against Cleveland to become the first Yankee since Don Mattingly from 1984 to 1986 to have consecutive 200-hit seasons, September 19, 1999

D.J. DATA: Although Derek Jeter would not necessarily classify 1999 as the best offensive season of his career because he didn't believe statistics ever told the whole story, he did have career bests in batting average (.349), homers, (24), RBIs (102), runs (134), hits (219), total bases (346), walks (91), intentional walks (5), on-base percentage (.438), slugging percentage (.552), and OPS (.989).

"So as the city ignites with both the Yankees and the Mets in the playoffs, in bars across New York, women will ask each other the tough question: Would you take the No. 4 [subway] to Jeter or the No. 7 to Shea Piazza? It's Jeter. The man is unadulterated gorgeous. God may have made a more perfect specimen, but not one who comes with cleats. Definitely worth a trip to the Bronx."

—**Sherryl Connelly, New York** *Daily News***, October 7, 1999**

"When Game 1 [of the ALCS] at Yankee Stadium was headed Boston's way, Jeter drew first blood [in his much-anticipated matchup with batting champion Nomar Garciaparra]. Down 3–2 in the seventh, one out and a man on second, Jeter hit an RBI single to center off Derek Lowe, ultimately allowing Bernie Williams to win it in the 10th with a homer off Rob Beck."

—**Ian O'Connor,** *The Captain***, 2011**

"Nomar leaped to steal a hit from the Yankees, then Derek leaped to swipe one back from the Red Sox, so Nomar leaped even higher to pilfer another. Derek made a sweet play in the shortstop hole, but then bounced the throw to second for an error. Then Nomar made an even sweeter play in shallow left field, but unintentionally mimicked Derek by bouncing his throw to second. The game was only three innings old, but the intense matchup between the Yankees and Red Sox already featured a marvelous duel between the dazzling shortstops whose surnames are not necessary."

—**Jack Curry, about the first official postseason game between New York and Boston, won by the Yankees 4–3,** *New York Times***, October 14, 1999**

"Whenever I hear my name in the same sentence as [Derek's], I think that's an honor. I think he's absolutely tremendous."

—**Nomar Garciaparra, Boston shortstop, October 13, 1999**

"Man, people were animals out there. . . . It was like dodging grenades. That stuff hasn't even happened in New York since I've been there."

—**D.J., shaken by Red Sox fans who littered the field in Game 3 because of poor umpiring, shoddy Sox fielding, and a six-run Yankees' ninth inning featuring Jeter's single and Ricky Ledée's grand slam in their 9–2 victory**

"We wanted to end it here. We didn't want to give them any life or confidence."

—D.J., whose two-run first inning home run off Kent Mercker was enough for Orlando Hernández to beat the Red Sox, 6–1, in Game 4 of the 1999 ALCS, to give the Yankees their 36th pennant, October 18, 1999

"People ask me about Derek Jeter all the time, about the fact that we're both shortstops, about the fact that I play for the Red Sox, and he plays for the Yankees. I won the American League batting title this year [by hitting .357], finishing one place ahead of Derek [who hit .349], and some people [asked] if there was any special meaning for me in beating him. Honestly, I found that question to be really kind of amusing. After all, I'd rather have his 1999 world championship."

—Nomar Garciaparra, Red Sox shortstop, as told to Tony Massarotti, *Derek Jeter: A Yankee for the Millennium,* **2000**

"This time around against Atlanta [in the World Series], Jeter turned Game 1 in the Yankees' favor when his RBI single off Greg Maddux in the eighth made it 1–1 before the Yankees scored three more. In Game 2, Jeter singled and scored in the first inning, doubled and scored in the fourth."

—Ian O'Connor, *The Captain,* **2011**

"This is what you've worked for; this is what you've been wanting for so long. Now go out and get it done."

—D.J., giving words of encouragement to Yankees starter Roger Clemens before he pitches a 4–1 victory over Atlanta to complete the Yankees' four-game sweep in the 1999 World Series, the team's 25th championship and Clemens's first

"Derek Jeter, to me, happens to be one of the top two or three ballplayers in the game."

—Bobby Cox, Atlanta manager, whose team was swept by New York in the 1999 World Series

> ## "PEOPLE LOOKED AT [JETER] AS THE BEST PLAYER IN BASEBALL, EVEN THOUGH HE DIDN'T HAVE THE BEST SKILLS, WHICH IS A VERY HARD THING TO PULL OFF."
> ### —REGGIE JACKSON, YANKEES HALL OF FAMER

"The media can't get to him. He's so good at avoiding everything. That whole year, he was the best player on a winning team, and he finishes sixth [in the voting]."

—Jorge Posada, Yankees catcher, on why Jeter never could win the MVP award

"I want to win, that's it. It doesn't get any more complicated than that."

—D.J., who showed no disappointment that he didn't receive more consideration for the MVP award

"I'm trying to catch Yogi. He has 10 rings. You set your goals high."

—D.J., *Tim McCarver Show*, May 9, 2000

"Yogi [Berra] started teasing me after we won our third one [in 1999]. We won back-to-back, and he said, 'You've got three more to catch me: five in a row.' . . . I get on him all the time. 'Yogi, it doesn't count. You went straight to the World Series.'"

—D.J., about how Berra's dynastic Yankees didn't have to first win division and league championship series when they captured five straight world titles from 1949 to 1953, to Tom Verducci, *Sports Illustrated*, November 25, 2009

D.J. DATA: After 1999, Derek Jeter had 795 career hits. Only five major leaguers had accumulated more hits in their first four seasons: all-time hits leader Pete Rose and Hall of Famers Babe Ruth (who began his career as a pitcher), Stan Musial, Hank Aaron, and Willie Mays.

"Before his career is over, he's going to be recognized as one of the best who ever played the game; I really believe that. You're talking about a guy who batted .349. It's hard to believe he can get better, but I really believe he can."

—Tim Raines, Yankees outfielder

"If you've been successful, why not improve?"

—D.J., *Tim McCarver Show*, May 9, 2000

"YOU CAN ALWAYS IMPROVE. I JUST WANT TO BE CONSISTENT. THAT'S ALL I WANT TO BE REMEMBERED AS."
—D.J., QUOTED BY ROBERT CRAIG, *DEREK JETER: A BIOGRAPHY*, 1999

"Derek Jeter had the ideal reaction to questions about his [deserving to] start in the 71st All-Star Game. The New York Yankees' shortstop ignited a 6–3 American League victory. Jeter was AL manager Joe Torre's choice to replace injured elected starter Alex Rodriguez in the starting lineup. Torre said he took his own man over an equally deserving Nomar Garciaparra of Boston because Garciaparra started last year, and this year Jeter had more votes. Jeter also had more hits—three, including a double, two RBI, and a run scored—before he yielded to Garciaparra after five innings. That effort won him the MVP award—the first Yankee to do so."

—Rod Beaton, *USA Today*, July 12, 2000

"Nice play by Palmer to knock it down! He's got a strong arm . . . and he did not get him. Well, we'll see how they score that. It was hit sharply. If it's scored a hit, it will be a memorable one."

—Jim Kaat, Yankees broadcaster, about Derek Jeter's 1,000th career hit, a grounder off Detroit's Steve Sparks that knocked the glove off the hand of third baseman Dean Palmer, September 25, 2000

D.J. DATA: On October 1, 2000, Jeter became the third Yankee in history to have three consecutive 200-hit seasons following Lou Gehrig (1927–29) and Don Mattingly (1984–86). Since 1950, only three other American Leaguers had accomplished this feat: future Hall of Famers Jim Rice, Wade Boggs, and Kirby Puckett.

"Jeter finished the 2000 regular season with a .339 batting average, but given his added muscle, he was disappointed in his number of homers (15) and RBI (73)."

—Ian O'Connor, perhaps guessing wrong about Jeter being disappointed in his power numbers, *The Captain*, 2011

"Those 30 exhibition games in the spring and 162 regular-season games don't mean a thing if we don't get the ring. It doesn't make a difference that we won the World Series in 1996, 1998, and 1999. I want to win it again and again."

—D.J., whose New York Yankees would have to beat the A's in the ALDS and Mariners in the ALCS before they could face the New York Mets in the 2000 World Series, *Game Day*, 2001

"Who cares if you won 10 in a row or lost 10 in a row?. . . . When you start the postseason, it's 0–0. Oakland could care less if we were struggling at the end of the year. If you're a hot team, you have to go out and try to perform well in a short series."

—D.J., about the Yankees' September struggles prior to playing the hot A's in Game 2 of the 2000 ALDS, which the Yankees would win by taking three of the last four games

BORN FOR THE POSTSEASON

"His self-assuredness made him a transcendent postseason player; his performance spiking in the most crucial moments. Jeter found the postseason games to be more fun: The stakes were greater, more people were watching, and he loved the spotlight; perhaps his concentration was more acute. . . . He seemed born to play in October, [Joe] Torre once said."

—**Buster Olney,** *The Last Night of the Yankee Dynasty,* **2004**

"You don't see a change in him between a playoff game and the third game of the season. He's always taken the same approach. He's hit the same way. He's stayed with his strengths."

—**Don Mattingly, Yankees first baseman (1982–95) and coach (2004–07)**

"I approach a game day in the postseason the same way I do during the regular season. The preparation is exactly alike. What I do during the daytime, how I work out and warm up at the stadium, doesn't really change. There is a lot I have to try and ignore, though. There is more media hype surrounding the play-offs and especially the World Series. There are cameras everywhere you turn and large groups of reporters asking you for interviews. The season is on the line, too, whether it's the first game of the American League Championships or the World Series. But I don't let any of that get to me. I just continue to go about things at my own pace and keep my focus as sharp as I would during the regular season."

—**D.J.,** *Game Day,* **2001**

"Jeter's 20 postseason homers, 200 hits, .308 average and .465 slugging percentage came against many of the best pitchers of his generation, some of the best all-time [including 42 starters who had or would win the Cy Young Award]. By any measure, his postseason career is one of the best seasons any major leaguer has ever had."

—**Steve Buttry,** *Hated Yankees* **blog, 2012**

"I don't like to say you focus more in the postseason, because it sounds like you're focusing less during the season. But in the postseason, you are more focused. You can't help it. Every pitch, every grounder, every inning means more."

—D.J.

"[Jeter's] the guy critics declare overrated in every month of the baseball year but the last."

—Dave Buscema, *Game of My Life: 20 Stories of Yankees Baseball*, 2004

"He's played in so many postseason games, it's like a regular-season game for him."

—Jason Giambi, Yankees teammate

"From 1996 until the 2001 World Series, the Yankees played .746 baseball in the postseason, an outrageously great record over 71 games, playing against the best teams under the most pressure. They were 53–18 while winning 14 of 15 series. It ranks as one of the most astounding stretches ever of October greatness. Jeter batted .319 in that run and, like some comic book superhero, always seemed to show up exactly the right time to save the day."

—Tom Verducci, *The Yankee Years*, Joe Torre and Tom Verducci, 2009

"I say I'll let him have it; I'll let him have Mr. October II. He is The Man in this era. He's going to be remembered by the Yankees fans that way. He's going to get cheered and held in reverence not because he hit .350 and made All-Star teams. He's going to be remembered because of his clutch postseason performances. There you have it. Now there are officially two Mr. Octobers."

—Reggie Jackson, Yankees Hall of Famer known as Mr. October because of his postseason heroics, to Kevin Kernan, *New York Post*, October 8, 2004

"There was a lot of pressure on us. We played Seattle [in the ALCS], and Seattle was tough. Going into Game 5 against Seattle, we had to win, otherwise we had to travel back to Seattle for Games 6 and 7. And the Mets had already won [the NLCS], so it put pressure on us to go ahead and get it over with. Then you get so excited you beat Seattle, the next thing you know, you've got to get your mind right because that means absolutely nothing unless you beat the Mets."

—D.J., quoted by Dave Buscema, *Game of My Life:*
20 Stories of Yankees Baseball, 2004

"THE BIGGEST STAGE YOU COULD HAVE IN NEW YORK SPORTS IS YANKEES AND METS IN THE WORLD SERIES."
—D.J., ABOUT THE SUBWAY SERIES IN 2000

"All you heard about in New York, everywhere you went . . . Yankees fans saying, 'You have to win, you have to win, you have to win.' Mets fans tell you how bad you are. That was a pretty big series in terms of *I would have had to move out of the city if we lost to the Mets.*"

—D.J., quoted by Dave Bucsema, *Game of My Life:*
20 Stories of Yankees Baseball, 2004

"One of those Derek Jeter moments."

—**Bobby Valentine, Mets manager, on cutoff man Jeter taking a throw, pivoting in the air, and throwing a strike to catcher Jorge Posada to cut down speedy Timo Perez at the plate, in the Yankees' victory over the Mets in Game 1 of the 2000 World Series**

"First pitch, 8:31. . . . And Jeter swings . . . it's a high drive to left. It is high . . . it is far . . . it is gone! First-ball fastball! Deep into the bleachers in left field . . . and on the first pitch of the game, the Yankees take a 1–0 lead!"

—**John Sterling, Yankees radio broadcaster, on Jeter's leadoff at-bat against the Mets' Bobby Jones in Game 4 of the 2000 World Series, which was won by the Yankees to put them ahead in the Series 3–1**

"We're not getting a lot of production from our leadoff guys (they are 0 for 12 in the three games), so Mr. T decides to move Derek up to the top spot for Game 4. Bobby Jones is the Mets starter, and his first pitch of the game, Derek drives it over the left-centerfield wall at Shea Stadium. It's a single run that feels like 10, for the way it fires us up and coldcocks the Mets. It is Derek Jeter at his best, providing just what we need, when we need it."

—**Mariano Rivera, Yankees reliever, about Game 4 of the World Series versus the Mets,** *The Closer,* **2014**

"Everyone seems to ask if I'm changing my approach when I'm the leadoff hitter. But I'm aggressive, and I've been known to swing at the first pitch. With runs tough to come by in the postseason, you want to score early."

—**D.J., October 26, 2000**

"It was, perhaps, the single most emphatic symbol of the Yankees' dominance of the era: *Nice try, but we'll take it from here.*"

—**Tyler Kepner, about Jeter's leadoff homer, introduction,** *Derek Jeter: From the Pages of The New York Times,* **2011**

"Jeter did not stop at one moment, though. In his next at-bat, he unearthed enough speed to turn a double into a triple and went on to score his second run of the game—his fifth of the World Series."

—**Selena Roberts, about Jeter's vital contribution to the Yankees' 3–2 victory in Game 4,** *New York Times,* **October 26, 2000**

"THIS KID, RIGHT NOW, THE TOUGHER THE SITUATION, THE MORE FIRE HE GETS IN HIS EYES. YOU DON'T TEACH THAT."
—JOE TORRE, YANKEES MANAGER

"Imagining the Mets in the victory parade kept us focused on winning the series."

—**D.J.,** *Game Day,* **2001**

"Derek Jeter's gone deep again!"

> **—Joe Buck, Fox broadcaster, calling Jeter's home run off Al Leiter in the sixth inning of Game 5 of the 2000 World Series that tied the Mets 2–2**

"Once we tied 'em, I thought we pretty much had 'em after that."

> **—D.J.**

"[Luis Sojo's hit to put us ahead in the ninth inning] was huge. He got that hit, Jorge scored. In our minds, 'Bring in Mo. It's over.' . . . Before Piazza came out [to hit in the bottom of the ninth with two outs and a runner on base], I went to the mound and I said [to Rivera], 'Well, you know what he's trying to do, so don't just groove it in there.' And then when he hit that ball, I thought for a minute it was gone. But it's pretty deep out there. I mean you look at Bernie, I knew we had won."

> **—D.J., about the final out of a 4–2 Game 5 victory which gave the Yankees the 2000 World Series title, quoted by Dave Buscema, *Game of My Life: 20 Stories of Yankees Baseball*, 2004**

"This, by far, was the best team we played in the five years I've been here. All five games could have gone either way."

> **—D.J., praising the Mets team that he batted .409 against in the 2000 World Series**

"The 2000 World Series games were the most thrilling games I've ever played, better than my first World Series, better than the Series the year we won 125 games. All of New York was involved, and the excitement surrounding the city was amazing. . . . You can just tell from your teammates' eyes that everyone feels the same way—exhilarated. All of your hard work has paid off, and you made it there with your team, the people you see more than your families. We spend a lot of time together, and when we win, it's really a feeling that's difficult to describe. It's a sensation unlike any other."

> **—D.J., *Game Day*, 2001**

"He's allowed."

—George Steinbrenner, Yankees owner, about how Jeter was the one employee who could get away with pouring champagne over his head to celebrate the team's third consecutive World Series victory

"Jeter's one of the most classic winners ever to play the game. Every time, we said, 'OK, now we've got it going,' Jeter did something to change the game."

—Steve Phillips, Mets GM, about the first player to be named the MVP of both the All-Star Game and World Series in the same year

"Every year is a different story . . . but I'd be lying if I said this one wasn't more gratifying. I mean, we struggled this year. We've had rough times. . . . Winning isn't easy. We made it look easy. It's something very difficult to do. We've had our bumps in the road."

—D.J., about winning the world championship in three consecutive years, 1998–2000

"You fans should really enjoy watching this team because you're not going to see many like it."

—D.J., to the crowd at the 2000 World Series victory celebration

TORRE AND JETER: THE TEAM COMES FIRST

"I was with [Joe Torre as my manager] since I was 21 years old, and I pretty much grew up with him."

—D.J., 2007

"I feel privileged to have managed Derek Jeter for 12 years. During his first year in 1996, the team concept instilled in him was apparent. . . . He came to work every day."

—Joe Torre, Yankees manager from 1996 to 2007

"THE BOND BETWEEN TORRE AND JETER WAS UNSHAKABLE. . . . IT WAS A REMARKABLE RECORD OF DECORUM: TWELVE YEARS TOGETHER AND THE MANAGER NEVER HAD A PROBLEM WITH HIM."
—TOM VERDUCCI, *THE YANKEE YEARS*, JOE TORRE AND TOM VERDUCCI, 2009

"From the start, it was clear that we had the same set of values. We had the same respect for the game. The only thing that was important to either one of us was winning, all the stuff that went into winning."

—Joe Torre, Yankees manager, February 17, 2014

"Derek was the kid Joe took under his wing. Joe loved the people who were somewhat perfect, who did the right things and said the right words. Derek was that kind of player."

—Jim Leyritz, Yankees catcher

"What you love about him is that he doesn't make excuses, he doesn't showboat, he doesn't do any of that stuff. He just goes out and plays."

—Joe Torre, *The Yankee Years*, Joe Torre and Tom Verducci, 2009

"Mr. T was like a father to me."

—D.J.

"Jeet believed in Joe's way, and everyone kind of felt, 'If Jeet believes in it, we have to believe in it.' Jeet and Joe were both positive thinkers, they didn't overreact to anything, and they didn't show their emotions until the very end. It was a perfect marriage."

—Mike Borzello, Yankees bullpen catcher

"I learned something from watching Mr. Torre for all these years. You always hear the phrase *you treat everyone the same*. But that's not correct. You treat everyone fairly."

—D.J., to Brian Williams, *NBC Evening News*, September 25, 2014

"He continues to push the right buttons. He's got a magic wand. You can't say enough about him as a manager. He's a player's manager. He lets you play. He doesn't get on you unless you make mental mistakes. He has a lot of confidence in everybody."

—D.J.

"There is a lot you can say about a team just by looking at their manager. Joe Torre happens to be the best in the majors. Everyone loves him and wants to do right by him. . . . Mr. Torre never panics, and he always stays positive. That's why the Yankees continue to play great, confident baseball, and why we continue to make it to the postseason. Mr. Torre is really calm during the year, but when we win the Series, he gets pretty emotional. He doesn't need to say much to us; we know how he feels."

—D.J., *Game Day*, 2001

"Derek played in an age when individual achievements received a lot of glory, but that's not how he was raised by his parents, and that's not what he played for. Winning and exemplifying that Yankees pride transcend everything else. Derek made immeasurable contributions to a dynasty, and he did it all with unfailing class and leadership. Derek Jeter is the ultimate team player and an even more extraordinary person."

—Joe Torre, Yankees manager from 1996 to 2007, February 11, 2014

"DEREK JETER IS THE BEST PLAYER I'VE EVER MANAGED. I DON'T THINK THERE'S ANY QUESTION. IT'S MORE THAN JUST HIS ABILITY. IT'S HIS DEDICATION TO THE CITY OF NEW YORK, THE NEW YORK YANKEES. . . . I MAY BE BIASED, BUT HE'S AS GOOD AS ANY PLAYER I'VE EVER BEEN AROUND."

—JOE TORRE, YANKEES MANAGER FROM 1996 TO 2007

"He is a friend for life, and the relationship we have shared has helped shape me in ways that transcend the game of baseball. His class, dignity, and the way he respected those around him—from ballplayers to batboys—are all qualities that are easy to admire, but difficult to duplicate. I have known Mr. Torre for a good majority of my adult life, and there has been no bigger influence on my professional development. It was a privilege to play for him in the field, and an honor to learn from him off the field."

—D.J., in a statement released by the Yankees organization after Torre turned down a one-year contract from the team and concluded a 12-year run as manager that would get him into the Hall of Fame

"I always treasured the relationship and always will."

—Joe Torre, Yankees manager from 1996 to 2007

"Through the years in baseball, I've seen a lot of guys change with success. In Jeter's case, he hasn't changed one iota in the five years he's been in New York. This is [a] special guy, and it's a credit to his upbringing that all the success, money, and adulation he's gotten as a celebrity ballplayer in New York never went to his head."

—Don Zimmer, Yankees bench coach, *Zim: A Baseball Life*, 2001

"Even a guy like Derek, it's going to be hard for him to break that [$252 million barrier] because he just doesn't do the power numbers. And defensively, he doesn't do all those things. So he might not break the 252. He might get 180. I don't know what he's going to get. One-fifty? I'm not sure."

—Alex Rodriguez, Texas shortstop, explaining why his friend won't be able to negotiate a better contract than Rodriguez's major league record-high $252 million for 10 years, to Dan Patrick, ESPN Radio, December 2000

"A-Rod [Alex Rodriguez] had violated an unwritten law of the big league land. Ballplayers rarely attack and marginalize each other in the middle of high-stakes contract negotiations, especially when those ballplayers are supposed to be dear friends."

—Ian O'Connor, *The Captain*, 2011

"A-Rod's statements lend further credence to the suspicion he is green not with money but with envy. He appears to be jealous of Jeter's address and his jewelry. Jeter, by playing in New York and winning four championships in his first five seasons, has a higher profile than Rodriguez."

—Tom Keegan, *New York Post*, December 21, 2000

"He's a great player with four World Series rings and a World Series MVP. He has things everybody dreams of. I think everybody is jealous of a winner."

—Tino Martinez, Yankees first baseman, supporting Jeter
after Rodriguez's unflattering statements

"You'd have to ask him."

—D.J., responding to a reporter who asked if Rodriguez
is jealous of him, March 3, 2001

"Maybe after I've talked to him, I could comment on it, but it doesn't bother me."

—D.J., WFAN, December 20, 2000

"I'm not trying to beat Alex's [highest-salary] record anyway. The only record I'm concerned with is Yogi's record, and that's the [10] championships."

—D.J.

"After Yankees president Randy Levine completed talks on a 10-year deal [worth $189 million] with Derek Jeter's agent, Casey Close, Steinbrenner waited a week before formally approving the contract. In the interim, he met with Jeter and reminded the shortstop of the responsibilities inherent in the longest deal in club history. . . . Jeter had served the organization well, earned a contract that fell within market value, waited through negotiations, and then Steinbrenner treated him like a teenager who had asked for the keys to the family car. With the completion of the deal in sight, it seemed to others that Steinbrenner wanted to show off his own power to Jeter and give him a last lecture."

—**Buster Olney,** *The Last Night of the Yankee Dynasty,* **2004**

"Derek Jeter embodies everything the Yankees are about."

—**George Steinbrenner, Yankees owner, after making the Yankees'
new contract with Jeter official**

"This is the only organization I've played for, and the only one I want to play for. Hopefully I'll be with the Yankees for my entire career, and this is a giant step toward that."

—**D.J., about his new contract**

JETER AND RODRIGUEZ: A TENUOUS FRIENDSHIP

"Alex and I met [when he was a senior] in high school. We talked on the phone [in 1993] about whether to go to college or go with teams. Then we got really close during the rookie-development program that Major League Baseball runs. In the off-season, we play in the MTV Rock 'n' Jock softball game. We talk all the time."

—**D.J., about his close relationship with Seattle shortstop Alex Rodriguez
when they were young ballplayers,** *Seventeen,* **1999**

"The first thing when I wake up in the morning, I check the box score to see how Derek Jeter did."

—**Alex Rodriguez,** *Inside Sports,* **August 1997**

"On the field, there's a rivalry between New York and Seattle, but I'm Alex's biggest fan. Like he says, every morning I check the stats, watch him on TV. Off the field we're friends. We hang out, do whatever we want. People say, 'How are you that close if you compete all the time?' But off the field, we're just like regular people."

—**D.J.,** *Inside Sports,* **August 1997**

"Playing against Derek makes me work that much harder. Hell, there's nothing I like better between the lines than kicking his butt."

—**Alex Rodriguez, Mariners shortstop, on his friendly rivalry with his best friend on the Yankees**

"I brag on him so much that my teammates are sick of me talking about him."

—**D.J., to Tom Verducci,** *Sports Illustrated*

"He's like me. He wants to have a good time and be a good person. . . . It's like we're looking in the mirror."

—**Alex Rodriguez**

"Jeter slept at Rodriguez's house when the Yankees were in Seattle, and Rodriguez would find a bunk in Jeter's apartment when the Mariners traveled to the Bronx. Rarely have two higher-profile opponents been as close."

—**Jack Curry,** *New York Times,* **February 16, 2004**

"At this point, Derek has become like my brother,"

—**Alex Rodriguez, Mariners shortstop**

"A rift developed in spring training 2001 with the publication of a story in *Esquire* magazine by Scott Raab about [agent Scott] Boras and Rodriguez [by then a Texas Ranger]. In the piece, Rodriguez went out of his way to take shots at Jeter. Indeed, it was Rodriguez who brought Jeter into his conversation with the writer, doing so without any polish whatsoever."

—Tom Verducci, *The Yankee Years*, Joe Torre and Tom Verducci, 2009

"JETER'S BEEN BLESSED WITH GREAT TALENT AROUND HIM. HE'S NEVER HAD TO LEAD. HE CAN JUST GO AND PLAY AND HAVE FUN. AND HE HITS SECOND—THAT'S TOTALLY DIFFERENT THAN THIRD OR FOURTH IN THE LINEUP. YOU GO INTO NEW YORK, YOU WANNA STOP BERNIE [WILLIAMS] AND [PAUL] O'NEILL. YOU NEVER SAY, 'DON'T LET DEREK BEAT YOU.' HE'S NEVER YOUR CONCERN."
—ALEX RODRIGUEZ, TEXAS RANGERS SHORTSTOP, SAYING CRITICAL WORDS ABOUT JETER'S TALENTS THAT WOULD FOREVER DAMAGE THEIR RELATIONSHIP, TO SCOTT RAAB, *ESQUIRE*, APRIL 2001

"It was [Rodriguez's agent Scott] Boras who added fuel to the fire that Jeter never had to carry a ball club. Alex was asserting these things, but Boras was playing the role of reinforcing this idea that Alex was at a totally different level than Derek Jeter."

—Scott Raab, writer who interviewed Rodriguez for the
April 2001 issue of *Esquire*

"You go into a series against the Yankees with a plan to pitch to Jeter, and you might get him out in that first game pitching to that hole you think you've seen. But by the last game of the series, that hole isn't there anymore because he will make the adjustments."

—Brad Ausmus, Tigers catcher, contradicting Alex Rodriguez's assertion
that opposing teams didn't worry about Jeter's bat

"You can throw [Jeter] inside as much as you want, and he can still fist the ball off. You can throw the ball low and away, and he can hit with power the other way. We have pitchers' meetings, and he's one of those guys where you just stay on the subject for a while. What do you do?"

**—Jesse Orosco, Baltimore Orioles left-handed reliever, contradicting
Alex Rodriguez's contention that teams didn't prepare to face Jeter**

"Sure, it hurts anytime someone you're close to says something you question. But Alex was coming from Seattle and had signed this megadeal. He was on a platform that maybe he'd never been on before. I think he found himself having to defend the reason he got paid so much. Or he was asked, 'If you get this, what's Derek going to get?' So he was comparing us, which I told him shouldn't even be an issue. I said, 'You didn't pay yourself. You shouldn't have to answer that question. Let them ask the owner.' I think he was saying things that maybe other people had said to him."

—D.J., to Diane K. Shah, *Playboy*, June 2004

"[Alex] called so we had an opportunity to talk. It's a situation where he clarified what he said and what his intentions were. That's about it. I gave him the benefit of the doubt."

—D.J., March 3, 2001

"I don't anticipate him saying anything else. I've known him for a long time. We'll be friends after this."

—D.J., March 3, 2001

"We weren't as close as we had been. We were still friends."

—D.J., to Diane K. Shah, *Playboy*, June 2004

"How could I ever dog Derek Jeter? It's impossible. There is nothing to knock. He's a great defensive player. He's a great offensive player. He's one of the top three players in the game, for the greatest team of my era."

—Alex Rodriguez, Texas shortstop, saying his words in *Esquire* were misinterpreted

"Of course, Rodriguez would say the quotes were taken out of context . . . but from that day on, Alex Rodriguez and Derek Jeter would always be compared. And, A-Rod—though he was statistically the better player—would suffer in the comparisons."

—Joe Posanski, NBCSports.com, February 12, 2013

"Yankees: Shortstop Derek Jeter was cleared Sunday to resume working out after his ailing right shoulder was examined by a team doctor."

—*Chicago Tribune*, about Jeter, whose shoulder inflammation in spring training and strained right quad would force him to miss his only Opening Day until 2013 and contribute to a rough start in 2001, March 5, 2011

"Derek Jeter is off the disabled list, and Chuck Knoblauch is not throwing the ball away. All is right with the world."

—Sarah Jessica Parker, actress and New York baseball fan, about Jeter's return to the Yankees and his rejoining his troubled double-play partner Knoblauch, who had developed a mental block that prevented him from making accurate throws to first base

"It's a good day today."

—D.J., who informed Yankees manager Joe Torre, a prostate cancer survivor, that doctors had declared his sister, Sharlee, was cancer-free, May 11, 2001

"While she was going through [six months of chemotherapy], I didn't feel the need to let everyone know. It was more difficult for her. I don't want to make it out to be it was difficult for me."

—D.J., about his sister's often painful battle with
Hodgkin's disease, to reporters, May 12, 2001

"Yesterday morning, Jeter discussed the situation at length with reporters for the first time, calling his sister's situation 'a success story.' Out on the field later, he made sure it was another good day. Jeter's three-run homer with two outs in the eighth inning gave the Yankees an 8–5 victory over Baltimore at the Stadium."

—Michael Morrissey, *New York Post*, May 13, 2001

"He's an incredible talent. I'm a lifetime Baltimore Orioles fan, so he's like my worst nightmare."

—Ed Norton, actor

"Yogi [Berra] played well in 1959. . . . His season's highlight probably came on August 3 in the second All-Star game, when he hit a home run off Don Drysdale. . . . Oddly enough, this would be the last home run by a Yankee in an All-Star game until 41 years later when Derek Jeter hit one in the 2001 game."

—Allen Barra, *Yogi Berra: Eternal Yankee*, 2009

"[Yogi Berra] never tired of reminding Derek Jeter of his team's failure to win the 1997 World Series. . . . When he wasn't chiding Jeter about collective achievements, he might rag on him about a personal failure. Once he stopped by to tell him that he looked terrible striking out on a high 3–2 pitch the night before. 'Why did you swing at that?' Berra asked. 'Well, you swung at those pitches,' Jeter replied. Berra, the epitome of the bad-ball hitter, thought about that for a moment and snapped, 'Well, I hit those; you don't.'"

—Harvey Araton, *Driving Mr. Yogi*, 2012

"I turned on the TV, and I saw what everyone else saw. It was on every channel, so it didn't really make a difference what channel you had on. You watch to see what is happening, and then you go from there. I don't think it was any different for me than it was for anyone else."

—D.J., about first learning that terrorists flew two hijacked planes into the World Trade Center on September 11, 2001

"It was tough, but we had an opportunity to talk to a lot of people and make them smile, which is a good thing. It really makes it hit home even more, because though you realize how bad it is, you meet with all of the firemen, rescue workers, and volunteers, then go to the Armory and see the families grieving over the people they lost; it really hits you."

—D.J., who along with Bernie Williams, Chuck Knoblauch, and several coaches went with Joe Torre to visit the Jacob Javits Center in Manhattan, which was being used as an emergency staging area; St. Vincent's Hospital, where survivors (if there were any) were expected to be treated; and the New York Armory, September 15, 2001

"You meet people who just lost family members. What do you say?"

—D.J.

"Some things you keep to yourself."

—D.J., about personal conversations and experiences he had meeting people who had lost family members on 9/11

"IT WAS GREAT FOR THE FANS. . . . IT GAVE THEM SOMETHING TO CHEER FOR, EVEN IF IT WAS JUST A COUPLE OF HOURS EACH DAY."
—D.J., AFTER THE YANKEES PLAYED THEIR FIRST HOME GAME SINCE 9/11, SEPTEMBER 28, 2001

CLASSIC MOMENT:
OCTOBER 13, 2001, NETWORK ASSOCIATES COLISEUM, OAKLAND

"The Yankees are down, two games to none, in their best-of-five first-round playoff series against the Oakland A's. With New York clinging to a 1–0 lead in the seventh inning of Game 3 and A's designated hitter Jeremy Giambi on first base, Oakland's Terrence Long . . . ropes a shot into right field. By the time the ball rolls to the outfield wall, it's clear that Giambi is going to try to score. Yankees outfielder Shane Spencer unleashes a throw that sails over the heads of two cutoff men and bounces along the first-base line . . . where Jeter, in full sprint, scoops it up and laterals it to catcher Jorge Posada, who tags Giambi out."

—Seth Mnookin *GQ,* April 2011

"Everyone knows that Giambi is gonna score, and there is nothing to be done— everyone except the artist at shortstop, Derek Jeter."

—**Bernie Williams, Yankees outfielder,** *Rhythms of the Game***, 2011**

"I ignored Jeter's movement. It was like 'Where is he going?' I was so convinced that we had scored. You're thinking, 'There's no way Jeter's connecting these dots on this play to make it work.'"

—**Billy Beane, Oakland A's GM**

"I was supposed to be in that position. I'm the third cutoff man. I'm supposed to cut it off and redirect the throw."

—**D.J., expressing his much-argued-about contention that he didn't improvise but simply completed a relay play that the Yankees practiced**

"Jeter's intervention was instantly hailed as one of the great improvisational plays in postseason history, but he refused credit for his intuitive positioning. He said the idea of stationing the shortstop near the first-base line on balls hit to deep right field was Don Zimmer's."

—Harvey Araton, *Driving Mr. Yogi*, 2012

"To me, it's not important whether the Yankees practice that play or not. The fact of the matter is [Jeter's] good enough to make that play. You can practice that play until you're blue in the face; he's probably the only guy who makes that play. He sees the field better than anyone."

—Terry Francona, major league manager and ESPN analyst, February 2012

"My job, basically, is to read the play. You practice positioning in spring training; you don't work on backhand flips."

—D.J.

"It had to be in one motion. I didn't have time to set up, plant, and throw. I just got it on one hop, and it was more of a reaction thing. It wasn't like I thought it through."

—D.J.

"That son of a bitch . . . knew it would tail back in. He threw it so all Posada had to do was catch and tag."

—Ron Washington, A's third base coach

"Jeremy Giambi is out. Our 1–0 lead is intact. Derek Jeter pumps his fist. Mussina pumps his fist. I feel like running out of the bullpen and pumping my fist. Half the dugout, it seems, is charging out on the field, a spontaneous burst of emotion for a player who never stops thinking or hustling. It's the greatest instinctive play I have ever seen."

—Mariano Rivera, Yankees reliever, *The Closer*, 2014

"We didn't want to admit it, but Jeter's play was pretty amazing. You watch it, and you say to yourself, *What just happened?* Of course, we all wanted Jeremy to slide, but I'm not sure it would have made any difference. What was Jeter doing on the first base line intercepting that ball? I don't know. How did he make a backhand flip with enough accuracy to get Jeremy? I don't know. Jeter is the one guy who amazes me. He's always in the right place at the right time, and you can't teach that. Ordinarily, his running over like that would have been a huge waste of time and energy, but that play was a momentum shifter and game saver. I hate to think it, but that play may have unhinged us."

—**Johnny Damon, A's outfielder,** *Idiot*, **2005**

"The Oakland players are aghast, speechless. The crowd is still trying to process what just happened. The announcers are trying to comprehend it, too, and multiple replays are shown. . . . Jeter's play on that October day was nothing short of a masterwork of art."

—**Bernie Williams, Jeter's teammate,** *Rhythms of the Game*, **2011**

"What was he even doing in that spot?"

—**Johnny Damon, A's outfielder**

"He had no business there whatsoever!"

—**Terrence Long, A's outfielder**

"I don't have a clue as to how or why he was even involved in that play. Shows what kind of player he is."

—**Art Howe, A's manager**

"You ever have a death in the family?"

—**Art Howe, A's manager, on what it was like in the clubhouse
after losing Game 3**

"We definitely win the series if Jeter doesn't make that flip play."

—J.P. Ricciardi, Oakland's director of player personnel

"YOU'RE NEVER GOING TO SEE THAT PLAY EVER AGAIN."
—LUIS SOJO, YANKEES INFIELDER

D.J. DATA: Despite making the errant throw over two cutoff men that Jeter had to retrieve while crossing the first baseline before flipping the ball to Posada to tag out Jeremy Giambi, Shane Spencer was, like Jeter, credited with an assist on the play.

"Got beer spilled on me. Nobody caught me. I think people were just reaching for their drinks."

—D.J., about going over the rail to catch a foul ball hit by Terrence Long in the eighth inning in the Yankees' 5–3 win over Oakland to clinch the Division Series 3 games to 2, quoted by Ian O'Connor, *The Captain*, 2011

"1–1 to Terrence Long. Popped up, third base side, Brosius and Jeter both over. Jeter. . . . Did he get it? Did he get it? Did he get it? He got it! He got it! They throw to second; the runner tags, and he's safe. Or are they saying he didn't get it? Now they're appealing; the first base umpire didn't know if Jeter caught it, had to ask the second base umpire, and they said he caught it."

—Thom Brennaman, broadcaster, Fox, October 15, 2001

"Just as he caught the ball, Jeter smashed into the padded concrete wall with his hip and flipped into the stands, landing hard. The Yankees won the game, but Jeter, just like that stopped hitting. He was 2-for-17 against the Mariners [in the ALCS] and then 4-for-27 against the Diamondbacks [in the World Series], making him a .136 hitter after falling hard into the stands. If he was hurt, Jeter, of course, told no one, not even Torre."

—Tom Verducci, *The Yankee Years*, Joe Torre and Tom Verducci, 2009

"Derek is very comparable to [Joe DiMaggio] in that they both have that sixth sense. They both play the game so naturally and beautifully. Never out of place and always heading for the right spot. Joe never made a mistake, and Jeter doesn't, either. I mean, the kid has a gift. Joe's gift."

—Phil Rizzuto, Yankees Hall of Fame shortstop and broadcaster, quoted by Ian O'Connor, *The Captain*, 2011

"I've never seen an athlete dominate any sport—football, basketball, or baseball—the way he did in this playoff series."

—George Steinbrenner tearfully speaking to a reporter about Jeter, who hit .444 and made two remarkable fielding plays after the Yankees defeated the A's in the 2001 ALDS

"Seven weeks after 9/11, it would send a powerful signal for the president to show up at Yankee Stadium. I hoped my visit would help lift the spirits of New Yorkers. We flew to New York on Air Force One and choppered into a field next to the ballpark. I went to the batting cage to loosen up my arm. A Secret Service agent strapped a bulletproof vest to my chest. After a few warmup pitches, the great Yankees shortstop Derek Jeter dropped in to take some swings. We talked a little. Then, he asked, 'Hey, President, are you going to throw from the mound or from in front of it?' I asked what he thought. 'Throw from the mound,' Derek said. 'Or else they'll boo you.' I agreed to do it."

—George W. Bush, United States President in 2001, about throwing out the ceremonial first pitch prior to Game 3 at Yankee Stadium of the 2001 World Series, *Decision Points*, 2010

"DON'T BOUNCE IT. THEY'LL BOO YOU."
—D.J., GIVING ADDITIONAL ADVICE TO PRESIDENT GEORGE W. BUSH BEFORE HE THREW A PERFECT STRIKE PRIOR TO THE YANKEES' 2–1 VICTORY OVER ARIZONA IN GAME 3 AND GOT A HUGE OVATION FROM THE EMOTIONAL CROWD AT YANKEE STADIUM, OCTOBER 30, 2001

"It's over—this game is over this inning."

—D.J., confidently to teammate Tino Martinez prior to the 10th inning of Game 4 of the 2001 World Series, in which Jeter was due up third, October 31, 2001

"Mr. T's contract was up. It expired on October 31. He used to hold my bat. And I told him when I got my bat from him, 'This is the last time I have to listen to you because after midnight, you're no longer employed by the Yankees.'"

—D.J., about coming to bat with two outs in the 10th inning as the clock was about to strike 12

"And up came Jeter. He fouled off pitch after pitch [thrown by sidearming Arizona's Byung-Hyun Kim], running the count to 3–2. In the stands, a fan held a sign up. 'Mr. November.' The clock had just run past midnight, turning Halloween to November 1; the first time major league baseball had been played in November. Jeter lived for these moments. This stage. He'd own it."

—Dave Buscema, *Game of My Life: 20 Stories of Yankees Baseball,* 2004

"Three-two pitch swung on and drilled to right field. Going back Sanders, on the track . . . at the wall. . . . See ya! See ya! See ya! A home run by Derek Jeter."

—Michael Kay, Yankees broadcaster, on Jeter's 10th-inning home run off Arizona's Byung-Hyun Kim to win Game 4 of the 2001 World Series 4–3, November 1, 2001

"Jeter raced around the bases, his arm forever shooting into the night in victory as he rounded first. He came around third, took a few steps home, then one . . . two . . . and a leap onto home plate, grinning like a little kid as he disappeared under a pounding, pinstriped wall of teammates. Yankees 4, Diamondbacks 3."

—**Dave Buscema,** *Game of My Life: 20 Stories of Yankees Baseball,* **2004**

"This was the first time I faced [Byung-Hyun] Kim. It takes a while to pick up his release point. I had seen a lot of pitches. To be honest with you, I was just trying to get on base. He left a slider over the plate. The only thing that could have made it better was if it was Game 7. Everyone dreams of playing in a World Series, of hitting a home run in a World Series. A walk-off home run in a World Series? It doesn't get any better, especially in New York, and after 9/11."

—**D.J., who had earned the nickname Mr. November**

"I've never hit a walk-off home run. Not even in Little League."

—**D.J.**

"I don't know if the attacks added to the desire and need for us to win for [our sakes]. . . . We felt as though we were playing for more than the Yankee organization. We felt as though we were playing for all New Yorkers."

—**D.J., ESPNNewYork.com, October 28, 2010**

"I remember [that Curt Schilling and I nodded at each other before my first at-bat in Game 7]. It was fun. I always look at it as fun. Schilling was as big a big game pitcher as there was. There were others, but you can't say there was anybody bigger than him since I was playing. So Game 7 of the World Series and you're facing the best? It's fun."

—**D.J., to Tom Verducci,** *Sports Illustrated,* **November 25, 2009**

GRACE UNDER PRESSURE

"You're playing a game, whether it's Little League or Game 7 of the World Series. It's impossible to do well unless you're having a good time. People talk about pressure. Yeah, there's pressure, but I just look at it as fun."

—D.J., to Tom Verducci, *Sports Illustrated*, November 25, 2009

"See, Jeter *wants* to be in the spot that has you quivering even from the comfort of your couch. The spot that forces you into a paralyzed state, save the incessant nervous tapping of your leg against the floor, your heart unable to take the tight score with your team's season on the line."

—Dave Buscema, *Game of My Life: 20 Stories of Yankees Baseball*, 2004

"Jeter, as far as handling the pressure, is the best I've ever seen."

—Joe Torre, Yankees manager, *The Yankee Years*, Joe Torre and Tom Verducci, 2009

"I think pressure is what you put on yourself. Nobody else can put pressure on you—no matter what the media says."

—D.J., *New York* magazine, April 7, 1997

"The hubris was a necessity, really, to sustain his performance in the face of such extraordinary expectation and pressure."

—Buster Olney, *The Last Night of the Yankee Dynasty*, 2004

"I'm stressed out just watching [Jeter take a wild swing in a clutch situation in a postseason game], and he's laughing, and I'm thinking . . . 'How can any human being be that relaxed in that spot?'"

—John Flaherty, Yankees catcher

"Other players would be fully focused, almost in a trance, and he would be making jokes. His behavior was possible, some teammates thought, only because Jeter was absolutely certain that the Yankees would find a way to win, and if the pivotal opportunity fell into his hands, he would succeed."

—Buster Olney, *The Last Night of the Yankee Dynasty*, 2004

"Big games and big situations don't scare him."

—Joe Torre, Yankees manager

"Anybody asks me who you want up at the plate, in all the years I've played, he's the man. He loves it. You can see it in his eyes. He embraces the situation."

—Andy Pettitte, Yankees pitcher, who Jeter said was a gamer and was relied on more than any other starter

"Defensively, he's the guy you want the ball hit to when it's a pressure situation, last out of a game, you know he's going to catch it and make a good throw to first base."

—Cal Ripken Jr., Hall of Fame Orioles shortstop

"I get nervous watching my teammates. When I'm on the bench and someone's in a big spot, I'm nervous. But I enjoy being in those situations. It doesn't mean I'm going to be successful. I've failed plenty more times than I've been successful, but I'm not afraid of failing so I just look forward to those big moments."

—D.J., to Michael Kay, *CenterStage*, December 2003

"It was amazing how relaxed he was. He could be 0-for-4 that day, but if he needed a hit that fifth time, with men on base and the game on the line, he got it."

—Tino Martinez, Yankees first baseman

"In big games, the action slows down for him where it speeds up for others."

—Reggie Jackson, Yankees Hall of Famer

"The bigger the situation, the more the game speeds up. That's all mental. It messes people up. You think, 'I've got to do this. I've got to do that.' When in reality, all you have to do is the same thing you've always been doing. Slow it down. Realize you've been . . . successful in this situation before. Be calm. The more you can do that, the more pressure you take off yourself, and the easier it is to perform."

—D.J.

"I think that's where people get in trouble, when they start complicating things. It's really not that complicated. The more complicated you make it, the more difficult it is on you. You're playing a game where you fail more than you succeed. You've got to try to keep it as simple as possible."

—D.J.

"He's a player who doesn't seem scared to succeed, and he really wants to find how high he can take his game. . . . Not being afraid of success is one attribute that's the difference between a star and superstar."

—Roger Clemens, Yankees pitcher, quoted by John Delcos, *Derek Jeter: A Yankee for the New Millennium,* 2000

"New York is a place that can swallow you up if you're not able to handle the pressure of success—and of failure. [Derek] handles it with class and dignity."

—Darryl Strawberry, Yankees outfielder, on avoiding the pitfalls that plagued him as a young player

"I admire the fact that he can control his emotions in an emotional setting."

—Cal Ripken Jr., Hall of Fame Orioles shortstop

"I would take the chance to be the hero or the goat in every game I play for the rest of my life. Those moments are what make playing sports so exhilarating. . . . I love being in those situations with the Yankees, those tense moments during the regular season as we chase another title. To me, that's fun."

—D.J., *Game Day,* 2001

"I like the thrill of competition. I love dangling off that cliff, not knowing whether I'm going to fail or succeed."

—D.J., *The Life You Imagine*, 2000

"He's amazing; he's calm in situations when other players are nervous."

—Jason Giambi, Yankees first baseman

"He exuded this confidence that when he was in a big spot he was going to do something."

—John Flaherty, Yankees broadcaster and former catcher

"[Derek's] the best clutch player in baseball. It's tough to describe it to people that don't see him all the time because the stats aren't there. But if you see the day-in, day-out performances, he's the best."

—Tino Martinez, Yankees first baseman, April 6, 2005

"OF ALL THE PLAYERS I PLAYED WITH, ALL THE PLAYERS I MANAGED OR COACHED, HE'D BE THE GUY I'D WANT UP THERE IN THE NINTH INNING OF AN IMPORTANT GAME."
—LARRY BOWA, YANKEES COACH IN 2006–07, APRIL 5, 2009

"Every time Jeter had something to do with the outcome of a game, it made me nervous."

—Terry Francona, manager of the Red Sox (2004–11) and Indians (2013–present)

"The electricity in [Bank One Ballpark] is off the charts as [Arizona's Luis] Gonzalez fouls off [Mariano Rivera's] first pitch [with the bases loaded and the score tied with one out in the bottom of the ninth inning in Game 7]. The next pitch is a classic Rivera cutter, veering in on [the left-handed batter's] hands. He swings, cracking the bat, just below the trademark. 'I got jammed, but I knew I didn't have to hit it hard. I knew I just had to put the ball in play.' The ball floats toward shortstop, spinning in the air, like a cue shot and the backpedalling Jeter, who was playing in to cut off the run at the plate. Jeter races back and lunges in vain as the ball floats over him and lands on the lip of the outfield grass. [Jay] Bell—the first free agent signed in Diamondbacks history—races across the plate with the Series-winning run as absolute bedlam breaks loose on the field and in the stands."

—Rick Weinberg, ESPN.com

"Jeter sat on the bench, staring out onto the field—believing he should watch the other team celebrate and remember how he felt about losing."

—Buster Olney, about Jeter's reaction after losing Game 7 of the 2001 World Series, 3–2, *The Last Night of the Yankee Dynasty*, 2004

"Losing never entered our minds. Not for a second."

—D.J., who had trouble believing the Yankees had lost in a World Series to what he considered an inferior team, having won the previous four Series in which they'd played, November 4, 2001

"I don't want to hear people say, 'We had a successful season; we made it to the World Series.' It doesn't mean a thing unless you win. You don't play to get to the World Series. You play to win a World Series."

—D.J., whose Yankees teams would reach the World Series only twice more after being defeated by Arizona in 2001, losing in 2003 and winning in 2009

"You didn't want to say it was the end of the book, but it was the end of a chapter."

—D.J., after the three-time defending Yankees lost the 2001 World Series to Arizona in seven games

"BEFORE LOSING IN GAME 7 OF THE 2001 WORLD SERIES, THE YANKEES HAD WON 14 OF THEIR FIRST 15 POSTSEASON SERIES IN DEREK JETER'S CAREER."
—TOM ROBINSON, *DEREK JETER: CAPTAIN ON AND OFF THE FIELD*, 2006

"Of all the shortstops today, New Yorkers are fortunate to see Derek Jeter play every day. Other guys might hit more home runs, but he keeps winning every year. I always said he has a distorted view of the world."

—Ozzie Smith, newly elected Hall of Fame shortstop for the Padres and Cardinals, anointing Jeter as the major's best current shortstop, quoted by Bill Madden, New York *Daily News*, January 10, 2002

"I have no comment. There is no need to fuel the fire."

—D.J., after Yankees outfielder Ruben Rivera, Mariano Rivera's cousin and Jeter's friend since their days together in the minors, confessed he had stolen Jeter's glove with the intention of selling it to a memorabilia dealer during spring training in 2002

"Even though this '02 team is hands-down more focused and talented than any I've ever seen . . . by *no* means are we perfect. Case in point: Derek Jeter, who's right now standing in his locker singing at the top of his lungs. Headphones in place, he bobs to a thumping hip-hop beat, sounding an awful lot like Jay Z . . . if Jay Z was tone-deaf. . . . Derek may be an amazing shortstop, but he's also an amazingly bad singer."

—David Wells, *Perfect I'm Not*, 2003

"Sports today is very much about athletes 'giving back,' and Derek Jeter epitomizes this with the life he is leading."

—John Rawlings, senior VP and editorial director of the *Sporting News*, announcing that Jeter had been selected as its 2002 No. 1 Good Guy in Pro Sports, primarily for his work with his Turn 2 foundation

"I would love to win the Gold Glove. . . . People say, 'Well, you had one year when you only made nine errors.' But you don't make errors on plays if you don't get to the ball. I think this year, I have a lot more range."

—D.J., who had 10 errors through August 2, 2002, after doing more stretching and agility drills during the off-season, August 3, 2002

"He's always been really good. The most impressive part of his defensive game is he has a very accurate arm and very good feet; he's very fleet-footed. He has a nose for the baseball, and that's a gift you can't teach. He's always had phenomenal range, and he's always trying to be at the top of his game."

—Alex Rodriguez, Texas shortstop, quoted by Tyler Kepner, *New York Times*, August 4, 2002

"New York 10, Texas 3—[Texas Rangers shortstop] Alex Rodriguez hit his major league-leading 46th home run on an eephus pitch from Orlando Hernández (7–3), but everything else went the Yankees' way at New York. Alfonso Soriano hit his 31st homer, setting a team record for second basemen, and drove in three runs. Jason Giambi reached 100 runs batted in, Derek Jeter made a headfirst slide home to score his 100th run, and Bernie Williams had three more singles, extending his hitting streak to 17 games."

—*Associated Press*, failing to mention that Jeter's successful slide on August 26, 2002, made him just the third player in major league history to score 100 runs in his first seven seasons, joining Earle Combs of the Yankees (1925–32) and Ted Williams of the Red Sox (1939–49)

"It just shows it's tough to do. Not bad [company] at all. Of course, I'd like to hit 50 home runs and drive in 200 runs, but my job hitting second is to move guys over, get on base, steal bases, and score runs. It just says I've been consistent in doing that."

—D.J., after tying the record of scoring 100 runs in his first seven seasons, August 26, 2002

"The Angels were a mere four outs away from a 5–4 win when the hero(es) came to the rescue. Angels reliever Ben Weber replaced starter Jarrod Washburn to start the eighth and got the first two batters before walking both Alfonso Soriano and Derek Jeter. In came [Scott] Schoeneweis, who gave up a two-out, game-tying single to Jason Giambi. Then [Brendan] Donnelly surrendered the biggest of the Yankees' four home runs, a three-run blast by Bernie Williams that sent the Angels into the big city muttering to themselves. 'It was a great feeling,' Williams said. 'Everything happened so quick at that moment. I don't think I remember running the bases. I remember shaking Derek's (Jeter) and Giambi's hands.' Washburn gave up four runs and six hits through seven innings. All four runs scored on home runs, one each by Jeter [in the first inning], Giambi, and Rondell White."

—**Chuck Richter, about the Yankees' 8–5 victory in Game 1 of the ALDS, their final victory of 2002, Angelswin.com**

"It's a different group. Some of us have [won sudden death games], the ones that have been here. But this is a new group, so we'll find out."

—**D.J., prior to a do-or-die Game 4 for the Yankees in the 2002 ALDS series**

"The play of the whole division series was Garret Anderson catching that ball [Jeter hit] down the left-field line, and . . . I don't know how that happened."

—**Joe Torre, Yankees manager, about Jeter's fly near the fence being caught by Anderson with men on second and third and no outs in the fifth inning of Game 4, preventing a big inning by the Yankees in what would be a 9–5 ALDS-clinching victory by the Angels**

"Jeter played today with a stressed right arm, and he took a hard foul off his leg, but he managed two singles to give him 101 career hits in the postseason. That is the most in major league history, accomplished, of course, in this age of triple-tier playoffs. But his .500 average was not enough."

—**George Vecsey, *New York Times*, October 6, 2002**

"No team has ever played better against us than that team has. . . . They did everything better than we did. . . . I don't see anyone beating them."

—D.J., about the victorious Anaheim Angels, who would defeat the Giants in the 2002 World Series

"What really caught everyone by surprise was Steinbrenner's criticism of Derek Jeter [for going out to a late-night birthday party]. By now Jeter was a virtual deity in New York, already acknowledged as right up there with Phil Rizzuto as the greatest shortstop in Yankees history, with four championship rings and a .317 average in seven seasons in the big leagues. Not only that [but] he'd just hit .500 (8 for 16 with two homers) in the losing Division Series to the Angels."

—Bill Madden, *Steinbrenner: The Last Lion of Baseball*, 2010

"As far as trying and being a warrior, I wouldn't put anyone ahead of him. But how much better would he be if he didn't have all his other activities? . . . When I read in the paper that he's out until 3 a.m. in New York City going to the birthday party, I won't lie. That doesn't sit well with me."

—George Steinbrenner, Yankees owner, sparking the only (and very short-lived) controversy over Jeter's behavior during his entire career, to Wayne Coffey, New York *Daily News*, December 29, 2002

"BY 2002, [JETER] HAD ALREADY DATED MORE BEAUTIFUL WOMEN THAN HUGH HEFNER COULD COUNT."

—IAN O'CONNOR, *THE CAPTAIN*, 2011

"Derek dated singer Mariah Carey in 1997–1998 . . . .They eventually split, with both blaming media attention as being the main cause. . . . Jeter and former Miss Universe Lara Dutta were an item in the early 2000s. . . . Jeter began dating singer and actress Joy Enriquez shortly after. . . . Alex Rodriguez introduced the two at the All-Star Game in July, 2001. . . . Jeter and actress model Jordana Brewster first appeared as a couple when they went out clubbing together for Derek's 28th birthday."

—Zimbio.com

BASEBALL'S MOST ELIGIBLE BACHELOR

"There were many crushes on Derek Jeter."

—Chris Oosterbaan, Jeter's creative writing and history teacher
at Kalamazoo Central High

"I was in love with the *Price Is Right* girls when I was young. All of them."

—D.J., to Brandon Steiner, Derek Jeter Day Steiner Sports event,
December 6, 2014

"I've been here 42 years, and I've never seen girls go fanatical about a ballplayer
like this."

—Kenneth Spinner, Yankee Stadium vendor

"Hanging out with him sucks because all the women flock to him."

—Chili Davis, Yankees outfielder

"Teenage girls shrieked each time his name was announced (a reaction that was
often teasingly reproduced in the Yankees' clubhouse)."

—Buster Olney, *The Last Night of the Yankee Dynasty*, 2004

"If the Yankees are the Beatles, Derek is the cute one."

—Charlie Steiner, Yankees broadcaster

"I was only 22 when I first came up, but I didn't have to go through what he goes
through. I didn't have all those girls screaming at me all the time. I wasn't as
good-looking as him."

—Yogi Berra, Yankees Hall of Famer

"What of those women who brought placards bearing their offers of marriage for Derek Jeter?"

—**Mark Kriegel, about female fans at the Yankees World Series victory parade in 1996, New York** *Daily News,* **October 30, 1996**

"I think that he's most popular with the ladies. Last ticker-tape parade, they were lined up and down Broadway, screaming and holding up signs: I WANT TO MARRY YOU, DEREK! What can you say? He's handsome, and he plays well. Everyone wants to be near him."

—**Jaswinder Singh, New York City cabdriver**

"I was the youngest one, and everyone else was pretty much married so I think they were stuck with me."

—**D.J., about why female fans were attracted to him, to Michael Kay,** *CenterStage,* **December 2003**

"He blushes when asked about the teenyboppers who worship him and scream his name when he's at bat, as if Brad Pitt himself were stepping up to the plate. At 6'3", 185 pounds, Jeter is long and lean, and his pale-green eyes change with the sunlight like a kaleidoscope. While Bernie Williams has bashful brown eyes that avert when a compliment is paid him, Jeter has James Dean eyes, narrow and cool—dangerous eyes for a shy bachelor in the big, bold city. Truth is, he can barely walk more than a few steps outside his apartment building [in New York City] before he's stopped, usually by a young woman."

—**Kelly Whiteside,** *Sports Illustrated Presents: The Champs! 1996 New York Yankees: A Special Collector's Edition,* **November 13, 1996**

"He's a hunk, and I don't even like that word. Women like guys who have a big presence but sort of play it down. It's very appealing."

—**Kim Basinger, actress**

"His name appeared regularly in the gossip pages of the *Post* and the *Daily News*, and when he dated pop singer Mariah Carey in 1998, one of the tabloids sent a writer to Tampa specifically to dig out information on the two."

—**Buster Olney,** *The Last Night of the Yankee Dynasty,* **2004**

"It was the longest night of my life."

—**Kristilee Wilcox, makeup artist after spending a night in jail because she failed to appear in court for a hearing on trespassing charges resulting from her running onto the field during an April 2002 game to hand Derek Jeter her phone number, 2002**

"My experience is that public figures don't really like to read poetry about themselves. Or poetry at all."

—**Elinor Nauen, New York poet, about why she didn't expect her baseball crush Derek Jeter to read the 600 stanzas she devoted to him in her anthology,** *So Late into the Night,* **October 6, 2011**

The '99 team was great—Williams, Cone,
And my fave, Derek Jeter, the shortstop,
Who not only hits to the awesome max
But has a grin sweet as a lollipop.
But it's also true that he doesn't drop
Balls, he makes every play with grace, he acts
Swell to fans, calls the manager Mister
Torre, not Joe, But his big plus? His keister.
Of course, Jeter's more than just a cute ass
For years he has been one of the premier
Players, improving all the time. A mass
Of stats proves this—good arm, hitting a "mere"
.349, flashy fielding, speed. Doodads
Like these do nicely ornament his rear.
Oh, there I go again about Butt-Man.
No, really, I'm a truly serious fan.

—**Elinor Nauen, poet, "Derek and the Boys," 1999**

"Why he'd make a great date: Kind of boy you'd bring home to Mom—and hope she doesn't steal him. Where he'd take you for a weekend getaway: To meet his mom."

—**Sherryl Connelly, New York** *Daily News*, **October 7, 1999**

"I wanted to tell Jeter that the reason I got into journalism was so that I could interview him in the locker room (which never happened)."

—**Jennifer Amato, managing editor with Greater Media Newspapers,** *Suburban*,
October 9, 2014

"You're so goddamned handsome."

—**Helen Beller, 103-year-old great-great-grandmother and big Yankees fan
who got to meet Derek Jeter on her first visit to Yankee Stadium
in 50 years, September 1, 2006**

"Jeter . . . puts the 'Oy!' in playboy: The green-eyed bachelor reportedly has dated Scarlett Johansson, Jessica Alba, Jessica Biel, Mariah Carey, and former Miss Teen USA . . . Vanessa Minnillo. And those are just the famous ones."

—**Nicole Blades,** *Women's Health*, **March 5, 2008**

"WILL YOU MARRY US"

—FOUR FEMALE FANS, EACH CARRYING ONE WORD OF THEIR MESSAGE

"Independent; intelligent; driven; happy."

—**D.J., describing his ideal mate, to Steve Serby,** *New York Post*, **July 8, 2007**

"He'd better pay more attention to the ball game than he does to women. . . . I want him completely devoted to the team during the season."

> —George Steinbrenner, Yankees owner, explaining his criticism of Jeter to Ed Bradley, *60 Minutes*, September 25, 2005

"He's told me that every year I've been here."

> —D.J., to Ed Bradley about Steinbrenner's reasons for criticizing him, *60 Minutes*, September 25, 2005

"If I'm paying a guy $16 million, I want him to listen."

> —George Steinbrenner, Yankees owner, February 2003

"No, I don't need any extra motivation. My motivation is to win."

> —D.J., when asked if Steinbrenner's criticism motivated him, to Ed Bradley, *60 Minutes*, September 25, 2005

"Does somebody push him to do it? He pushes himself."

> —Jorge Posada, Yankees catcher, confirming Jeter doesn't need anyone to motivate him, 2003

D.J. DATA: Early in 2003, to show the public that their relationship wasn't strained by Steinbrenner's criticism of Jeter not focusing on baseball 24/7, the two of them agreed to do two Visa commercials together, each set in Steinbrenner's office. In the first, an angry Steinbrenner asks Jeter how he can afford to go out every night. Jeter simply holds up a Visa card. Steinbrenner says, "Oh" and joins Jeter in a conga line at a club. Jeter would tell journalist Diane K. Shah for the June 2004 issue of *Playboy*, "I was the one who had to persuade him to do it. It wasn't easy. He did it a couple of times, and then he called it quits. Fortunately they got a good take."

(continued)

D.J. DATA (CONTINUED): The script for the second Visa commercial:

George Steinbrenner: "I hear you're out dancing, eating, and just carousing with your friends. Is it true that you're going out every night?"

Derek Jeter: "Absolutely not."

George Steinbrenner: "Good!"

They are interrupted by a beautiful young woman at the office door. She is dressed for a night on the town.

Young Woman: "Derek, we are running late . . . sorry."

"PARTY ON!"

> —Newspaper headline with the subheading "Jeter says he won't change lifestyle, despite rips from the Boss," New York *Daily News*, February 4, 2003

"If I was a fan and was looking at the 'Party On' article, then I may question it."

> —D.J., upset that fans might wrongly believe George Steinbrenner's public criticism and the misleading headlines to be true

"He's the boss, and he's entitled to his opinion, right or wrong, but what he said has been turned into me being this big party animal. He even made a reference to one birthday party. That's been turned into that I'm like Dennis Rodman now. I have no problems with people who criticize how I play. But it bothers me when people question my work ethic. That's when you're talking about my integrity. I take a lot of pride in how hard I work. I work extremely hard in the offseason. I work extremely hard during the season to win. My priorities are straight."

> —D.J., *Associated Press*, February 13, 2003

"It's one of the most foolish things I have come across. Derek can take the hits he deserves [about his play on the field]. But to attack his character is something that he isn't going to stand for, and I applaud him for that."

—**Casey Close, Jeter's agent, February 13, 2003**

"Don't get me wrong; it's not like I didn't go out and have fun. But there's been a lot of players that come to New York and get caught up in the lifestyle, and before you know it, they're sent away to another team because it affected their performance. My number one priority was on the field. I've had fun. It's not like I've never gone out; I've done a lot of things. But I've always kept sight of my number one priority."

—**D.J.,** *GQ,* **April 2011**

"THERE'S NEVER A WORRY ABOUT DEREK. EVEN THOUGH HE'S A YOUNG, FAMOUS PLAYER WHO LIVES IN MANHATTAN AND GOES OUT ON OCCASION, I'VE NEVER SEEN HIM OUT OF CONTROL. HE HANDLES HIMSELF SO WELL IN PUBLIC."
—DAVID CONE, FORMER YANKEES PITCHER

"People might be surprised to hear that I'm a real homebody. Fans may think I'm out partying every night, but that's not true. Other than going out to eat and to a movie, I am home 90 percent of the time."

—**D.J.,** *Game Day,* **2001**

"As a sports person, you're always saying there is no switch you can turn off and on. Derek Jeter, to me, had a switch where he could do everything all day and then hit a switch when it was time to play the game."

—**Paul O'Neill, Yankees broadcaster and former outfielder, 2014**

"Jeter's still a young man. He'll be a very good candidate for the captaincy. But he's got to show me and the other players that that's not the right way. He's got to make sure his undivided, unfettered attention is given to baseball. I just wish he'd eliminate some of the less important things, and he'd be right back to where he was in the past."

—George Steinbrenner, Yankees owner

"He is just trying to go out and be a 28-year-old kid, but I know one thing about Derek Jeter, and that is he comes ready to play, and his performance is very consistent. We would not be sitting here with the four rings without him."

—Joe Torre, Yankees manager, February 11, 2003

FIVE

The Captain

"Leadership: I don't think is something that's appointed; it's something that's earned."

—D.J., to Brian Williams, *NBC Nightly News,* September 25, 2014

"He always has been the leader of this team; he's always been the guy that we look to. He's our captain. If there's anybody who's going to be the captain of this team, it's Derek Jeter."

—Jorge Posada, Yankees catcher, February 17, 2003

"I know I can do a lot better than last year. The issue was focus, and that's what I met with [Mr. Steinbrenner] about."

—D.J., prior to the 2003 season

"I know the young man will come through for me this year."

—George Steinbrenner, Yankees owner, prior to the 2003 season

"Throughout his career, Jeter had stayed free of serious injury. [On Opening Night] in the 2003 season, Jeter took a headfirst slide into third base against Toronto. He dislocated his left shoulder [in a collision with Toronto Blue Jays catcher Ken Huckaby] . . . [and] was out of action for more than a month."

—Ken Rappoport, *Super Sports Star: Derek Jeter*, 2004

"OH, NO!"

—Newspaper headline, accompanied by a picture of Jeter lying on his back in pain and holding his dislocated left shoulder after Toronto catcher Ken Huckaby dove into him while making the tag at third base, New York *Daily News*, April 1, 2003

"This kid never shows any pain. He's played with pain I can't tell you how many times, and not let on. But this was something he couldn't hide."

—Joe Torre, Yankees manager

"I thought maybe I'd broken my collarbone, because I felt a pop. . . . I just wanted to get off the field, because you have 50,000 people looking at you. It took a while for them to get the golf cart out there. Then finally, we went inside, and they popped it back in."

—D.J., to Diane K. Shah, *Playboy*, June 2004

"He was hustling. I was hustling. There were a bunch of bad factors all rolling together at once. It would have made a big difference if I didn't have shin guards. I could have slid more conventionally."

—Ken Huckaby, Toronto catcher, on the tag play at third in which he injured Jeter

"He doesn't have my cell phone number."

—D.J., telling reporters Ken Huckaby hadn't called him to apologize as he claimed

"[Ken Huckaby] said he left me a message, and I didn't call him back. That never happened. I see all these [negative things being written about me]—Oh, I 'treated the poor *kid* [wrong]'—he's older than me! . . . I don't think he intended to jump on me and dislocate my shoulder. I don't think he purposely hurt me, but I think he was a little out of control."

—D.J., to Michael Kay, *CenterStage*, December 2003

"Taking a shower is kind of hard. You can only clean one side."

—D.J., about having his left arm in a sling, April 2, 2003

"That period of watching and waiting positively killed Jeter, who had never played fewer than 148 games. He was going stir-crazy inside the home he purchased in 2001, a $12.6 million apartment in the upper reaches of Trump World Tower."

—Ian O'Connor, *The Captain*, 2011

"I'm good enough."

—D.J., when he returned to action after six weeks, May 2003

"When I was managing in Trenton and he was on rehab and he came into my office because he knew me and said, 'Stump I'm here to help your club win.' I said, 'Derek you're here to get healthy and get you back to New York.' And he said, 'No, I'm here to help your club win.'"

—Stump Merrill, Trenton manager

"The Yankees officially named Derek Jeter captain on June 3, 2003, at a hastily arranged news conference on a road trip to Cincinnati, of all places. It was one of the last truly impulsive acts of the principal owner, George Steinbrenner, whose influence would soon begin to wane. But the Yankees were slumping at the time, and Steinbrenner felt the urge to formally recognize what everyone had known for years."

—Tyler Kepner, *Derek Jeter: From the Pages of the New York Times*, 2011

"I know the timing was strange, but I felt the team . . . needed a little spark."

—**George Steinbrenner, Yankees owner, who made Jeter captain while the team was on the road and without even informing manager Joe Torre, June 3, 2004**

"An honor is an honor regardless of where you get it."

—**D.J.**

"He stops being everyone's kid brother now, the perpetually respectful youngster who called his manager 'Mr. Torre' and his owner 'Mr. Steinbrenner' from the moment he showed up for good in the spring of 1996. Hard as it is to believe, Derek Jeter will turn 29 years old in another 22 days, an age when you really should be looked at less as a boy-band pin-up and more of a grown up. He has no choice now, of course. Because wearing the captain's 'C' for the New York Yankees is about as grown-up as it gets."

—**Mike Vaccaro, *New York Post*, June 4, 2003**

"I think that was the Boss's decision. I don't know how much input anybody else in the organization had."

—**D.J.**

JETER THE LEADER

"It's something I'll always treasure, and I'll do it to the best of my ability."

—**D.J., about George Steinbrenner making him the 11th captain in Yankees history**

"I'm not knocking any other team. But it's not like [Captain's] a title that's just thrown around lightly in this organization."

—**D.J., to Steve Serby, *New York Post*, May 6, 2004**

"When The Boss told me I was captain, he told me not to do anything differently than I'd done in the past. . . . Maybe there were certain personality traits that he saw in me."

—D.J., 2012

"He's the captain of that team for a reason. It's because he is the leader of that team."

—Jim Leyritz, Yankees catcher, to Peter May, *Boston Globe*, October 8, 2003

"I think there's a lot of guys in the clubhouse and throughout baseball who might not understand the job the same way I do, only because I grew up a Yankees fan, and I know exactly what that means. I know about Lou Gehrig. I know all about Thurman Munson. I saw first-hand what Don Mattingly was all about, and how important being captain was to him. Maybe if you didn't follow the Yankees as closely as I did, you wouldn't appreciate what being captain of the Yankees means."

—D.J., 2005

"When [Derek] first came here, the other players seemed to gravitate toward him. So I thought this day would eventually come."

—Joe Torre, *Associated Press*, June 3, 2003

"He's exceptional in so many ways. The one thing that strikes you—and it struck me—is that older guys look up to him. You don't ever see that."

—Joe Torre, Yankees manager, as told to Marty Noble, *Derek Jeter: A Yankee for the New Millennium,* 2000

"To Derek. Read and study. He was a great leader just as you are and will be a great leader. Hopefully of the men in pinstripes."

—George Steinbrenner's inscription in his book present to Derek Jeter after the Yankees won the 1999 World Series, Alan Axelrod's *Patton on Leadership: Strategic Lessons for Corporate Warfare*

"A lot of what's in [the book] are things [Mr. Steinbrenner] says: 'If you're going to lead, you've got to sit in the saddle.'. . . You've got to be willing to go out and do the things you ask of the people you're leading.'"

—**D.J., to Diane K. Shah,** *Playboy*, **June 2004**

"He represents all that is good about a leader. I'm a great believer in history, and I look at all the other leaders down through Yankee history, and Jeter is right there with them."

—**George Steinbrenner, Yankees owner**

"I think that people tend to watch some of the guys who have been here a long time. I think you lead by example, that's the biggest thing you can do."

—**D.J.**

"I think I'm a mixture of leading by example and leading by tweaking guys. . . . I think I know when to push the right buttons with different players because I watch my teammates, and I know how far guys will let you go. I'm always playful, never too personal."

—**D.J.,** *The Life You Imagine*, **2000**

"Derek leads by great example. I don't think there's a guy in the big leagues that works harder than him."

—**Jason Giambi, Yankees first baseman, 2003**

"If he could do it, then I could, too. If one guy does something the right way, that means I can, too."

—**Russell Martin, Yankees catcher in 2011 and 2012, quoted by David Waldstein,** *New York Times*, **March 1, 2015**

"If I had a problem with someone or had a problem with what someone said, I'll tell him. I don't think it has to be a bigger story than necessary by going through the media."

—**D.J., on his behind-the-scenes leadership**

"He makes everyone better because he exports his confidence that he will succeed to this teammates, that the team will prosper, find a way."

—Joel Sherman, *New York Post*, February 12, 2014

"Derek brings out a humanity in managers that makes everybody comfortable with them."

—Mike Borzello, Yankees bullpen coach

"Over the years, Torre would use people like [Joe] Girardi and [David] Cone to deliver messages to teammates on a peer-to-peer basis. No one filled the role more than Jeter, especially once he was named captain in 2003. It was never Jeter's nature to be loud and extroverted. But if it meant speaking up for the good of the team, especially under the advisement of Torre, Jeter was all in."

—Tom Verducci, *The Yankee Years*, Joe Torre and Tom Verducci, 2009

"I don't do things through the media, but that doesn't mean I don't say things or I'm not vocal. You guys maybe don't know about it. But you don't have to know about everything."

—D.J., telling reporters that some things he did as a captain were private

"A lot of the things that Derek does go unseen. He does talk to guys on the side, but he doesn't make it a media thing."

—Jason Giambi, Yankees first baseman, who Jeter supported, despite his antidrug stance, when he apologized after it was revealed he had taken steroids and human growth hormone

"If you didn't know he was captain, you'd know he was the captain. It's how he treats kids up from the minors. It's how he greets rivals who've been traded here, or signed here. It's how he finds a player who's been released, or traded, or sent down, talks to them, offers them counsel. Almost all of that not only absent from your eyes, but my eyes, too."

—Joe Girardi, Yankees manager

"I think everyone who comes in here knows it's Derek's team. Derek's the captain of the greatest franchise in sports."

—**Johnny Damon, Yankees outfielder, 2006**

"He's not intimidated by any situation, and to be a leader you have to be like that. . . . He's able to make light of a lot of situations, to keep guys relaxed."

—**Joe Girardi, Yankees manager**

"When he was leading you out there, you felt like you were on a better team than maybe you actually were."

—**John Flaherty, Yankees catcher**

"A lot of people say he's a quiet captain, and maybe he is, but he's a guy that leads by example, and that's the kind of guy I want to follow."

—**Brett Gardner, Yankees outfielder, September 23, 2008**

"I think I've always been the way I am now. I think maybe I've become a little bit more vocal as I've gotten older. Through time, you learn from experiences. I think I've learned to deal with people a little better over time. That in particular has developed a bit."

—**D.J., 2012**

"It was my first camp, 2011. My locker was close to his, and I was sitting there, first or second day of camp minding my own business, and he comes by and says, 'What's up, buddy?' And I was like, 'OH MY GOD! That's Derek Jeter!' There have been only a few times that I've ever been star-struck here, and that was definitely one of them. In 2012, when I was making my debut (in a relief appearance), he just comes up, puts his arm around me, and says, 'Listen, it's the same [as you've been pitching your whole life].' That's why he's as great as he is. He is such a great leader and captain for our team. It's the one thing we're definitely going to miss when he's gone."

—**David Phelps, Yankees pitcher, to Sweeny Murti,**
SportsNet New York, **September 22, 2014**

"I try to treat our young players the same way I hoped to be treated when I was a rookie."

—D.J., *The Life You Imagine*, 2000

"*Fortune* magazine may have taken Jeter-worship to a ridiculous new level by naming the Yankees shortstop the 11th greatest leader in the world. Not just the sports world, mind you, but the entire planet. Perhaps we can take comfort in the fact that Jeter failed to join the likes of Pope Francis (No. 1), Bill Clinton (No. 5), and the Dalai Lama (No. 9) in the top 10."

—Chuck Schilken, *Los Angeles Times*, March 27, 2014

"As far as I'm concerned . . . that captaincy should be retired with No. 2. . . . It's always ownership's call, but I'm not interested in giving the captaincy out anytime soon."

—Brian Cashman, Yankees GM, ESPN Radio, March 5, 2015

D.J. DATA: Jeter was the 11th team captain for the Yankees and served the longest: Hal Chase, 1912; Roger Peckinpaugh, 1914–21; Babe Ruth, 5/20/22–5/25/22; Everett Scott, 1922–25; Lou Gehrig, 1935–41; Thurman Munson, 1976–79; Graig Nettles, 1982–84; Willie Randolph, 1986–88; Ron Guidry, 1986–88; Don Mattingly, 1991–95; Derek Jeter, 2003–14

"Let me get 1,501 first before I think of 3,000. I've got seven years left on this [contract], so I'll be around for awhile."

—D.J., joking to reporters after his fifth-inning single off the Orioles' Pat Hentgen at Camden Yards gave him 1,500 career hits in only his eighth full season, August 17, 2003

"I'm more pleased with this season than any other season, because it's been tougher, injury-wise. It's probably more satisfying than any year before."

—D.J., after going 0-for-3 on the final day of the season
but expressing no disappointment that his .324 average, a 27-point
improvement from 2002, fell just short of beating Boston's Bill Mueller
for the AL batting title, September 29, 2003

"It was just one game. We'll be fine."

—D.J., after the Yankees lost Game 1 of the ALDS to the Minnesota Twins

"Derek Jeter is as good a player as there is in the league. He leads that baseball team and does a very good job of it."

—Ron Gardenhire, Minnesota manager, praising Jeter after he led the Yankees to a
four-game victory over the Twins in the ALDS, getting hits
in every game and batting .429

"We've probably been the two most consistent teams in the league. Why would you want to face an easier team? If you want to be the best, you have to beat the best."

—D.J., looking forward to the Red Sox–Yankees matchup in the 2003 ALCS

THE RIVALRY

"Jeter was raised in the Yankees organization to hate the Red Sox and everything they stood for."

—Ian O'Connor, ESPN.com, September 29, 2014

"Do I hate the Boston Red Sox? Do I hate the players? No."

—D.J., prior to Game 1 of the 2003 ALCS between the Yankees and Red Sox

"[Red Sox fans] hated him because he was the most recent incarnation of Yankees' evil, the symbol for everything they wanted but couldn't have. Come the postseason, the Yankees always seemed to end the game with another win and a pump of the fist from Jeter."

—**Dave Buscema,** *Game of My Life*, **2004**

"Not one player on any of my Boston teams ever had a single negative thing to say about him."

—**Johnny Damon, Boston outfielder, about the respect the Red Sox had for the Yankees shortstop with four championship rings**

"You hear all these glowing things said about him, and your natural inclination is to think that that it can't be all true, and that he's built up by the media. You come and see him play 20 times a year against you, and you realize, hey, he's the real deal."

—**Theo Epstein, Boston Red Sox GM**

"The rivalry has gotten more intense each year I've been in the major leagues. You have respect for the other team, I think, but it's gotten to the point where in the postseason, you've got guys throwing at each other's heads and charging the mound. It's almost like the old days, when they used to fight all the time."

—**D.J., to Diane K. Shah,** *Playboy*, **June 2004**

"This rivalry is a rivalry that, what can I tell you, the fans are involved in it, but it's not like the fans personally hated him. It was like, 'This is my team, that is yours.' But everybody has much respect for Jeter."

—**David Ortiz, Red Sox DH and first baseman, 2014**

"Give it a rest, Sox fans. Jeter was the man. The only thing that sucks is that he had to play for the Yankees."

—**Perry Eaton, BDCwire.com, February 13, 2014**

"You don't want to be the team that allows Boston to go to the World Series."

—**D.J., to Michael Kay,** *CenterStage*, **December 2003**

"The two hated rivals had faced each other 25 times in '03 leading up to Game 7 of the ALCS. . . . In squaring off against each other so many times, the Yankees and Red Sox had generated some disdain for one another. Earlier in the season on July 7 in the Bronx, Pedro Martínez, Boston's ace, had plunked both Alfonso Soriano and Derek Jeter—bean balls that were so intense they sent the two hitters at the top of the Yankees' batting order to the hospital. Jeter was hammered on his right hand while Soriano suffered a shot on his left hand. The after effects of the HBPs were so great that, after more than two weeks later, both hitters felt the pain of Martínez's missed location; the captain's hand was still swollen, and Fonsy felt some aches just by checking his swing."

—A.J. Martelli, MLB.com, 2014

"Pedro was the ace, so [manager Grady] Little stuck with him to start the eighth. And he looked fine when Nick Johnson popped out to [Nomar] Garciaparra at short. Five outs to go. Forever. Jeter doubled to right. Bernie Williams singled. Jeter scored. Red Sox 5, Yankees 3."

—Dave Buscema, on the beginning of the Yankees' three-run game-tying rally against fatigued Pedro Martínez in Game 7 of the 2003 ALCS, *Game of My Life*, 2004

"The Yankees would not have [reached the World Series] except for Jeter's performance in the seventh game of the American League Championship Series. With the Yankees trailing Pedro Martínez by three runs [in the eighth inning], Jeter whacked a double off the wall and reached second base and clapped his hands, in joy and anticipation. All eyes are on Derek Jeter in October. . . . All we heard this past summer was that Derek Jeter had found his level. Limited power. Limited range. And perhaps even slightly passé in the new century of the slugging shortstops. Ah, yes, we heard those bleats, quite often emanating from Yankees fans themselves, morbidly fearful that somehow a 39th pennant was impossible because Jeter would not slug 40 home runs or steal 40 bases. Since then, we have seen [Oakland's Miguel] Tejada pull a rock on the basepaths in the first round. We have seen Nomar blow hot and cold in the ALCS. And here was Derek Jeter, standing on second base, clapping his hands. All eyes are on Derek Jeter."

—George Vecsey, *New York Times*, October 23, 2003

"There's just something about [Derek]. When he's on the field, good things happen. I can't even describe it."

—**Aaron Boone, Yankees third baseman**

"I thought they were going to pull Pedro in the seventh. And their bullpen was doing good. . . . I say, 'OK this is a sign' . . . Jeter, Then Bernie, Then Matsui, Then Jorge gets that little [score-tying] blooper."

—**Mariano Rivera, Yankees reliever, as quoted by Dave Buscema, *Game of My Life*, 2004**

"LIKE DEREK TOLD ME, 'THE GHOSTS WILL SHOW UP EVENTUALLY.'"
—AARON BOONE, WHO, WITH POSSIBLE HELP FROM THE GHOSTS OF YANKEES LEGENDS BABE RUTH, LOU GEHRIG, AND JOE DIMAGGIO, SMASHED AN 11TH INNING WALK-OFF HOMER OFF BOSTON KNUCKLEBALLER TIM WAKEFIELD IN GAME 7 OF THE 2003 ALCS TO GIVE NEW YORK THE AMERICAN LEAGUE PENNANT

"I believe in ghosts. And we've got some ghosts in this stadium."

—**D.J., in the winning team's clubhouse after Aaron Boone's homer sunk the Red Sox 6–5, October 16, 2003**

"In the first inning of Game 3 of the World Series against the Florida Marlins, Josh Beckett . . . strikes out Derek Jeter on three pitches. Jeter spends the next three hours and eight innings doing more than anybody else on the team to make sure we win the game. . . . Jeter doubles to left and scores in the fourth inning. He singles to center to lead off the sixth inning. He doubles to right [off Beckett] and scores the go-ahead run in the eighth inning [on Matsui's single off reliever Chad Fox]. Beckett pitches seven and a third and strikes out 10 and gives up just three hits and two runs. All three hits, and both runs, come from Derek Jeter, a man who never stops competing [and who in the ninth inning, would be hit by a pitch and score on Bernie Williams's three-run homer]. He gives his personal all but always wants it to be about the team."

—**Mariano Rivera, Yankees reliever, about Jeter's contributions in a 6–1 victory over the Marlins in Game 4 of the 2003 World Series to give the Yankees a 2–1 lead—before losing three straight games and the title, *The Closer*, 2014**

"It makes you sick. How else can you feel?"

—D.J., about having to watch the Marlins celebrate winning
the world title at Yankee Stadium

"The series with the Red Sox was emotionally draining because all seven games were intense. But I don't think that's why we lost [in the World Series]. We lost because Florida played better than we did."

—D.J., to Diane K. Shah, *Playboy*, June 2004

"There's no sugarcoating it. They pitched better than us; they had more clutch hits. People need to stop saying it's a big shock."

—D.J., after the heavily favored Yankees lost the 2003 World Series to the Florida
Marlins in six games despite outscoring them 21–17

"For a while, I didn't like to be out and around a lot of people. I pretty much kept to myself. But you never forget it. I still think about us losing. You want to remember what it feels like, because you don't want to have that feeling again. That's what drives you to try to be better."

—D.J., to Diane K. Shah, *Playboy*, June 2004

"In his first eight full seasons in the major leagues, 1996–2003, Jeter played on Yankees teams that won 64 percent of their games, won 16 of 20 postseason series, played in six World Series, won four world championships, and came within three games of winning six titles in eight years. It was and remains the greatest dynasty . . . since the expansion era began in 1961."

—Tom Verducci, *The Yankee Years*, Joe Torre and Tom Verducci, 2009

"This is a great day for the New York Yankees and for the city of New York. In acquiring Alex Rodriguez, we are bringing to New York one of the premiere players in the history of the game. . . . I'm delighted that Alex really wanted to be a Yankee and to play side by side with our team captain Derek Jeter, who has shown himself to be a tremendous leader both on and off the field."

—George Steinbrenner, Yankees owner, making sure to praise Jeter after a blockbuster trade brought his ex-friend and the reigning AL MVP, Alex Rodriguez, to the Yankees, February 16, 2004

"WE HAVE ARGUABLY THE BEST LEFT SIDE OF THE INFIELD IN THE HISTORY OF BASEBALL, AND THIS IS WHAT IT'S GOING TO BE: DEREK JETER AT SHORTSTOP, ALEX RODRIGUEZ AT THIRD BASE."
—BRIAN CASHMAN, YANKEES GM, TO REPORTERS AT RODRIGUEZ'S PRESS CONFERENCE FOLLOWING HIS TRADE TO NEW YORK, FEBRUARY 17, 2004

"If Derek Jeter was feeling the heat from the newest star in the Yankees' expanding galaxy, he didn't show it. If he was feeling defensive about remaining the shortstop of the team he captains, he didn't sound it. . . . 'The measuring stick is how many championships you win,' Jeter said, the implicit message serving as a reminder that in this statistical category, it is Jeter 4, Rodriguez 0."

—Harvey Araton, about how Jeter welcomed new Yankees' acquisition Alex Rodriguez to the team at a press conference but had no thoughts about changing positions to accommodate him, *New York Times*, February 18, 2004

"[Derek] would tell me, 'When we're 38, 39, 40, we'll play a year or two together and go into the sunset.' . . . I never thought at 28, we'd be playing together."

—Alex Rodriguez, Yankees third baseman, *Tim McCarver Show*, July 11, 2004

"Everyone's pretty excited. You're adding one of the best all-around players in the game to your lineup, so it's only going to make us a better team. . . . Neither of us has had problems getting along with teammates before, so I don't see why we'd have problems now. It gives the media something to write about though."

—D.J., to Diane K. Shah, *Playboy*, June 2004

"The worst thing that could happen for the media, I think, is for me and Alex to get along. I think everyone wants us to disagree, to battle over who's doing this and who's doing that. But that's not the case."

—D.J., February 2004

"I hope all the writers lay off on this thing, A-Rod versus Jeter. . . . Let them go about playing baseball. It's going to be tough enough as it is in the American League East. . . . Jeter should take him to dinner. . . . He'll show that kind of great leadership. I would bank on it."

—George Steinbrenner, Yankees owner, February 2004

"I think they have to see us hold hands and go to a movie so they know we've made up. When we're 50 years old, they're going to say, 'Well, Alex and Derek: Are they arguing? Are they best friends? Are they brothers?' We're just having fun with it."

—Alex Rodriguez, *Today*, 2004

"Alex pretended to be thrilled to talk about his relationship with Jeter, while Jeter mostly demurred. Alex happily reminisced about sleepovers the two had had during their first years in the league and earnestly referred to Jeter as his 'brother.' Jeter was clearly feeling less fraternal, and his responses to questions about A-Rod were polite but guarded."

—Selena Roberts, *A-Rod*, 2009

"I know I'm going to get a hit again."

—D.J., while going 0-for-32 in April 2004 as pundits suggested the reason for the worst slump of his career was his discomfort having Alex Rodriguez as his teammate

"This is a long time for anybody, especially a guy with his ability."

—Joe Torre, Yankees manager about the worst hitless streak by a Yankee since 1977

"A streak like that, you wouldn't wish on anyone, even other teams. Guys on other teams even have been giving me support."

—D.J.

"I would boo myself, too. I wouldn't want to play on a team where if you're playing bad, they don't care."

—D.J., on being booed for the first time ever at Yankee Stadium

"They probably started feeling sorry for me a little bit. But even when they booed me before, they were still cheering when I went to the plate."

—D.J., after home fans started giving him ovations to try to encourage him out of his slump

"He's doing everything that a captain does. He's on the top step of the dugout when a guy gets a hit. When a guy's in a slump and you notice he's the first guy to pull for his teammates, that's a special player. A lot of guys go into slumps, and they go in a shell. They're not thinking about anyone else but themselves. His head is still in the game."

—Gary Sheffield, Yankees outfielder, April 2004

"It's like a bad dream is over with."

—D.J., after homering off Oakland's Barry Zito and rediscovering his stroke, paving the way for a .400 average and 9 homers in June, April 29, 2004

**"WATCHING [DEREK] UP CLOSE THIS YEAR, I TOLD HIM, 'BOY YOU'RE A LOT GREATER PLAYER THAN I THOUGHT, AND I THOUGHT YOU WERE GREAT.'"
—ALEX RODRIGUEZ, YANKEES THIRD BASEMAN, 2004**

"Me and my sister cooked for her. I cooked the steak. I almost burned my sister's house down."

—D.J., about what he and Sharlee gave their mother on Mother's Day, to Steve Serby, *New York Post*, May 16, 2004

"I knew that I wanted to say hi to him, to tell him how much I respected him. Before I could say anything [after I doubled], he came over and said hi to me. Actually, he said it in Spanish. That's something you don't really see often: someone who you know doesn't speak Spanish trying to make an effort to communicate with you. That really surprised me. . . . I wanted to tell him I admired him. I think all I said was that I was a great fan of his."

—Adrian Beltre, Los Angeles Dodgers third baseman, one of many young players who idolized Jeter from afar, about meeting Jeter on the field during an interleague game on June 19, 2004, 2014

CLASSIC MOMENT: JULY 1, 2004, YANKEE STADIUM, NYC

"Yankee Stadium. It's the top of the 12th, and the Yankees and Red Sox have been tied, 3–3, since the seventh inning. With runners on second and third and two outs, Boston's Trot Nixon lofts a pitch into shallow left field. Jeter catches the ball on a dead sprint, saving two runs in the process, before his momentum carries him straight into the stands."

—Seth Mnookin, *GQ*, April 2011

"Greatest catch I've ever seen. It was unbelievable. He's just so unselfish. He put his body in a compromising situation."

—Alex Rodriguez, Yankees third baseman

"When he's helped back onto the field, his chin is bruised, and his face is bloodied. He spends the rest of the game in the hospital."

—Seth Mnookin, *GQ*, April 2011

"He looked like he got punched by Mike Tyson."

—**Alex Rodriguez, Yankees third baseman**

"Derek Jeter, who seems to get better and better every year, made a play that amazed all of us. There was a short fly ball down the left field line. His job was to make the catch and beat the Boston Red Sox, and without worrying or caring whether he was going to get hurt, he ran toward the stands, put his glove up, stretched out, and somehow caught the ball. That play impressed me, yeah, but I was even more impressed the next day when I saw his face. It was all bruised and scarred from colliding with a railing or the seats, or whatever he ran into making that catch. The next time I got to speak to Derek, I told him, 'Hey, that was absolutely an amazing catch, and it's even more amazing you considered playing the next day.' I give the guy a lot of respect."

—**Johnny Damon, *Idiot*, 2005**

"I'VE NEVER SEEN A GUY OF HIS CALIBER GO ALL OUT. IT PROVED TO YOU HOW IMPORTANT THESE GAMES ARE. IT TOOK OUR CAPTAIN TO PROVE IT TO US AGAIN." —GARY SHEFFIELD, YANKEES OUTFIELDER

"You know, the thing is, in 2001, I fell in the stands in the same area, but it was in the photographers' pit, which is all cement, and it didn't feel too good. So, when I was catching that ball, I knew I was going to fall in the stands because I was too close, but I figured if I jump over the photographers' pit maybe I'll run into someone and feel a little bit better. . . . Fifty-seven thousand people and I picked the seat that no one was in. So that didn't feel too good either."

—**D.J., to Ed Bradley, *60 Minutes*, September 25, 2005**

"I always play hard. That's your job, to lead by example. If it makes other people want to play hard and win more, I guess it's worth it."

—**D.J., July 3, 2004**

"The juxtaposition between Jeter and Red Sox shortstop Nomar Garciaparra, who sits out the game with a sore Achilles,' is jarring. Garciaparra . . . is traded later that month."

—Ken Rosenthal, FoxSports.com

"For years, Jeter had been known for his clutch play and his uncanny baseball instincts, not to mention his cover-boy good looks. His toughness, by contrast, was largely unheralded, yet it was the quality his teammates appreciated most about him. Jeter would sooner reveal the identity of his latest girlfriend to the gossip-page editors than admit being bothered by an injury. . . . Sure enough Jeter was back at shortstop the night after his bloody dive as the Yankees and Mets met for Part II of the annual Subway Series. Doctors had sewn seven stitches into Jeter's chin . . . and his right cheek was still puffy and discolored. . . . But Jeter . . . couldn't understand why anyone would think he wouldn't play."

—John Harper, *A Tale of Two Cities*, Tony Massarotti and John Harper, 2005

"You have to put a gun to his head to get him out of the lineup."

—Reggie Jackson, Yankees Hall of Famer

"I hate excuses. I don't want to hear them. I don't make them. In my opinion, you either play or you don't. If you play, no one wants to hear what's bothering you. I've taken a lot of pride in going out there every day and doing my job."

—D.J.

"I don't like to watch baseball. I think it's boring for me to watch it. I like to play."

—D.J.

"The 2004 All-Star Game in Houston marked Jeter's sixth appearance and second start in the Mid-Summer Classic, and also saw Jeter start in the infield with two Yankees teammates (Jason Giambi and Alex Rodriguez) and Alfonso Soriano, who had been the captain's keystone combo mate for the previous few years before being traded for A-Rod in the winter of 2003–04. Jeter had a great game, going 3-for-3 with three singles and a run scored, but he was . . . overshadowed for the MVP award by Soriano, who was 2-for-3 overall and hit a three-run homer in the first inning that set the tone for the AL's 9–4 win."

—Lou DiPietro, YESNetwork.com

"Derek Jeter homered in the first inning for his 1,000th career run, then stole a pair of bases in the ninth inning and scored on Hideki Matsui's two-out single to lead the New York Yankees over Cleveland 5–4 Tuesday night in Cleveland, the Indians ninth straight loss. New York, which rallied from a 4–1 deficit, has won two straight after losing six of seven and remained 6½ games ahead of second-place Boston in the AL East. It was the Yankees 48th come-from-behind win, the most in the majors. . . . Jeter, hit on the left elbow by a pitch from Bob Wickman (0–2) on Monday, showed no signs of lingering problems. He hit his 16th homer in the first inning, then walked against Wickman with the score 4-all in the ninth and stole his 19th and 20th bases."

—*Associated Press*, August 26, 2004

"It means I'm getting old."

—D.J., about becoming the 11th Yankee to score 1,000 runs

"A-Rod and Jeter [did] enough as a tandem [in 2004] to lead the Yankees to their third consecutive season of more than 100 victories and their seventh consecutive division crown. . . . To the rest of baseball, it seemed another simple case of the Yankees steamrolling the competition with their checkbook. . . . The Yanks were laying out $184 million in wages, almost $60 million more than the second-highest payroll (Boston's)."

—Ian O'Connor, about the difference in payroll between the teams that would meet again in the 2004 ALCS, *The Captain*, 2011

"Jeter doesn't have the most hits in playoff history for nothing. He's Mr. October. He comes up big. Maybe you take A-Rod over a 162-game schedule, but in one game I'd go with Jeter any time."

—Johnny Damon, Red Sox outfielder, *Idiot*, 2005

"He's special. He's been brought up on this stage, which I think has been very helpful for him. When the game is on the line and the bright lights are on, I've never seen a player grow his game to above superstars. He plays above himself; he really does. He has a magical way about him in big moments."

—Alex Rodriguez, Yankees third baseman, *Tim McCarver Show*, July 11, 2004

"After Game 3 [of the 2004 ALCS], I told the players, 'Guys, we've got a little more work to do.' Everybody was so businesslike, especially Derek Jeter, who was reminding his teammates that even though they'd just kicked the heck out of those guys, it was not over."

—Joe Torre, Yankees manager, about the concern he shared with Jeter that Boston might become the only team in major league history to come back from a 3–0 deficit and win a postseason series

"We know they're not going to give up, but we're exactly in the position we want to be in."

—D.J., after the Red Sox beat the Yankees in Game 4 to prevent being swept in the 2004 ALCS

"Nothing surprises me at this point."

—D.J., after the Red Sox withstood his three-run double against Pedro Martínez, tied the score in the ninth inning, and won Game 5 in 14 innings

"THE MORE I FACED HIM, THE MORE I RESPECTED HIM,"
—PEDRO MARTINEZ, BOSTON PITCHER

"With one out and Derek Jeter on first [in the eighth inning of Game 6 of the ALCS], [Alex] Rodriguez hit a grounder to the right side. Red Sox pitcher Bronson Arroyo picked up the ball and ran toward Rodriguez, who used his left hand to bat the ball out of Arroyo's glove. Jeter scored as the ball rolled away. But the Red Sox protested, and the umpires huddled and ruled Rodriguez was out. Jeter was ordered back to first base. Yankees fans threw trash onto the field, but when play resumed, Gary Sheffield fouled out to end the inning."

—**Mel Antonen, *USA Today*, October 20, 2004**

"That was freakin' junior high baseball at its best. Let me ask you something: Does Derek Jeter do that? . . . You know for a fact he doesn't because Derek Jeter is a class act and a professional, that's why."

—**Bronson Arroyo, Boston pitcher, objecting to Alex Rodriguez's unsuccessful attempt to get away with slapping the ball out of his glove on a tag play near first base, a key interference call in the Red Sox's 4–3 Game 6 victory, evening the ALCS at three games apiece**

"I can't say, 'Oh we were the better team and oh, if this happened or that happened.' They played better than us. That's all I can say. We couldn't stop them. . . . When you look back, it's shocking."

—**D.J., to reporters about Boston crushing the Yankees 10–3 in Game 7 of the ALCS to become the first team ever to come back from a 3–0 deficit in the playoffs**

"It's not the same team [as in 1998–2000]. I've said it time after time; it's not the same team."

—**D.J., to reporters after the Game 7 loss at Fenway Park about the Yankees' change in personnel since 2000**

"They were better than us. Bottom line, they didn't give up."

—**D.J., who always gave credit to the other team for winning, even it was the archrival Red Sox**

"I've been on the other end of a few of 'em. I was a little jealous, but they deserve it. You respect what they accomplished. You know how hard it is to do. They've waited a long time, so I'm sure a lot of thought and effort went into it."

> —D.J., on standing on the top step of the third base dugout at the 2005 home opener at Fenway Park and watching the Boston Red Sox receive their 2004 world championship rings

"I've always respected Terry [Francona, Boston's manager]. I know his players loved playing for him, and I got to know him throughout the years. I always admired him from afar. He always seemed to me like he was pretty even-keel. He never seemed to overreact. He never had a look of panic on his face, and I think that rubs off on teams."

—D.J.

A MAN OF HABIT

"By 2009, part of his routine in Red Sox games involved acknowledging [Boston manager Terry] Francona before his first at-bat of each game. Approaching home plate, Jeter would look over into the Boston dugout and gesture toward the Sox manager with his hand or bat. If Francona was momentarily distracted, Jeter would step back and wait for a response before proceeding with his work."

> —Dan Shaughnessy, *Francona: The Red Sox Years*, Terry Francona and Dan Shaughnessy, 2013

"Whenever Joe Torre went to the mound to make a pitching change, Jeter loped in from his position and slapped him on the chest with his glove. Playoffs, World Series, ugly blowout of the Yankees, it didn't matter; he'd always hit his manager."

—Buster Olney, *The Last Night of the Yankee Dynasty*, 2004

"Every morning before a game, I eat pancakes and an omelet."

—D.J.

"Every day, the captain walks into the clubhouse with his grande skim cappuccino from Starbucks, answers questions at his locker, goes off to the training room, takes batting practice, takes the field on a sprint ahead of the rest of the guys, plays baseball without much more emotion than an occasional pumped fist."

—T.J. Quinn, New York *Daily News*, September 17, 2006

"Here is what [former Yankees catcher Russell] Martin best remembers: Jeter arriving at the clubhouse each day, a cup of Starbucks coffee in hand and a wisecrack on his lips. Jeter going through his pregame routines and batting practice, patterns that almost never wavered. Jeter eating a peanut butter and jelly sandwich before each game."

—David Waldstein, *New York Times*, March 1, 2015

"The scene has played out countless times in stadiums across the country; you can almost set your watch to it. About three hours before the scheduled first pitch, Derek Jeter walks into the clubhouse, a coffee cup nestled in his right hand. The Yankees captain approaches the laptop computer set up for ticket requests, punches in a few names, slings a pair of white sanitary socks over his shoulder and begins to prepare for the nine innings ahead. While he does, Jeter's java is a constant companion."

—Bryan Hoch, MLB.com, September 16, 2014

"Like every ballplayer, Jeter believes in routine. He has used the exact same model bat [a Louisville Slugger] for every professional plate appearance over his multiple decade career. He is famous for stepping out of the batter's box and arching his back between pitches."

—Dan Shaughnessy, *Francona: The Red Sox Years*,
Terry Francona and Dan Shaughnessy, 2013

"Derek never starts a game until he finds where his parents are seated. It's a habit he has had since Little League. And as soon as he spots his mom, he says hi."

—Ed Bradley, *60 Minutes*, September 25, 2005

"Everything I do is pretty much a routine. I wouldn't say I'm superstitious; it's not like if I don't have it, I'm flipping out. But I'm a creature of habit, I guess is the best way to put it. . . . I've got the same routine. I don't need to try to break it. Well, I guess I'll have to—fairly soon."

—D.J., with his career winding down, 2014

"IT IS A PASTIME AMONG BASEBALL STATISTICIANS TO MALIGN DEREK JETER'S DEFENSE. TWO YEARS AGO, WHEN JETER SAID HE WANTED TO WIN A GOLD GLOVE AT SHORTSTOP, HE WAS ROUNDLY RIDICULED. BUT YESTERDAY, RAWLINGS ANNOUNCED THAT JETER HAD WON HIS FIRST GOLD GLOVE AWARD, VOTED ON BY AMERICAN LEAGUE MANAGERS AND COACHES."
—TYLER KEPNER, *NEW YORK TIMES*, NOVEMBER 3, 2004

"It's a great honor. I take pride in my defense, and I work hard each year to improve in the field. There were a number of fantastic defensive shortstops in the American League—too many to count—and to be recognized with the Gold Glove makes it that much more of an accomplishment. I also want to thank our pitching staff for having so many of our opponents hit balls in my direction."

—D.J., upon winning the first of what would be five
Rawlings Gold Gloves, November 2, 2004

"I don't know what the defensive-stat stuff is going to say, because there are so many variables. It all adds up to: what? I don't particularly know. But I do know that he has contributed to our success both offensively and defensively for years, and it's nice for him to be officially recognized on the defensive end."

> —Brian Cashman, Yankees GM, about Derek Jeter winning his first
> Gold Glove, November 2, 2004

"Derek Jeter is a great, inspired leader and captain. He certainly deserves this honor."

> —George Steinbrenner, Yankees owner, about Jeter's first Gold Glove,
> November 2, 2004

THE ATTACK OF THE SABERMETRICIANS

"I play in New York, man. Criticism is part of the game; you take criticism as a challenge."

> —Derek Jeter in response to criticism of his defense, including by sabermetricians

"The sabermetric crowd was ganging up on Jeter . . . who was number 1 in the hearts of Yankees fans, number 2 in their game programs, and number 30 or so in the sabermetric rankings of everyday shortstops."

> —Ian O'Connor, *The Captain*, 2011

"Jeter has long been baseball's most polarizing defensive player. In the right crowd—a mix of sabermetricians and the regulars at Stan's Sports Bar—it takes just three words ("Derek Jeter's defense") to touch off a debate between people who are equally convinced that the Yankees captain is either one of the best or one of the worst defenders of all time."

> —Ben Lindbergh, Grantland.com, August 27, 2013

"One of their conclusions was that Derek Jeter was probably the least effective defensive player in the major leagues at any position."

—Bill James, Boston Red Sox advisor and author of *The Historical Baseball Abstract*, on the findings of John Dewan and others at Baseball Info Solutions when comparing Jeter's fielding to Houston shortstop Adam Everett's, *The Fielding Bible*

"OK, so Adam Everett is a better defender than Jeter; that's useful enlightening information. But for heaven's sake, which shortstop would you rather have on your team. Polarizing as the discussion has become, pretty much everyone can agree that Jeter has been delivering big plays at opportune moments from the start of his career."

—Ken Rosenthal, FoxSports.com

"It would make intuitive sense that Derek Jeter is the worst defensive shortstop of all time. . . . The worst defensive shortstop in baseball history would *have* to be someone like Jeter who is unusually good at other aspects of the game."

—Bill James, Boston Red Sox advisor and pioneer sabermetrician,
The Fielding Bible

"In 2003, a Monmouth University mathematics professor named Michael Hoban wrote a book, *Fielder's Choice: Baseball's Best Shortstops*, that ranked Jeter as the worst in the game at his position because of the dramatic decline in his range."

—Ian O'Connor, *The Captain*, 2011

"Because Jeter looks like the perfect shortstop in the field, and because he is fundamentally sound and makes dozens of heads-up plays, there is no middle ground in the argument about his defense. Those who go by their eyes swear he is a good or even a great defender; those who go by the results [stats?] say that Jeter's limited range cannot be an illusion. There will never be a middle ground."

—Gary Gillette, ESPN.com, May 2, 2006

"In 1997 (before his decline), Derek Jeter led all shortstops in chances (assists plus putouts). His range [according to my formula for assessing fielding performance] compared to the other shortstops was a very good 39 points above the league average."

—**Michael Hoban, mathematics professor and author of the influential 2003 book** *Fielder's Choice: Baseball's Best Shortstops***, BaseballGuru.com, 2005**

"From 1998 through 2002, Jeter's fielding range was—in a freefall pattern— culminating in 2002 when his range factor was 75 points *below the league average* (the worst of any shortstop in the majors)."

—**Michael Hoban, mathematics professor and author, BaseballGuru.com, 2005**

"I'm the worst? I don't think I would say that. But I couldn't really care less what some mathematical equation comes out with. . . . How do you rank defensive shortstops? I don't see how a formula can evaluate how somebody plays. [For example] you get a strikeout pitcher on the mound as opposed to a ground-ball pitcher, it's going to affect the statistics you use to evaluate defense. So I don't really think you can."

—**D.J.**

"Apparently, some readers of my articles felt that because Jeter was awarded the Gold Glove in 2004 this means that my assessment of his fielding skills through 2002 must be faulty. Or perhaps they feel that Jeter may have improved his fielding in order to have received the award. Well . . . the second conclusion is accurate. That is, Derek did indeed improve his fielding in 2004. In fact, it was his best fielding season in his nine years in the major leagues. However, that does not mean that he was the best fielding shortstop in the American League and deserved to win the Gold Glove."

—**Michael Hoban, mathematics professor and author, BaseballGuru.com, 2005**

"You can't automatically figure out how everybody plays defense; otherwise you're just playing Nintendo. You're playing on a computer. You can't mathematically figure that out. That's impossible to do . . . because everybody doesn't play the same position and doesn't have the same pitcher. The ball's not hit in the same spot, and you don't have the same runner. . . . One day, he's got a leg problem, the next day, he doesn't. . . . There are too many factors that go into it."

—D.J., giving his negative opinion of sabermetrics

"They think they have a mathematical equation that figures everything out. . . . It seems like once somebody says one thing about you, people tend to run with it, and we never hear the end of it."

—D.J.

"Mathematical equations and statistical analysis had long been suggesting Jeter was a below-average fielder despite his soft hands and his unmatched ability to come in on slow grounders and run down pop flies over his head. . . . Of course, the sabermetricians could not account for the fact that Jeter played hurt as often as any other position player in the game."

—Ian O'Connor, *The Captain*, 2011

"According to the number crunchers who charted batted balls, he never conquered his difficulty ranging to his left. Part of the problem was that he often played with leg injuries without making it known publicly. If limited range was Jeter's Achilles' heel, Torre was more than willing to live with it because of everything else Jeter gave the Yankees. After all, the Yankees did win four World Series and six pennants with Jeter manning the shortstop position. Torre still wanted the ball hit to Jeter with the game on the line, as great a cut-to-the-chase test of a shortstop's value as anything."

—Tom Verducci, *The Yankee Years*, Joe Torre and Tom Verducci, 2009

"Jeter gets more outrageous and patently false praise than any other player."

—Bill James, Red Sox advisor and author of *The Historical Baseball Abstract* and *The Bill James Handbook*

"JETER IS A TREMENDOUS PLAYER, FOR REASONS THAT I SHOULDN'T HAVE TO EXPLAIN."
—BILL JAMES, RED SOX ADVISOR AND AUTHOR OF *THE HISTORICAL BASEBALL ABSTRACT*, GAVE A WISHY-WASHY REASON FOR WHY HE'D WANT JETER ON HIS TEAM DESPITE THINKING HIM THE WORST DEFENSIVE SHORTSTOP IN BASEBALL

"One guy I'll never criticize if the metrics don't match up with the player is Derek Jeter. It's like someone saying they don't like the mole on Cindy Crawford's face. . . . As someone who believes in metrics, I'm here to give you the good news: I still think Jeter is an incredible talent."

—Billy Beane, A's GM and metrics student

"The stat-heads scoffed at him, but then the stat-heads never figured out a way to measure the things he did. Some guys would lean over a wall in foul territory to make a catch. Jeter would launch himself over it, sometimes two rows deep. He'd come out a bruised face, a cut chin, and the ball."

—Rick Reilly, ESPN.com, May 28, 2014

"Whereas baseball writers used to live and die by batting average, runs batted in, and home runs, now it's WAR, WAR, WAR. Keith Olbermann's recent diatribe about Jeter's presumed place in baseball history, for example, was structured almost entirely around Jeter's failure to rank high in this category. (Baseball-Reference has him at #88 in all time WAR [wins above replacement], sandwiched between luminaries like Larry Walker and Raffy Palmeiro.) But WAR, of course, includes the defensive metrics that, basically, might not work. So there's a chance we have over-corrected; Jeter may be better than we now think."

—Elijah Wolfson, *Newsweek*, September 25, 2014

"Jeter's lifetime negative WAR ranks somewhere between wrong and extremely hard to believe. Jeter was very good going to his right, coming in and going back and only had an issue going to his left. He had good speed, a very good arm, and immaculate instincts. He was also very sure-handed. At a key spot there's almost no one more likely to make the routine play. No real baseball person would claim Jeter was a poor defensive shortstop as his defensive WAR suggests."

—Jon Heyman, *CBS Sports*, September 28, 2014

"[Keith] Olbermann's well-researched harangue [on ESPN] relied, of course, on the cherry picking of stats. . . . Olbermann pulled out the WAR [wins above replacement] category to suggest Jeter perhaps wasn't even as great a Yankee as Thurman Munson, Willie Randolph, Mike Mussina, or Red Ruffing, either. Now that's just plain silly. What that tells you is that the WAR stat is imperfect, not that Jeter is. . . . Jeter stacks up a lot better if you use other measures. Jeter's offensive WAR is 95.3. That is superb and ranks him ahead of Ripken among shortstops. Jeter's 95.3 mark, in fact, is higher than that of Ken Griffey Jr., Albert Pujols, Manny Ramirez, Al Kaline, Frank Thomas, Chipper Jones, Mike Schmidt, and Jimmie Foxx. The problem with Jeter's total WAR is that his defensive WAR is somehow negative, dragging his overall number down. . . . Even sabermetric experts will admit the defensive metrics are at the very least imprecise. In this case, they are an out-and-out injustice. . . . But even on the stats, Jeter is still great by any fair measure. For the record, Olbermann concluded Jeter's 'nowhere near an immortal.' Of course that's wrong. . . . Even if you put the popularity aside, Jeter isn't just near an immortal, he obviously is one. Anyone saying otherwise is simply looking for an argument or attention."

—Jon Heyman, *CBS Sports*, September 28, 2014

"The score was tied in the last of the 12th inning at Yankee Stadium in Game 2 of the 2004 American League Division Series. Derek Jeter was at third base with one out. Hideki Matsui hit a bullet line drive directly at Twins right fielder Jacque Jones. Maybe Jones didn't think Jeter would tag up—a poor assumption—or, more likely, Jones didn't have a chance to get his feet set and get behind the ball because it was hit so hard. Flat-footed, leaning backward, he made a weak throw to the plate. Jeter tagged up and scored the winning run. 'You made your decision to go as soon as the ball was hit?' Jeter was asked. 'I made my decision to go *before* the ball was hit,' Jeter said. That's why Jeter is such a great baserunner; that's why he's our pick for the best baserunner in the game. There are other candidates, including Larry Walker and Roberto Alomar, but we'll take Jeter because of intelligence, aggressiveness, experience, and speed."

—Tim Kurkjian, about *ESPN The Magazine* naming Jeter baseball's best baserunner, *ESPN The Magazine*, January 19, 2005

"He has something in him that a lot of guys don't have; it's instinct. I give a guy five years to become a good baserunner. If he's no good after five years, he has no chance. If you're bad after five, you'll be bad after 12; run until they tag you out. This guy was really good his rookie year, and things haven't changed."

—Don Zimmer, Tampa Bay coach, to Tim Kurkjian, *ESPN The Magazine*, January 19, 2005

"ON THE BASEPATHS, HE'S ONE OF THE BEST BASERUNNERS YOU'LL FIND. HE'S NEVER SATISFIED WITH JUST ONE BASE; HE'S ALWAYS LOOKING TO TAKE THE NEXT ONE."
—NOMAR GARCIAPARRA, RED SOX SHORTSTOP, QUOTED BY TONY MASSAROTTI, *DEREK JETER: A YANKEE FOR THE NEW MILLENNIUM*, 2000

"He's so sound fundamentally. He cuts the bags so well and has a great feel for the overall game."

—Omar Minaya, Mets GM

"How smart and skilled a baserunner was Jeter? Excluding steal attempts and force plays, over one two-year period, he was tagged out once."

—Tim McCarver, to Danny Peary, 2015

"After '01 we lost some guys and after '02 we lost some guys, and after '03 we lost the pitching staff. Whatever semblance of that [championship] team there was, it certainly was gone after '03. It started phasing out after '01, but after '03 it was just Derek and Posada and Mariano and Bernie who were left. Everybody else was new. The mix wasn't the same."

—Mike Mussina, Yankees pitcher, about why so many players on the 2005 team were unfocused and unprepared

"We're just going through the motions. It seems like we don't care."

—D.J., to reporters about the lackluster effort of the Yankees at midseason in 2005

"In some ways, I think a team like this is in more need of a captain than most teams, because new guys, no matter what they've done on other teams, they always seem a little awed by becoming a Yankee for the first time, whether it's the city, the fans, the history, whatever. I've seen kids up from the minors who fit in right away because they don't know any better. New guys like to have someone to talk to, someone they can trust."

—D.J., quoted by Mike Vaccaro, *New York Post*, March 6, 2005

"I wasn't thinking home run. I mean, I had thought that I would never hit one. Right at that moment, I just wanted to hit a fly ball to get the runner in from third. I was trying to avoid hitting a ground ball."

—D.J., after hitting a bases-loaded homer in his 5,770th career at-bat off the Cubs' Joe Borowski in a 7–1 victory at Yankee Stadium, his first grand slam after 156 home runs, ending the longest futility streak among active major leaguers, June 18, 2005

"While Jeter was a master of shrinking the biggest moments, Rodriguez [who would win his second MVP for the 2005 season] often made them too big to handle, and the [2005] Division Series loss to the Angels offered ample evidence of that. Jeter batted .333 with two home runs and five RBI in the series, and in the sudden-death fifth game, on the road, he had three hits, including a homer in the seventh inning and single to lead off the ninth with the Yanks down 5–3. Rodriguez finished the series with two hits in 15 at-bats, finishing hitless in Game 5, and all but killed the Yanks' last chance by following Jeter's ninth-inning single with a ground ball double play."

—**Ian O'Connor,** *The Captain,* **2011**

"Defense usually doesn't make many headlines, but it goes a long way toward winning ball games."

—**D.J., after winning his second straight Gold Glove, November 1, 2005**

"I don't care. I guess anything I do now is a plus."

—**D.J., responding to a 2006 poll of 470 players by** *Sports Illustrated* **in which his peers again named him baseball's most overrated player, ahead of Carlos Beltran and Alex Rodriguez**

IF ANYTHING, JETER WAS *UNDERRATED*

"There are things that go beyond ability. And I've said this about Derek in the past. He can't hit with A-Rod; maybe he can't throw with him. Can't throw with Garciaparra, can't do this with Garciaparra. But what I know is I wouldn't trade him for anybody. There is something special about Derek Jeter. What is it about him that makes him what he is? It's something that you can't put down on paper."

—**Joe Torre, Yankees manager**

"[In 1994], the year Paul Quantrill was with us, he came up to me one day, unsolicited, and said, 'I always knew he was a good player. I just didn't realize how good.'"

—Joe Torre, Yankees manager

"You really don't know how good he is—you don't know all the things he does—until you see him on an everyday basis."

—Gary Sheffield, Yankees outfielder

"Before I ever played against him, I thought he was overhyped because of the New York media. . . . But after playing against him, I think he's one of the best players of his generation. I think the players in the anonymous poll who said he was overrated are probably the same people like me, who didn't know until you played against him. Many times New York players are overhyped, but not in Jeter's case."

—Brad Ausmus, veteran catcher and future manager, who played against Jeter while on the Detroit Tigers in 1996, 2000, and 2001

"[My teammates on St. Louis and Tampa Bay] did have an appreciation of Derek, but they were really jealous of him. You know, like, 'What does he do that's so spectacular?' And you have to explain to them that you have to play with the guy every day to see how great he really is. You see him in a game or two, and you're not going to know."

—Tino Martinez, retired first baseman, who played for the Yankees (1996–2001, 2005), Cardinals (2002–03), and Tampa Bay (2004) during Jeter's career

"Derek is just Mr. Steady. . . . He's [doing] what he's done for so long so well that it's almost like you don't even notice him out there, because you're just so accustomed to him doing what he does."

—Tom Glavine, New York Mets pitcher, 2005

"If Derek [Jeter] is, as some have said, a 'baseball genius,' it's in the marriage of skills with that vision of the game that makes him so. There are players who are just as accomplished technically and conscientious professionally; he isn't even the very best shortstop playing the major leagues today, but none of those other players has exactly what Jeter has. The fusion of commitment and achievement give him an aura that, to many, is irresistible. He doesn't just play baseball; he lives and breathes it."

—Patrick Giles, *Derek Jeter: Pride of the Yankees*, 1998

"WHEN YOU TALK ABOUT A BRAIN, WHEN YOU TALK ABOUT A MIND, [SOMEONE] THAT ANALYZES EVERYTHING, THERE'S NOBODY BETTER."
—JORGE POSADA, YANKEES CATCHER

"For me, Derek is in the same position as [basketball Hall of Famer Bill] Russell. Bill Russell may not have been the most talented person. But he made everyone around him better. I'm still not sure people grasp that. I used to say that if you dropped somebody from Mars, and had him look at the shortstops who were around when [Jeter] was younger, had him look at [Miguel] Tejada and Nomar [Garciaparra] and Alex [Rodriguez], maybe he wouldn't think Derek fit in there. But that was why I was the lucky one. I got to watch him every day. I watched what he did and how he did it."

—Joe Torre, Yankees manager, looking back at how
Jeter was underappreciated, February 17, 2014

"All of a sudden, the talk about the greatness of Derek Jeter has intensified, and this is misguided. He's actually greater than that. . . . One of these centuries, when Jeter retires, historians will shake their heads and wonder why folks during his generation didn't realize that he was operating on a level beyond nearly everyone else around him."

—Terence Moore, MLB.com, September 2, 2011

"One game doesn't make a trend, much less a season, but how about a decade? On opening day at Yankee Stadium, there was Jeter, getting into an eighth-inning, first-pitch, split-finger fastball from a Kansas City reliever named Ambiorix Burgos, uncharacteristically pulling it into the left-field seats, making one more in a career of statements that he is the Yankees' captain, their leader, no matter where in the lineup he bats, no matter who bats and dresses around him. . . . It began with the welcome sight of Yogi Berra tossing a ball to Jorge Posada and climaxed with another grand Jeter moment."

—**Harvey Araton, about Jeter's game-winning home run with two outs and two men on in the bottom of the eighth with the Yankees trailing the Royals 7–6 on Opening Day in 2006,** *New York Times,* **April 12, 2006**

"We were all excited; we all had the feeling that something big was going to happen. . . . Derek's always been the right guy for that situation."

—**Jason Giambi, Yankees first baseman, April 12, 2006**

"I've watched this kid for 11 years. It seems when something needs to happen, he's at the start of it or the finish of it."

—**Joe Torre, Yankees manager, about Jeter's Opening Day heroics, April 12, 2006**

"People say, 'Are you more motivated now because you lost [last year]?' How could you be more motivated if you want to win all the time? You're not *extra*-motivated. It's the same thing."

—**D.J., about the Yankees not winning a title since 2000, 2006**

"Jeter helped create the Yankees' modern mentality, in which only championship seasons are considered a success. It is an all-or-nothing mind-set that, for some, creates a joyless, pressurized environment. But for Jeter, it is simply a fact. Every team wants to win as often as possible, so the goal must be a title every season. It is not like this everywhere, but for Jeter, it would be."

—**Tyler Kepner,** *New York Times,* **August 18, 2006**

"I don't know what it would be like, but I wouldn't change."

—D.J., about playing on a team that didn't expect to win every year

"It wasn't the first time that's happened. But a hit is a hit."

—D.J., about his 2,000th major league hit being a tapper to the left of the plate off Kansas City's Scott Elarton that catcher Paul Bako picked up and threw over the head of the first baseman, May 26, 2006

"I saw that. I guess it's a good thing she wasn't scoring."

—D.J., when he's told that television replay showed his mother turning toward his father after their son's questionably-scored 2,000th hit and saying "Error," May 26, 2006

"I finally got the ball during the rain delay [in the ninth inning]. I'll probably give it to my mom. She'll want it."

—D.J., who recorded his 2,000th hit in his 1,571st game to become the eighth Yankee to reach 2,000 hits, with a hit total behind only Lou Gehrig (with a team record 2,721 hits), Babe Ruth, Mickey Mantle, Bernie Williams, Joe DiMaggio, Don Mattingly, and Yogi Berra, May 26, 2006

"Now don't get me wrong, I do understand it's a game of numbers, and people are going to pay attention to your numbers, say you did this or did that. I would love to hit .400. That would be a lot better than .200. You take pride in how you play. But that shouldn't be your main focus. Your main focus should be whether you win or lose. . . . If you constantly sit around worrying about your stats, once you get in a funk, you'll never get out. Because all you're worried about is yourself. If you're worried about how we can win today, that's your only concern."

—D.J., 2006

"I don't worry about my statistics. I try to hit the ball hard or with more authority at any given time, but I don't sit around and focus on my numbers of home runs or doubles or RBIs. The minute you do that, you start to forget what's important. The object is to win ball games. I will help my team do that any way I can."

—D.J.

"The Yankees could have eliminated Boston from the playoff race by winning three of four games over the last two days. Instead it was the Red Sox who took three of four, including both games yesterday. In the process, they put an end to Derek Jeter's 25-game hitting streak, the longest by a Yankee in 64 years. In his fourth and final at-bat last night, Jeter swung at a 3–0 pitch for the first time since 2002, grounding out to first."

—**Tyler Kepner**, *New York Times*, **September 18, 2006**

"Jeter isn't just captain of the team, he's the captain of the infield at shortstop. But understand this even better: That area between second and third at Yankee Stadium is Jeter's turf, now more than ever. It doesn't matter to Yankees fans that some people think A-Rod might someday be called the best player of all time, or that he hits more home runs and knocks in more runs and might even have played a better shortstop once. That is Jeter's turf, his team, his town. His time. It doesn't change until he retires or A-Rod changes teams."

—**Mike Lupica, referring to a pop-up on which Jeter was charged with an error because after unsuccessfully trying to call off Rodriguez, he bumped him while going after the ball, too, causing the ball to drop, New York *Daily News*, August 19, 2006**

"As the team has gained control of the division, Jeter and Rodriguez have coexisted as suns in separate solar systems, mostly indifferent to each other, supportive on the field, always bland, always non-controversial, but always essential."

—**T.J. Quinn**, New York *Daily News*, September 3, 2006

"I'M NOT THINKING OF THE MVP RIGHT NOW. WE'RE THINKING ABOUT WINNING A DIVISION. NO ONE HERE'S FOCUSED ON INDIVIDUAL AWARDS."
—D.J., AFTER BOSTON'S DAVID ORTIZ TELLS REPORTERS HE'S MORE DESERVING THAN JETER FOR THE MVP AWARD IN 2006 BECAUSE HE HITS WITH MORE POWER, SEPTEMBER 11, 2006

"I'm going to choose my teammate, bottom line. I've seen the value of [Jeter] here."

—Johnny Damon, Yankees outfielder, choosing Jeter over his former teammate David Ortiz in the upcoming 2006 MVP vote, September 11, 2006

"There were others who starred in the Yankees' 8–4 victory over the Detroit Tigers in Game 1 of the A.L. Division Series, but nobody sparkled as brightly as Jeter, who tied a postseason record with five hits. Jeter, the Yankees' captain, has made a career of rising to meet the moment. This time, he topped himself. Jeter went 5 for 5 and capped his night with a home run over the center-field wall at Yankee Stadium in the eighth inning."

—Tyler Kepner, *New York Times*, October 4, 2006

"Jeter was about the only Yankee who escaped the first-round loss unscathed. He had a great statistical series, enhancing his legacy as a clutch October player."

—Ian O'Connor, *The Captain*, 2011

"He's a dream player; that's what he is. I don't think anyone in the history of the Yankees has handled New York any better than Derek Jeter."

—Jim Leyland, Detroit manager, whose Tigers defeated the Yankees in four games in the 2006 ALDS

"I sort of feel out of place. With Hank Aaron, the first thing that comes to mind is home runs."

—D.J., upon winning the Hank Aaron Award as AL's best hitter although he had only 14 homers, and the NL winner, Ryan Howard, slammed 58, October 25, 2006

"[According to Bill James's system for evaluating every player's value to his team, Win Shares] Derek Jeter had the best overall season in the American League in 2006, although David Ortiz had the best hitting season. And in the National League, Albert Pujols had both the best overall season and the best hitting season. As it turns out, Justin Morneau (American League) and Ryan Howard (National League) were voted the MVPs for 2006."

—Michael Hoban, university mathematics professor and author of the influential 2003 book *Fielder's Choice: Baseball's Best Shortstops*, BaseballGuru.com

"While I know that voting for these awards is primarily based on differing opinions and statistical debates, it's also part of what makes baseball such a great sport. I suspect this won't be the last time you will hear [Justin Morneau's] name mentioned when awards are being passed out. . . . You've heard me say it a thousand times, but winning the World Series for the New York Yankees continues to be my main focus. There is no individual award that can compare with a championship trophy, and I look forward to working towards that challenge again in 2007."

—D.J., after being edged in the MVP voting by the AL's batting champion, Twins first baseman Justin Morneau, despite his batting .344, scoring 118 runs, driving in 97 runs, banging 214 hits, and winning his third consecutive Gold Glove award, his first Silver Slugger award as the best offensive player at his position, and his first Hank Aaron Award, November 22, 2006

"I hope Jeter would embrace [Rodriguez] this year, in spring training, and bring him into the full circle as part of the Yankees family. If Jeter does it, I think everybody else will respond. . . . I think the Yankees' problem is that they just don't support each other enough."

—Darryl Strawberry, former Yankees outfielder, December 2006

"I faked it with [Wade] Boggs. And you have to fake it with Alex."

—Don Mattingly, Yankees coach, advising Jeter to pretend to get along with Rodriguez to help the team

"Don't you think I've tried? I try, and sometimes I've just got to walk away and come back and try again, but you know I've tried. And every time I try, he'll do something that pushes me away."

—D.J.

"The thing about [New York *Daily News* columnist] Mike Lupica that pisses me off is that he makes me look like the biggest ******** in the world, and then he takes a guy like Jeter and just puts him way up there."

—Alex Rodriguez, Yankees third baseman, on how he believed the New York press treated Jeter much better than they did him, quoted by Joe Torre and Tom Verducci, *The Yankee Years*, 2009

"The dynamic between Jeter and Rodriguez never was an open war that sent collateral damage flying about the rest of the clubhouse. Indeed, they operated more along the lines of a cold truce. But everybody in the clubhouse could feel the frost emanating from the Jeter-Rodriguez dynamic."

—**Tom Verducci,** *The Yankee Years,* **Joe Torre and Tom Verducci, 2009**

"Alex wanted to please everyone; Jeter suffered no fools. Alex put up stats that impressed even folks who didn't follow baseball; Jeter owned four World Series rings that he rarely wore in public. . . . Here, Alex was the better hitter, the superior athlete, the richest player—and on and on. He put his celebrity up against Jeter's. He would put his stats up against Jeter's. He had put his body through *everything* to best Jeter. Yet he was consumed by one gnawing, galling, undeniable difference between them: Jeter was clean."

—**Selena Roberts, who in the February 9, 2009 issue of** *Sports Illustrated* **was the first reporter to state, correctly, that Rodriguez had taken steroids,** *A-Rod,* **2009**

"Let's make a contract. You don't ask me about Derek anymore, and I promise I'll stop lying to all you guys."

—**Alex Rodriguez, Yankees third baseman, to reporters at spring training in 2007, indicating he no longer would try to pretend to be Jeter's friend**

"I cheer very hard for him, and he cheers hard for me. And most importantly we are both trying to win a world championship. . . . The reality is that there has been a change in the relationship, and hopefully we can put it behind us."

—**Alex Rodriguez, to reporters at spring training, February 19, 2007**

"I don't have a rift with Alex; let's get that straight. Like Alex said yesterday, when we're on the field, we support each other, and that's all that matters. What we do away from the field really has no bearing on us playing baseball."

—**D.J., to reporters at spring training, February 20, 2007**

"How would I characterize it? I would characterize it as *it doesn't make any difference.*"

—D.J., responding to a reporter's question about his relationship with Alex Rodriguez

"Not everyone can be friends. They help each other out. That's all you can ask for. They seem to get along fine to me."

—Jorge Posada, Yankees catcher

"You enjoy it, and you appreciate it. . . . He's as hot as I've ever seen a player."

—D.J., on Alex Rodriguez's record-breaking start in 2007 when he slammed 14 homers in his first 18 games

"It's not fair. He doesn't play; that's the bottom line. He puts the best team out there on the field and gives us an opportunity to win. We haven't gotten the job done. His job is something that shouldn't ever be talked about."

—D.J., about the possibility of Joe Torre's job being on the line if the Yankees didn't play better, to reporters, April 29, 2007

D.J. DATA: Derek Jeter was known for his consistency through his 20-year career, with few subpar years or even down periods during individual seasons. Writing for the *New York Times* on May 13, 2007, Tyler Kepner pointed out one of Jeter's greatest achievements: "At one point, from Aug. 20, 2006, through May 3[, 2007], [Jeter] had at least one hit in 59 of 61 games. The stretch began with a 25-game hitting streak, followed by a hitless game. A 14-game hitting streak followed that. Then, after another hitless game, Jeter ripped off 20 in a row. According to Trent McCotter of the Society for American Baseball Research, only one other player since 1900 had as many as 59 games out of 61 with a hit: Joe DiMaggio, who hit safely in 60 of 61 in 1941, when he had a record 56-game streak."

"I don't think about it, really. All I try to do, pretty much, is to be consistent. I don't try to overanalyze anything, I don't try to sit back and say, *You're doing this or that.* I just try to consistently help out every day. You look at it that way, especially when things are going bad, you're able to get out of it, because you're not concerning yourself with how you're doing individually."

—D.J., about getting a hit in 59 of 61 games and leading the league with 53 hits and a .376 batting average, to Tyler Kepner, *New York Times*, May 13, 2007

"When the season's over, you get a chance to reflect on what happened during the season. Once you sit around and start talking about what you've done, that's when you're in trouble. You always strive to do something better."

—D.J., to Tyler Kepner, *New York Times*, May 13, 2007

"He's gotten an awful lot of two-out hits. . . . When you get two-out RBIs, that's something that really deflates the opposition and perks up your team."

—Joe Torre, Yankees manager, about how Jeter has gone 9-for-15 with two outs and runners in scoring position early in 2007, to Tyler Kepner, *New York Times*, May 13, 2007

"THE GOOD, THE BAD, AND THE UGLY, HE THOROUGHLY ENJOYS ALL OF IT." —DOUG MIENTKIEWICZ, YANKEES FIRST BASEMAN, ON HOW JETER WAS COPING DESPITE THE TEAM'S EARLY SEASON STRUGGLES, TO TYLER KEPNER, *NEW YORK TIMES*, MAY 13, 2007

"Derek Jeter put himself in pretty good company with his three hits last night, passing Joe DiMaggio for sole possession of fifth place on the Yanks' all-time list with 2,216. Only Lou Gehrig (2,721), Babe Ruth (2,518), Mickey Mantle (2,415), and Bernie Williams (2,336) have more hits in franchise history."

—Mark Feinsand, about Jeter's second-inning historic 2,215th hit off Curt Schilling in the Yankees' 8–3 win over Boston, New York *Daily News*, May 24, 2007

"When you start putting those names up on the board, and I've been here the whole time Derek has been here, it's incredible. Every single year, he's been as consistent as you could ask for."

—Joe Torre, Yankees manager, May 23, 2007

"I was excited [even] when I caught him in [career] strikeouts in my [fourth year]. Any time you're on a list with Joe DiMaggio or any Yankee greats, it's a bit overwhelming."

—D.J., about passing Joe DiMaggio in all-time hits, May 23, 2007

"He's an absolute hitting machine, and he's been doing it for a long time."

—Andy Pettitte, Yankees pitcher, May 23, 2007

"Honestly, I'd be lying if I said it wasn't nice [to pass DiMaggio in career hits], but we're concerned with other things, like winning games."

—D.J., May 23, 2007

"Now is when you find out what kind of player you are."

—D.J., challenging his teammates at a meeting called by Joe Torre after the Yankees got off to a 21–29 start and were in danger of not making the postseason in what was likely Torre's last season as Yankees manager

"Starting today, every game is a playoff game. That's how we treat every game: like it's a playoff game."

—D.J., to his teammates at a clubhouse meeting after the 2007 All-Star Game to get them to focus and play harder so the Yankees could make the postseason

"People automatically assume, 'Well, your payroll is this, and you've got that player, that player, this all-star, that all-star . . . you should win.' No, it just doesn't happen like that. You have to have a lot of things go right."

—D.J., about how some of his teammates assumed they'd be in the playoffs again in 2007 just because they were Yankees

"You got people that are going through things they've never been faced with before. So, yeah, it's probably safe to say that I've done more [speaking out]."

—D.J.

"He's got to be more vocal. When things aren't going right, he's the guy we follow."

—Jorge Posada, Yankees catcher

"Torre called Jorge Posada 'Jeter's alter ego,' because Posada and Jeter were such good friends and believed in the same unselfish baseball methodology and had no tolerance for anyone who thought otherwise. Unlike Jeter, however, Posada had no problem getting in the face of a teammate."

—Tom Verducci, *The Yankee Years*, Joe Torre and Tom Verducci, 2009

"You could see that he was concerned. When Jeet talks, because he really doesn't talk all that much, he gets [his teammates'] attention."

—Larry Bowa, Yankees coach, about how Jeter's words contributed to the team snapping out of its funk and going 12–4 and scoring 151 runs coming out of the 2007 All-Star break

"If Derek said something, we knew he was frustrated or upset or bothered by what was going on. . . . He wouldn't pick out anybody. It was *we* are not getting guys over. *We* are not working counts like we do when we're successful. *We* are not playing good defense. Derek understood that he had to talk like the manager, that it had to be *we* and not *you*."

—Mike Mussina, Yankees pitcher, who said players listened to Jeter because he was a peer, quoted by Ian O'Connor, *The Captain*, 2011

"I've said a lot of things over the years. People assume I don't. . . . I always hear, 'Well, he's not vocal.' Yeah. Okay. I talk to everybody. But I don't do it when there is a camera around."

—D.J., quoted by Joe Torre and Tom Verducci, *The Yankee Years*, 2009

"I'VE SEEN JOE GO UP TO JEET MANY TIMES AND SAY, 'YOU WANNA HANDLE IT?' AND JEET WOULD ALWAYS SAY, 'I'LL TAKE CARE OF IT,' AND HE WOULD."
—LARRY BOWA, YANKEES THIRD BASE COACH

"Guys on [the Yankees] despised [Carl Pavano]. One day, Jeet walked by him and said, 'Hey Pav. You ever going to play? Ever?' Wow. That was a damaging comment coming from Jeter. He didn't say a whole lot, but when he said something like that, it was pretty piercing."

> **—Mike Borzello, Yankees bullpen catcher, about the captain's jab at the always-injured, high-priced pitcher for the team from 2005 to 2008, quoted by Joe Torre and Tom Verducci, *The Yankee Years*, 2009**

"He's got as much talent as anyone in the game, and he seems to be revitalized, enjoying himself. . . . He got off to a great start, and he's been riding that wave, and hopefully he'll continue."

> **—D.J., about Alex Rodriguez in 2007, when he'd hit 54 homers and drive in 156 runs in an MVP season, July 8, 2007**

"In their final meeting of the regular season, the Yankees nipped the Red Sox, 4–3, in Boston, getting two home runs off Curt Schilling and a strong return by Roger Clemens on Sunday night. Robinson Canó hit the first homer, and Derek Jeter the second—a two-out, three-run blast over the Green Monster in the eighth inning that will rattle around New England brains until the Yankees' season is over."

> **—Tyler Kepner, *New York Times*, September 17, 2007**

"He's got one good knee, and he's still the best clutch hitter I've ever seen."

> **—Roger Clemens, Yankees pitcher, after Jeter's home run gave him a victory over Boston, September 16, 2007**

"It's scary, but you expect it. He just finds a way to have his best at-bat when you need it most."

> **—Doug Mientkiewicz, Yankees first baseman, September 17, 2007**

PINSTRIPE PRAISE

"We can put on the uniform, and we can play in the stadium, but we're not the New York Yankees unless Derek Jeter is playing shortstop."

—Mike Mussina, Yankees pitcher, to Sweeny Murti, 2003

"We live in a time when we glorify too many bad things. Derek has always represented good things."

—Joe Torre, Yankees manager from 1996 to 2007

"Derek has got a lot of character. He has been a great role model."

—Joe Torre, Yankees manager from 1996 to 2007

"He never had the greatest ability. He just went out there, showed up at work every day, and always had a responsibility that he had to entertain the fans. He's so humble. There's nothing phony about him."

—Joe Torre, executive vice-president of baseball operations and former Yankees manager from 1996 to 2007, to Maria Bartiromo, Fox Business, September 26, 2014

"Derek Jeter has been a great representative of what the Yankees have stood for over the years. He has been a team player who has only cared about winning. He has also been a fine example both on and off the field over his long tenure as a Yankee. It has been a real pleasure to manage and play alongside him."

—Joe Girardi, Yankees catcher and manager 2008–present

"It has been an incredible honor having a front-row seat for one of the great players of all time. Derek has been a winner every step of the way."

—Brian Cashman, Yankees GM

"From the time he stepped on the field, I watched him. He kept getting better and better."

—Phil Rizzuto, Yankees Hall of Fame shortstop and broadcaster, 2006

"I played with Pee Wee Reese, and Jeter is better. I had a ton of respect for Ernie Banks, but Jeter is better than him, too, because he can do it all."

—Clyde King, Yankees aide

"I told him that he's influenced my life a heck of a lot more than I could ever have influenced his life."

—Brian Butterfield, Boston coach and former Yankees coach and minor league fielding instructor of Jeter's, quoted by Daniel Carp, *USA Today*, September 4, 2014

"Star player, yeah, a star person even more so."

—Chili Davis, Yankees outfielder

"The thing about him is that he's a real person. He's never changed. He's never been too big for anybody. He's never said anything about anybody. He's always had respect for any player he's played with, and he's always had respect for the game. I always tell parents and kids all the time, if you want to use somebody as an example of what you want your kid to be like, Derek Jeter is the model you want to use. He is the prime example of what an athlete is really all about. He stands out, he's classy, he's first class, and he treats everybody the same way."

—Darryl Strawberry, Yankees outfielder from 1995 to 1999

"I really like this kid. . . . He'll talk with you, work with you. If you can't play with this guy, then you can't play with anyone."

—Luis Sojo, Yankees infielder and coach, to Harvey Araton, *New York Times*, May 10, 2005

"I've been around a lot of great teammates, guys who had ups and downs and guys who showed emotion. With Derek, you couldn't tell from one day to the next whether he got four hits or struck out four times. He was always mentally prepared to play well. He knew how to turn the page better than anybody I've ever seen."

—David Cone, Yankees broadcaster and former pitcher, *Yankees Magazine's Homestand Blog*, June 29, 2014

"I expected a lot of a good things from him when I came [to the Yankees in 2003]. But everything I've seen about him as a player, as a teammate, and as a person has surpassed my expectations in every aspect."

—Aaron Boone, Yankees third baseman, October 8, 2003

"You knew that he was special [from the start]. You knew that he carried himself a little bit different than a lot of the other guys, a lot of class, a lot of charisma, a lot of confidence for as young as he was."

—Andy Pettitte, Yankees pitcher

"HE'S A GREAT PLAYER, PROBABLY THE BEST I'VE EVER PLAYED WITH AS FAR AS IF YOU NEED A BIG HIT, I WANT HIM UP THERE."
—ANDY PETTITTE, YANKEES PITCHER, MAY 23, 2007

"He's the best player I've ever played with, and I think a lot of people in the clubhouse are going to say that before he's done. What sets him apart is the number of ways he can affect a game."

—Paul O'Neill, Yankees outfielder, 1993–2001

"His popularity was so much bigger than anybody else's; he was the face of the Yankees—but he never put himself above anyone else. He was a great teammate and a fun guy to be around."

—Paul O'Neill, Yankees broadcaster and former outfielder, 2014

"Like a great jazz musician, Jeter has mastered the mechanics and basics of baseball to a point that, when he's on the field, he is thoroughly prepared and in command of any situation, able to use his intuitive and creative right brain to make his body do what it needs to in order to turn routine into artistry."

—Bernie Williams, Yankees outfielder, *Rhythms of the Game*, 2011

"He cares about people. He does everything the right way. It's tough not to like him."

—Jorge Posada, Yankees catcher

"It was an honor and privilege to have Derek next to me all those years. He made me a better player and a better person. I'm so proud of our friendship, and I love him like a brother. Derek was a true champion and the greatest teammate I ever had."

—Jorge Posada, 2004

"For me, he's number one."

—Jorge Posada, Yankees catcher from 1995 to 2011, 2014

"I saw Derek play for 19 years in the big leagues and some years in the minors, and all I saw was determination and desire to be the best. For me, as Jorge says, he's No. 1. I saw the man always want to bring the best and give the best for the team. He didn't say too much, didn't speak too much, but he said it all on the field. That's what you want from your captain, your shortstop, your main guy . . . to be in charge, especially in tough situations. You want the ball hit to him for the last out of the game."

—Mariano Rivera, Yankees pitcher from 1995 to 2013, who Jeter called the best reliever of all-time, 2014

"He's a good person. . . . He's not a false type of guy who says one thing and does the other. He's what he is. What you see is what you get."

—**Tino Martinez, Yankee first baseman**

"When I first met him [in 2003], he just had this aura of a superstar. He was a really cool, handsome-looking guy. But when you got to know him, he also had this side of him that was so down to earth—playful, always joking around. It was hard not to like him."

—**Hideki Matsui, Yankees outfielder, to Sweeny Murti,**
***SportsNet New York*, September 22, 2014**

"Jeet stepped up at a big time in my life, when I needed it. He said, 'He's my teammate, he's my friend, and we'll welcome him back.' It was a controversial issue for who he is and what he represents, and for him to do that, I'll never forget that. That's the type of guy Jeet is. He knew I was going through a tough time, and he wanted to lend a hand."

—**Jason Giambi, Yankees first baseman, on how Jeter, who was staunchly anti-steroids,
supported Giambi after it was disclosed in 2004 that he had used steroids
during his career, to Tyler Kepner, *New York Times*, September 25, 2008**

"Being able to stay with the organization and being able to play with him here for as long as I have is pretty special."

—**Brett Gardner, Yankees outfielder, to Sweeny Murti,**
***SportsNet New York*, September 22, 2014**

"Jeter is the best player I have ever seen in baseball. Not because his ability is better than everybody because you can find guys with more power, guys with more speed, but nobody is smarter than Jeter. When you see a guy with five rings, that means something. I came here, and I said, 'Wow, I'm playing with Derek Jeter. . . . I'm going to tell my kids.'"

—**Francisco Cervelli, Yankees catcher**

"Derek was the most low-maintenance star I've ever been around. He never told us he wouldn't do something, he had no entourage, he had no special interview rules. People loved him as a baseball superstar, and women loved him as a sex symbol, but he never carried himself like that."

—Rick Ceronne, Yankees PR man

"He might go down, when it's all over, as the all-time Yankee."

—Don Zimmer, Yankees coach from 1996 to 2003, September 13, 2009

"All his teammates from years past, all the guys who are playing with him to now, all appreciate what he has been able to do."

—Cecil Fielder, Yankees first baseman, 2014

"I say Derek Jeter is the greatest Yankee ever."

—Don Mattingly, Yankees first baseman and coach

"It's good being Derek."

—David Cone, Yankees pitcher

"There's only one manager in baseball who would've let us make the playoffs [in 2007], and it was Joe. And there was only one captain who would've let us make the playoffs that year, and it was Derek. That's because neither one ever panics. . . . Jeter never worried and always believed. He always said, 'We're one pitch or one play away from reeling off 18 of 20, and if you believe it, it's going to happen.'"

—Doug Mientkiewicz, Yankees first baseman, quoted by Ian O'Connor, *The Captain*, 2001

"True to the promise Torre gave Steinbrenner, the Yankees beat Tampa Bay, 12–4, to clinch a postseason berth. . . . The final out had the familiar patina of the good old days: Steinbrenner watching, Rivera pitching, Posada catching, Jeter, who had homered in the game, at shortstop, and Torre in the dugout. The Yankees, beset by injuries and a malaise that put them in [a] 21–29 hole [after which they went 73–39], unloosed a wild celebration in the Tropicana Field visiting clubhouse."

—Tom Verducci, on Joe Torre's Yankees reaching the postseason for the 12th consecutive and final time with the team in 2007, *The Yankee Years*, Joe Torre and Tom Verducci, 2009

"I said two things: 'This one means a lot to me,' and 'I'm proud of each and every one of you guys,' I wanted to say more, and I couldn't get it out, and then Jeter started soaking me."

—Joe Torre, Yankees manager, who was doused with champagne by Jeter when he became too emotional to talk, September 26, 2007

"This has definitely been the hardest one. We scuffled early on, but everybody here knew we had a good team; we were just playing bad. A lot of people counted us out, and everybody [here] sort of liked that."

—D.J., who went 3-for-5 with a homer as the Yankees routed Tampa Bay 12–5, making it the 29th (and final) time under Torre the team had clinched a regular season or post-season title, September 26, 2007

"I can have pure thoughts of him as a ballplayer without being corrupted and having to think about him as an owner. I can think of him as . . . a totally impressive ballplayer and a joy to watch as a fan. And as much of a pain in the a— as he's been to have to play against, you've got to be appreciative of it."

—Stuart Sternberg, Tampa Bay principal owner

"The joke around the guys was that we all had Derek Jeter's Driven on, and all the bugs were attacking us."

—Doug Mientkiewicz, Yankees first baseman, joking about Jeter's cologne being the cause of the strange bug infestation in Cleveland that contributed to the Yankees' 2–1 11th-inning loss to the Indians in Game 2 of the ALDS

"The Boss is the Boss. He's going to say what he wants to say."

—D.J., responding to ailing Yankees owner George Steinbrenner's final interview in the *Bergen Record*, in which he said manager Joe Torre's job was on the line if the Yankees didn't overcome a 2–0 game deficit to the Cleveland Indians in the 2007 ALDS

"You're from Los Angeles. It's a regular day in New York."

—D.J., about how in New York it was commonplace to have rumors such as George Steinbrenner threatening to fire Joe Torre if the Yankees didn't reach the ALCS, to *Los Angeles Times* reporter Bill Shaikin, *Los Angeles Times*, October 8, 2007

"We've done it so many times, I thought we were going to do it again."

—D.J., after grounding into a double play to end Game 4 of the ALDS, eliminating the Yankees from the 2007 postseason and ending Joe Torre's 12-year tenure as their manager

"Everyone knows I love Mr. T. He's the best, in my opinion. It seems like every season you're asking if this is his best year, and this by far is his best year. It goes without saying I support him."

—D.J., hoping his only major league manager, Joe Torre, would sign another contract with the Yankees, but he would leave to manage the L.A. Dodgers and be replaced by Joe Girardi

"Yankee shortstop Derek Jeter may not have his fifth World Series ring, but WFAN listeners did pick him as the top New York sports celebrity of the past 20 years. The was part of [the nation's first all-sports station's] celebration of its 20th anniversary."

—David Hinckley, pop culture reporter, about Jeter being selected the number one New York sports celebrity ahead of Mark Messier, Lawrence Taylor, Joe Torre, Patrick Ewing, George Steinbrenner, Mariano Rivera, Bill Parcells, Mike Piazza, Don Mattingly, Phil Simms, and Dwight Gooden, New York *Daily News*, November 7, 2007

"Jeter had made his eighth All-Star team, had won his second straight Silver Slugger award, and had become the first major league shortstop ever to collect six 200-hit seasons. But the sabermetric police had hauled in Jeter again, charging him with a number of fielding felonies. John Dewan of *The Fielding Bible* slapped Jeter with another minus 34 in 2007 ([meaning] he made 34 fewer plays than the average shortstop). . . . Jeter's 2007 Ultimate Zone Rating, according to FanGraphs.com checked in at minus 17.9, meaning his defense cost the Yanks 17.9 runs [in 2007] the average shortstop would have saved."

—Ian O'Connor, *The Captain*, 2011

"I FEEL SORRY FOR THE NEXT YANKEE MANAGER BECAUSE HE'S THE ONE WHO'S GOING TO HAVE TO TELL JETER HE CAN'T PLAY SHORTSTOP ANYMORE."
—JOE GIRARDI, FORMER YANKEES CATCHER AND BROADCASTER, WHEN SEEING JETER'S DIMINISHED RANGE, NOT KNOWING HE WOULD BE THE YANKEES' NEXT MANAGER AND NEVER TELL JETER TO SWITCH POSITIONS

"[In the fall of 2007]. . . general manager Brian Cashman took him to dinner and told him that the sabermetric crowd was right, that Jeter needed to improve his range for the sake of the team, or else."

—Ian O'Connor, about how Cashman spared Joe Girardi from having to talk to Jeter about his defense as his first act as the new Yankees manager, ESPN.com, February 20, 2014

"I don't think you should have a problem with trying to get better. . . . It's important to get better and to be willing to listen."

—D.J., confirming again that he was the ultimate team player by agreeing with Brian Cashman to improve his lateral movement by working with a fitness trainer

"Derek is . . . the greatest team player ever. Watching him made me wish I played team sports."

—John McEnroe, Hall of Fame tennis player

"Joe [Girardi] only cared about Derek's defense and his mechanics; he didn't care about anything else. Joe wanted him to play defense better, and I told him I had the program to make that happen."

—**Jason Riley, director of performance of the Athletes Compound training facility in Tampa's Saddlebrook Resort**

"With the Yankees paying the bills . . . Riley formulated a plan to increase Jeter's first-step quickness, particularly in fielding grounders to his left. Power lifting was diminished, agility—especially of the hips—was emphasized, weight was lost."

—**Joel Sherman, *New York Post*, February 10, 2010**

"When the shortstop met [Jason] Riley after the 2007 season, he told the trainer he wanted to play another eight to 10 years."

—**Ian O'Connor, ESPNNewYork.com, November 21, 2010**

"Baseball is a game of adjustments, and Jeter made monumental changes when it came to his training and conditioning. . . . Jeter began working with sports performance coach Jason Riley and parted ways with longtime trainer Rafael Oquendo. Riley helped Jeter create a training philosophy that focused specifically on lateral movements. Eventually, Jeter was able to learn new ways to strengthen the muscles in his legs and also create strategies on how to field ground balls by using efficient angles. Jeter was obtaining an all-encompassing education on the synchronization of his motor units and how to maintain powerful and explosive movements over the course of a 162 game schedule."

—**Wayne G. McDonnell Jr., about Jeter and Jason Riley figuring out how to extend Jeter's career, *Forbes*, August 31, 2012**

"I've been in the industry for 15 years, and I've never come across anyone like Derek."

—**Jason Riley, Jeter's fitness trainer, about his new client's astonishing work ethic**

AN ASTONISHING WORK ETHIC

"There may be people who have more talent than you, but there's no excuse for anyone to work harder than you do—and I believe that."

—D.J.

"My parents worked very, very hard."

—D.J.

"He took care of the same church, high school, and elementary school for 36 years, fixing the electrical wiring, repairing faulty pipes, and vacuuming the rugs around the altar. . . . He rarely sneaked away to see Derek Jeter, his grandson, play for the Yankees in person. Not when he had to wake up at 4:30 a.m. the next day. His name was William Connors, though everyone knew him as Sonny, and he was as much of a fixture at Queen of Peace Church in North Arlington, N.J., as the pews. . . . He worked diligently as the head of maintenance, a routine that his grandson observed as a boy and emulated as a man."

—Jack Curry, about Jeter's strong role model in regard to worth ethic,
New York Times, February 23, 2003

"He never missed work, if he was sick or he had a bad day. He always seemed to go and work every day. I think that's something I learned from him."

—D.J., about his maternal grandfather, William "Sonny" Connors, who passed
away on January 1, 2009, from a heart attack at the age of 68

"When Jeter was 10, his grandfather took him to work and showed him how to mow the football field. Jeter recalled that the grass was almost a foot high, and he had a mower with a bag, so he had to stop dozens of times and empty it. Once Jeter finished the job hours later, Connors told him to start over because the grass had grown back. 'I never worked with him again,' said Jeter."

—Jack Curry, about Jeter's role model in regard to worth ethic,
New York Times, February 23, 2003

> **"MY BIGGEST FEAR IN LIFE, ON OR OFF THE FIELD, IS TO BE UNPREPARED—FOR ANYTHING. I'VE ALWAYS RELIED ON PRACTICE, REPETITION, AND DISCIPLINE."**
> **—D.J., *JETER UNFILTERED*, 2014**

"Baseball is a sport where, until you hit 1.000 and make no errors, you always have something to work on."

—D.J.

"Working on his weaknesses is not beneath him. So many guys, if they do something well, that's all they do."

—Buck Showalter, Yankees manager in 1995, to Mark Herrmann, *Newsday*, March 29, 2014

"I worked hard, and I achieved my goal and my dream of playing shortstop for the Yankees."

—D.J., *Tim McCarver Show*, May 9, 2000

"We all consider rolling over and shutting the alarm off. Jeter never rolls over. He gets out of bed. It is never a consideration to take a day off. It is a responsibility to his team and to himself."

—Joe Torre, Yankees manager

"I like to hit the gym early in the morning. I feel better throughout the day when I get in a workout first thing in the morning."

—D.J.

"It is very impressive what he does to enhance his God-given ability when there are no reporters around and no cameras. He's working. Anyone would have understood if he didn't pick up a bat or glove after either of the championship years, and if he had gone on cruise control. But the taste of a championship and personal success only made him hungrier. That is why I think he's going to be even greater."

—Trey Hillman, Jeter's minor league manager, who hit him grounders in Tampa prior to the 1999 season

"I remember working out with him in 1996 in the winter in Tampa, and I kept telling him he was working too hard and to settle down. Then, I came back to the team in 1999, and I saw that his work ethic had not changed. And that impressed me. That told me something about the kid. They had just won three World Series, and he's out there, still working hard. Seeing that dedication he had after all the success he had had spoke a lot about Derek Jeter."

—Jim Leyritz, Yankees catcher, to Peter May, *Boston Globe*, October 8, 2003

"You know what statement bothers me? 'Overnight success.' There is no off-season anymore. People don't understand that. I'm down here [in Tampa] in November."

—D.J., who enjoyed the process of working out in the off-season

"I treat every spring training like it's my first ever and that I'm trying to make the Yankees all over again. I don't care that I've been starting shortstop for five years, or that I was the MVP of the World Series in 2000. Sure I am going to have a good time in Tampa and have fun preparing for the season, but I am going to work like I have to earn my job because I do."

—D.J., *Game Day*, 2001

"Derek made other players better simply by the way he showed up for work. He took the game seriously, and he was prepared to play every day. In those ways, he reminded me of Don Mattingly. Derek's work ethic and energy were infectious."

—David Cone, Yankees broadcaster and former pitcher,
Yankees Magazine's Homestand Blog, June 29, 2014

"JETER'S DEVOUT COMMITMENT TO HONING HIS CRAFT IS UNPARALLELED AND GREATLY ADMIRED BY TEAMMATES AND COMPETITORS THROUGHOUT BASEBALL."

—WAYNE G. McDONNELL JR., *FORBES*, AUGUST 31, 2012

"I love it when people doubt me. It makes me work harder to prove them wrong."

—D.J., who made it a point as a youngster to be the last player off the field during practices

"When you put a lot of hard work into one goal and you achieve it, that's a really good feeling."

—D.J.

"My whole thing is, you're only playing for three hours a day. The least you can do is play hard. You have what, four or five at bats? OK, it's not difficult to run, to give it 100 percent. It's effort. You don't have to have talent for effort."

—D.J.

"I'm fine."

—D.J., his familiar response when asked if he was too hurt to play, even when he wasn't fine

"You guys saw the outside of Derek for 20 years, but we saw the inside; you never saw the bumps and bruises he had in the trainer's room, but at the same time, when 6:45 came around, he was ready to play, and you wanted him to be there when it was time to make the final out. Those are the types of guys you want on your team, because they will never say, 'I can't play today because I don't feel good.'"

—Mariano Rivera, Yankees relief pitcher

"His willingness to work at his craft, despite all the siren songs of fame that call him particularly, is emblematic of the whole [Yankees] team."

—Joel Sherman, *New York Post*, 1996

"So many people are insanely busy nowadays, and it's easy to say, 'Ah, I'll work out tomorrow.' But you have to set aside a time and stick to that schedule."

—D.J.

"I love his work ethic. He has a great attitude. He has the qualities that separate superstars from everyday people, and a lot of it is attributable to his great family background."

—Michael Jordan, basketball Hall of Famer

"The big difference for me is that, as I get older, I find it's a lot easier to stay in shape than it is to get back in shape."

—D.J.

"The last thing you want to do is finish playing or doing anything and wish you would have worked harder."

—D.J.

"Derek Jeter arrived at his 16th Yankees spring training yesterday labeled as the worst shortstop in the majors by some statistics brainiacs over at [the University of Pennsylvania]."

—Kevin Kernan, *New York Post*, February 21, 2008

"Maybe it was a computer glitch."

—D.J., shrugging off an article about a University of Pennsylvania study showing the Gold Glover was rated 56th among 56 shortstops evaluated from 2002 to 2005, February 20, 2008

"It made me ill when I read that article. It's disgraceful. You have to use a scout's eye to determine range. [Jeter's range is] not as good at it was, but it's not bad. You might put some people ahead of him range-wise, but that doesn't mean they're better shortstops. Look how sure-handed he is; look how clutch he is. That makes up for a lot."

—Gene Michael, Yankees senior advisor and scout, February 20, 2008

"Workout-wise, I switched up a little bit. I focused on agility, legs, first step, and lateral movement. I really made some adjustments. I feel a lot quicker, I'm moving around a lot better."

—D.J., speaking about his off-season training regimen designed to improve his range, February 20, 2008

"Today it sunk in; Mr. T's gone and Joe's here. It's weird not seeing Mr. T. I've always said through the years I couldn't imagine playing without him. Now, I can."

—D.J., about being content with the new Yankees manager, his former teammate Joe Girardi, at spring training, February 21, 2008

"Yog, it's because he doesn't want to get booed."

—D.J., exhibiting his well-known sharp wit telling Yogi Berra why Reggie Jackson asked the popular Yankee Hall of Famer to accompany him to the mound when he threw out the ceremonial first pitch at Yankee Stadium to begin the 2008 season

D.J. DATA: Derek Jeter once told sportswriter Steve Serby of the *New York Post* who he would like to portray him in a movie. His choice was Will Smith because "He's kind of goofy; I'm goofy. You guys don't know, but I've got a funny side."

"Jeter did play better defense in 2008 and did improve his sabermetric scores. . . . But his body needed time to adjust to a new routine, and a quad injury limited the improvement in his range."

—Ian O'Connor, *The Captain*, 2011

"It's an unbelievable feeling to know that someone's over there [in Iraq] fighting for our country, and yet they find the time to write to me here at Yankee Stadium. It puts a lot of things in perspective, but also makes you appreciate the position you're in, in terms of playing for this organization . . . to get a chance to provide entertainment for people."

—D.J., about receiving letters from troops in a war zone, May 11, 2008

"I ain't talking about it. You guys can have fun with it."

—D.J., to reporters about again being voted baseball's most overrated player, ahead of pitcher Barry Zito and Alex Rodriguez, in a poll of 495 major leaguers by *Sports Illustrated*, June 19, 2008

"When *Sports Illustrated* did a survey of 'Whom would you pick to build a team around' just a week earlier, Rodriguez finished first and Jeter second. Make up your mind fellas."

—Brian Lewis, *New York Post*, June 20, 2008

"The players can't claim Jeter isn't a winner, with the highest winning percentage of any active player. . . . His .600 winning percentage (1,140-759-2) is the best among all players (min. 1,000 games) according to Elias Sports Bureau."

—Brian Lewis, *New York Post*, June 20, 2008

D.J. DATA: When speaking to reporters, Derek Jeter was known for being tight-lipped, particularly if the subject was not baseball. One of the few times he ventured into politics during his 20-year career, was on May 11, 2008, when Barack Obama and Hillary Clinton were vying to be the Democratic nominee in the November presidential election and Steve Serby of the *New York Post* asked him, "Is this country ready for a black or woman president?" He replied, "I think so . . . without question. You get to a point where you have to look beyond race, you have to look beyond gender, and you have to look at the top candidate."

D.J. DATA: On May 29, 2008, Jeter, arguably the best baserunner in baseball, was picked off first base by Baltimore's Dennis Sarfate. The last time he'd been picked off was by Oakland's Gil Heredia on September 2, 1998.

"I could never imagine it."

—D.J., before a 5–1 victory over the Blue Jays in which his go-ahead RBI single against Toronto's Jesse Litsch in the third inning was his 2,416th base hit, moving him past Mickey Mantle for third place on the all-time Yankees' hit list behind Lou Gehrig and Babe Ruth, June 4, 2008

"Nearly five years ago to the day, Derek Jeter recorded his 1,500th hit against the Orioles at Camden Yards. Friday night, Jeter reached another milestone, picking up his 2,500th hit in the very same ballpark with a first-inning single. Jeter is the 88th player in history to reach the mark, joining Ken Griffey Jr., Omar Vizquel, Gary Sheffield, Iván Rodríguez, and Luis Gonzalez as the only active players on the list. None of the others is younger than 36; Jeter is 34."

—Mark Feinsand, New York *Daily News*, August 23, 2008

"I guess if you play long enough, you're bound to get some milestones. . . . More importantly, we won. We needed this game."

—D.J., after recording his 2,500th hit against Baltimore's Radhames Liz, August 22, 2008

"[Alfredo] Aceves won his first big-league start with seven strong innings Tuesday night, leading the Yankees to a 7–1 victory over the Angels. Johnny Damon homered twice, and Alex Rodriguez went deep as well, but Derek Jeter stole the hitting headlines with two singles to move past Babe Ruth for sole possession of second place on the Yankees' all-time hit list. Lou Gehrig and Ruth had occupied the top two spots on the Yankees' all-time hits list for the last 70 years, but Jeter changed that with a first-inning single. Jeter's single in the seventh gave him 2,520 hits, 201 behind Lou Gehrig's 2,721."

—Mark Feinsand, about Jeter's monumental hit off Ervin Santana, New York *Daily News*, September 10, 2008

"That's the only voice I'd heard growing up, and that's the only voice I wanted to hear when I was announced at home. And fortunately he agreed to do it."

—D.J., about asking Bob Sheppard, the unofficially retired Yankee public address announcer, in 2008 to record his introduction of Jeter so he could always have it played when he batted at Yankee Stadium

"It has been one of the greatest compliments I have received in my career of announcing. The fact that ['Derek Jeter, Number 2'] wanted my voice every time he came to bat is a credit to his good judgment and my humility."

—Bob Sheppard, Yankee Stadium public address announcer

"The first hit I gave up was to Derek Jeter. . . . It was a slider down the middle, [and] that was all a little new to me because that pitch usually didn't get hit that way coming out of college and in the minor leagues, especially."

—David Price, Tampa Bay pitcher, who would give up Jeter's 3,000th hit in 2011, about giving up a home run to Jeter on September 14, 2008, in his major league pitching debut

"I was talking with my parents last night. They were saying, you know, you need to sit back and try to enjoy it while it's happening, because I'm always thinking about how we can win and things like that. But this is something that is pretty special. . . . Records are made to be broken, but this one at least will never be broken."

—D.J., upon breaking Lou Gehrig's record of 1,269 hits at Yankee Stadium five days before the last game would be played there, September 16, 2008

"Jeter's hit off Gavin Floyd was his 1,270th in the 85-year-old ballpark, scheduled to close Sunday. . . . The hit came in Jeter's 8,002nd major league at-bat, and he passed Gehrig for second on the Yankees' career list behind Mickey Mantle (8,102)."

—*Associated Press*, September 16, 2008

"He's a true Yankee. I think he embodies what baseball people want to see in a player: a guy that goes about his business the right way. He stays out of the headlines. He just does a lot of great things. He's important to the community. He gives back all the time, to children, to everyone."

—Joe Girardi, Yankees manager, after Jeter's record-setting day, September 16, 2008

"Two down. Everyone readied their cameras. At this point, Girardi took out Jeter, a dramatic flourish used on rare occasions when the manager clearly acknowledges the moment. He was allowing the captain to hear 'DE-REK JE-TER' one more time as he jogged to the dugout. He emerged briefly for one more curtain call. Wilson Betemit went out to play short. With flashbulbs popping, Rivera went 2-and-1 on Brian Roberts, and then delivered the final pitch in the history of old Yankee Stadium."

—Marty Appel, on Jeter's denouement at the first Yankee Stadium, September 21, 2008, won by the Yankees 7–3 over Baltimore, *Pinstripe Empire*, 2012

"TWO OUTS IN THE NINTH, I THOUGHT, 'I BETTER THINK OF SOMETHING.'"
—D.J., ABOUT HIS WINGING HIS FAREWELL SPEECH TO THE FANS AFTER THE FINAL GAME IN THE ORIGINAL YANKEE STADIUM IS PLAYED, SEPTEMBER 21, 2008

"For all of us out here, it's a huge honor to put this uniform on and come out every day to play. And every member of this organization, past and present, has been calling this place home for 85 years. It's a lot of tradition, a lot of history, and a lot of memories. Now the great thing about memories is you're able to pass it along from generation to generation. And although things are gonna change next year, we're gonna move across the street, there are a few things with the New York Yankees that never change. That's pride, tradition, and most of all, we have the greatest fans in the world. And we're relying on you to take the memories from this stadium, add them to the new memories to come at the new Yankee Stadium, and continue to pass them on from generation to generation. So on behalf of the entire organization, we just want to take this moment to salute you, the greatest fans in the world."

—D.J., delivering a heralded impromptu farewell speech following the Yankees final game at the first Yankee Stadium, September 21, 2008

"I was scared to death [about having to give a speech]. When I was younger, I used to get nervous when I had to do an oral report in front of 25 people. I guess I've come a long way."

—D.J., September 21, 2008

"He doffed his cap to salute the fans, and his teammates followed. Jeter always seemed to get it right. The familiar sight of his postgame interviews, the little cough into his fist, the squeezing of the nose, the small smile, had become familiar over the years. But it had taken his parents to tell him to enjoy it a little more. 'Make sure you enjoy this,' they told him. 'We don't want to look back and wish you'd done something different.' With that, led by Jeter, the team took a lap around the field, waving their caps, sharing the emotion. . . . All the while, Frank Sinatra's 'New York, New York' played over and over until the last fans had filed out, well past midnight."

—Marty Appel, on Jeter's personal post-speech farewell to the fans at the first Yankee Stadium on September 21, 2008, *Pinstripe Empire*, 2012

— SIX —

A Living Legend

"Everyone is disappointed, but we're here to support him and get him through it."

—D.J., on why he was among the Yankees present at Alex Rodriguez's press conference at which he confessed to taking steroids while he played for the Texas Rangers, February 18, 2009

"I think he cheated himself."

—D.J., about teammate Alex Rodriguez admitting to having taken steroids when he played for the Texas Rangers, to reporters, February 18, 2009

"One thing that's irritating and really upsets me a lot is when you hear people say it was the Steroid Era and that everybody is doing it, and that's not true. Everybody wasn't doing it. . . . I never took performance enhancers, and I never took steroids. . . . I understand a lot of big names are coming out [in the Mitchell Report]. But that's not everybody."

—D.J., on the day after Alex Rodriguez's press conference, to reporters, February 19, 2009

"I keep hearing about, 'Should the other 103 names come out?' Really, what is that going to do? It's just going to be another story, and it's going to be another black eye for the sport. I don't feel as though people should go around and ask everyone if they're on that list, because it's supposed to be anonymous. We have rights, and it was supposed to be anonymous."

—D.J., February 19, 2009

"My career's not over."

—D.J., to Ian O'Connor upon learning the sportswriter planned
to write a book about Jeter's career during the spring of 2009,
quoted by Ian O'Connor, *The Captain*, 2011

"Derek Jeter helped his temporary team defeat his regular team in an exhibition game
on Tuesday in Tampa, Florida . . . . His two hits and two runs batted in helped the
American team to a 6–5 victory over the Yankees at Steinbrenner Field."

—Joe Lapointe, about Jeter, the captain of the American team in the upcoming
World Baseball Classic, playing his only game ever *against* the Yankees,
New York Times, March 4, 2009

"It was weird the first time around, wearing a different uniform. I hadn't worn
another uniform that represented anything other than the Yankees since
high school."

—D.J., March 2, 2009

"Playing in New York, I've had the opportunity to learn from the likes of Derek
Jeter, who has been great to me since day one. Every time I get the chance to
see him, he comes over and congratulates me or gives me a piece of advice. If
there's one player who you're going to look up to as far as on-field ability, as far as
leadership, and as far as the way he carries himself, it is Derek Jeter. He's a proven
winner, a guy I have the utmost respect for and would pay good money to see play
on a daily basis."

—David Wright, New York Mets third baseman, about his World Baseball Classic
teammate, *Tim McCarver Show*

"They don't strike out. Everybody puts the ball in play. They all run. The left-handers
are halfway down the line when they put the ball in play. If I could do it, or teach it,
I would."

—D.J., about the offense of the Japanese team that crushed America 9–4 in the
semifinals of the 2009 World Baseball Classic

"While Derek Jeter and the Yankees have kept fans' heart rates up all season long—particularly over the team's current six-game winning streak—Jeter took some time yesterday morning to increase the heart rates of several children who participate in his Turn 2 foundation, which helps children attain healthy lifestyles as well as promotes academic achievement. Several high school students were chosen to participate in light exercise at the 24 Hour Fitness-Derek Jeter Gym in Midtown, which recently opened. Jeter watched as the students did jumping jacks, pushups, and other exercises with the help of a trainer. It is the second such gym Jeter has opened, with another set to open in the fall."

—David Satriano, *New York Post*, May 20, 2009

"One reason I decided to do this is because helping the kids is something that means a lot to me, and I want to share it with everybody. You don't have to be a professional athlete to keep yourself in great shape. . . . Our foundation throughout the years has preached prevention of drugs and alcohol to promote a healthy lifestyle. This is part of it; staying in shape, working out, and exercising help your health and make you feel good about yourself."

—D.J., about the Turn 2 event at his gym in New York City, May 19, 2009

"The Yankees . . . saw an entirely different human being in 2009. [Jason] Riley had loosened the tightness in Jeter's left ankle and hip. The trainer used a relentless series of resistance drills and cone drills to re-boot the communication center linking Jeter's brain, muscles, and nerves. The results were staggering. Suddenly, Derek Jeter had replaced Dick Clark as America's oldest teenager."

—Ian O'Connor, ESPNNewYork.com, November 20, 2010

"Jeter is Benjamin Button. . . . My God, it's amazing. My whole front-office career, I've been waiting for Jeter to slow down, and this year he's as good as ever."

—Billy Beane, Oakland A's GM

"Jason Riley's regimen was largely responsible for Jeter's defensive rebirth, and Kelleher's film work didn't hurt either. The former big league infielder spent his off-season studying every 2008 grounder that went Jeter's way and found the captain was playing too shallow and setting his feet too late. Jeter realized he could reach more balls by playing deeper, and by moving into a ready position earlier in the delivery. . . . As a result, Jeter's sabermetric scores [in 2009] finally lined up with his standing among Yankee fans. . . . Jeter ranked as the third-best defensive shortstop in all of baseball."

—Ian O'Connor, *The Captain*, 2011

"IF ANYONE'S GOING TO HIT A GAME-WINNING HOME RUN FOR THE FIRST WIN AT THE NEW STADIUM, IT'S GOING TO BE DEREK."
—MARK TEIXEIRA, YANKEES FIRST BASEMAN, AFTER JETER'S EIGHTH-INNING HOMER OFF THE INDIANS' JENSEN LEWIS GAVE THE YANKEES A 6–5 VICTORY, THEIR FIRST WIN AND SECOND GAME IN THE NEW YANKEE STADIUM, APRIL 17, 2009

D.J. DATA: Derek Jeter was never ejected from a game in his professional career. He came closest on July 6, 2009, when he got face-to-face with umpire Marty Foster after he slid into third base, eluded the tag, and was called out anyway.

"The ball beat you. He doesn't have to tag you."

—Marty Foster, umpire whose sorry explanation, according to Jeter, was why the Yankees captain argued emphatically and was nearly ejected, July 6, 2009

"I was unaware of that change in the rule."

—D.J., argued to umpire Marty Foster, July 6, 2009

"In my 27 years in the big leagues, [Jeter] is probably the classiest person I've ever been around."

—John Hirschbeck, umpire crew chief, to reporters after the game, suggesting he believed Jeter's account of what Marty Foster said to him, July 6, 2009

"I've been a big fan for a long time."

—President Barack Obama, to Jeter in the American League clubhouse during the 2009 All-Star Game

"This guy's like the old guy around here now, huh?"

—President Barack Obama, about Jeter to his American League teammates in their clubhouse during the 2009 All-Star Game

"I'm not the oldest."

—D.J., half-joking to the older President Barack Obama in the American League clubhouse during the 2009 All-Star Game

"I like Obama. . . . I really like the way he carries himself. . . . He just doesn't seem like he gets flustered much."

—D.J., to Steve Serby, *New York Post*, July 5, 2009

"For years, few have been as reliable as Derek Jeter has been at shortstop for the Yankees. And now, no one has been more productive. With a three-hit performance in the Bombers' 10–3 loss to the Mariners on Sunday at Safeco Field, Jeter surpassed Hall of Famer Luis Aparicio in becoming the all-time Major League leader in hits as a shortstop. Jeter entered the afternoon trailing Aparicio (2,673) by one hit, but tied the former 18-year big league vet with a first-inning single to right field off Seattle right-hander Doug Fister. The career Yankee stood alone after his next at-bat, a run-scoring double to right field off Fister that drove home Ramiro Pena with the first run of the game. Jeter also added a bloop single to right field off Fister in the seventh inning to finish the afternoon 3-for-4 and with 2,675 hits as a shortstop. He also has 13 hits as a designated hitter."

—Bryan Hoch, MLB.com, August 16, 2009

"It's amazing what he's been able to accomplish, and he's still got a lot of baseball left. A lot of guys, when they try to get that [kind of] record, it takes them a while. It didn't take him long today."

—**Joe Girardi, Yankees manager, August 16, 2009**

"I didn't even know about that record until two days before. We were in Seattle. A reporter asked me about it. I said, 'What are you talking about?' I had no idea whatsoever. I was unaware of it. But it's hard to believe, when you think about it."

—**D.J., about becoming the all-time hits leader for shortstops, to Tom Verducci, *Sports Illustrated*, November 25, 2009**

"You see a Manny Ramirez, you seen an A-Rod, you see Jeter. . . . Guys that I played against and with, these guys you're talking about cannot compare. We didn't have baggy uniforms. We didn't have the dreadlocks. It was a clean game, and now they're setting a bad example for the young guys."

—**Jim Rice, Red Sox Hall of Famer, *Associated Press*, August 21, 2009**

"I didn't know I was like that. . . . I don't wear baggy pants or have dreadlocks."

—**D.J., responding to Jim Rice's bizarre criticism, New York *Daily News*, August 2009**

CLASSIC MOMENT:
SEPTEMBER 11, 2009, YANKEE STADIUM, NYC

"[Derek] Jeter passed [Lou] Gehrig for the most hits recorded by a Yankee, 2,722, a record held by Gehrig for 72 years. His Yankees teammates leaped out of the dugout to embrace him, and even the Orioles' players applauded from the dugout. The charter franchises in the major leagues all had their hit leaders, and they had names like Cobb, Aaron, Lajoie, Banks, Musial, Mays, Rose, Yastrzemski."

—**Marty Appel, *Pinstripe Empire*, 2012**

"It was vintage Derek Jeter; stay inside the ball and hit it the other way. He's been doing it a long time."

—**Joe Girardi, Yankees manager, after Jeter laced a fastball by Baltimore's Chris Tillman past diving first baseman Luke Scott for a team-record career hit 2,722**

"The players on the Yankees' bench poured from the dugout to greet him, taking turns giving hugs. Alex Rodriguez was the first to arrive, before Robinson Canó, Mark Teixeira, Joba Chamberlain, and the rest. . . . The fans chanted Jeter's first and last names, and Jeter waved his helmet to all corners of the new Yankee Stadium. As he did on Wednesday, when he tied the record, Jeter pointed to the box with his parents, sister, and friends on the suite level above the Yankees' on-deck circle. Jeter's girlfriend, the actress Minka Kelly, stood beside his mother, Dorothy, and both smiled widely. The crowd continued to chant for Jeter, and Nick Swisher, the next batter, stepped out of the box to make the moment last. As the cheers cascaded over Jeter, he waved his helmet again and then clapped a few times in Swisher's direction: back to work."

—**Tyler Kepner,** *New York Times*

"FOR THOSE WHO SAY TODAY'S GAME CAN'T PRODUCE LEGENDARY PLAYERS, I HAVE TWO WORDS: DEREK JETER."
—GEORGE STEINBRENNER, YANKEES OWNER, PUBLICITY RELEASE, SEPTEMBER 11, 2009

"Forty, 50, 60 years from now, fans are going to read the back of his baseball card and see a lot of hits. That's pretty amazing, but that won't capture even 50 percent of it."

—**Alex Rodriguez, Yankees third baseman**

"When you talk about Gehrig, you're suddenly in church; it's a hushed tone, it's respectful. Who was greater than Gehrig? And then he blows by him!"

—**Billy Crystal, comedian**

"Lou Gehrig, being a former captain and what he stood for, you mention his name to any baseball fan around the country, it means a lot. I think passing him makes it stand out that much more."

—D.J., about what he believed was his finest individual
achievement so far in his career

"It's still hard to believe. . . . Being a Yankees fan, this is something I never imagined. Your dream is always to play for the team, and once you get there, you just want to stay and try to be consistent. This wasn't part of it. This whole experience has been overwhelming."

—D.J.

"The fans. It wasn't ideal conditions tonight, and for the fans to stick around, it really means a lot. Since day one, they've always been very supportive. They're just as much a part of this as I am."

—D.J., his response when asked what he would remember most years later about
the rainy day on which he passed Gehrig's Yankees' hit record

"This is a day everyone will continue to remember forever in our country, and I'm sure people's thoughts were elsewhere. But at least for a little while, they had a chance to cheer today."

—D.J., remembering the eighth anniversary of 9/11

"Come on, man, you're talking about another 1,500 hits."

—D.J., scoffing at the idea he could pass Pete Rose's major league record of 4,256
hits, despite being ahead of Rose's pace at the age of 35

"I don't think [Derek's] ever played any better than he's playing right now, which is awesome. He's running really well, he's playing great defense, he's hitting, he's hitting for power. Where he takes it from now, we're all having fun watching him."

—Alex Rodriguez, Yankees third baseman, praising his teammate who was batting .331

"Jeter and Rodriguez had learned to function together—never close, but no longer icy. They had made different choices and discovered that they did not, in fact, have much in common except what mattered most: They were talented players who could help each other win."

—Tyler Kepner, introduction, *Derek Jeter: From the Pages of the New York Times*, 2011

"For me, playing next to him I've learned so much. He's motivated me and inspired me. . . . Derek is the ultimate grinder. He's the ultimate winner."

—Alex Rodriguez, Yankees third baseman, who hoped to win his first championship in 2009

"I've had conversations with Derek, [and he] understands Alex's positives and negatives. He loves the statistical return he gets from Alex, and he's come to understand the way Alex is."

—Buck Showalter, who managed Jeter on the Yankees and Rodriguez on the Rangers

"When the Yankees clinched the AL East title, the papers ran photos no enemy of the Yankee state ever wanted to see. . . . The photos captured a beaming Jeter lifting A-Rod's cap off his head with his left hand and pouring a bottle of bubbly over A-Rod's bowed scalp with his right. At last, the captain had baptized Rodriguez a Yankee."

—Ian O'Connor, *The Captain*, 2011

"The captain elevated his traditional stats along with his sabermetric scores, finishing [2009] with a .334 batting average, [212 hits and] a .406 on-base percentage, and more steals (30) than he had in 2007 and 2008 combined as the 103–59 Yanks won the AL East by eight games. Jeter nailed down his 11th division title and 13th postseason appearance in 14 years as a full-time shortstop."

—**Ian O'Connor,** *The Captain,* **2011**

"The new Yankee Stadium hosted its first playoff game in style Wednesday night. . . . [The Yankees] snuffed the Minnesota Twins, 7–2, in the first game of their division series. . . . Alex Rodriguez shook his playoff slump with two run-scoring singles. Both times, he drove in Derek Jeter, who hit the first postseason homer at the new stadium in the third inning. . . . Jeter, who reached base in all four of his at-bats, now has as many postseason homers (18) as Mickey Mantle and Reggie Jackson. That he has done it in many more games does not diminish his reputation."

—**Tyler Kepner, about Game 1 of the Yankees' three-game sweep of Minnesota in the 1999 ALDS,** *New York Times,* **October 8, 2009**

"Back in the ALCS for the first time in five years, New York built a 2–0 lead in the first. Derek Jeter and [Johnny] Damon singled, and left fielder Juan Rivera threw to the shortstop position for an error that put runners on second and third. Alex Rodriguez's one-out sacrifice fly . . . gave the Yankees the lead, and Hideki Matsui followed with a short popup . . . [that] fell for a single as Damon came home."

—*Associated Press,* **about Jeter igniting a two-run rally in the first inning that would be enough for CC Sabathia to beat the Angels, 4–1, in Game 1 of the 2009 ALCS, October 16, 2009**

"It wasn't fun under these conditions."

—**D.J., who scored the first run and drove in the last run as the Yankees prevailed 4–1 over the Angels on a freezing, windy night in the Bronx**

"Coming through under pressure once again, [Alex] Rodriguez hit a tying homer in the 11th inning, and the New York Yankees edged Los Angeles 4–3 Saturday night on Maicer Izturis' error in the 13th for a 2–0 lead in the best-of-seven series. . . . Derek Jeter also homered, and [Robinson] Canó had an RBI triple for the Yankees. Mariano Rivera threw 2⅓ shutout innings, his longest outing since May 30, 2006. . . . Jeter's third-inning homer [off Joe Saunders] was his second of these playoffs and No. 19 of his postseason career, breaking a tie with Yankees Hall of Famers Mickey Mantle and Reggie Jackson for third place behind ex-teammate Bernie Williams (22) and Manny Ramirez (29)."

—*Associated Press*, **October 17, 2009**

"The Angels did survive Jeter's leadoff homer and A-Rod's fourth-inning blast to win Game 3 in 11 innings, and they did barely overcome A-Rod's Game 4 pounding to win a topsy-turvy Game 5 and send the series back to New York. . . . Game 6 was an efficient Pettitte-to-Joba-to-Mariano execution, and when the clock struck midnight, the great Rivera secured the last of his six outs, a strikeout of Gary Mathews Jr. that sent Jeter and Mark Teixeira into Rodriguez's arms to celebrate A-Rod's first trip to the World Series."

—Ian O'Connor, about the Yankees winning their first American League pennant since 2003, *The Captain*, 2011

"I can't tell you how much I admire Derek Jeter, everything about him. He's a symbol of everything that's right about the game, as far as I'm concerned. He's a great role model for other players. When I tell my kids or grandkids about the great players from my time, I'll be proud to say I was on the same field with Derek Jeter."

—Howie Kendrick, Angels second baseman

"You're a wonderful role model not only for the youth of America but also our players. You have been the face of baseball for many years, and you're truly deserving of this award."

—Bud Selig, MLB commissioner, when presenting Jeter with the prestigious Roberto Clemente Award for community service because of his work with the Turn 2 Foundation prior to the Yankees' victory in Game 2 over Philadelphia in the 2009 World Series

"I'm well aware of what he did on and off the field. I think every player should be aware of that. If they are not aware of it, they should learn about it."

—D.J., when presented the Roberto Clemente Award by his widow Vera Clemente

"Any award that's named after Hank Aaron to me is very special [because of] what he has represented, not only in his playing days but how he handled himself when he was off the field and to this day. I have the utmost respect for him. This is an award that means a lot to me."

—D.J., when presented with the award for being the best offensive player in the American League prior to the Yankees' victory over Philadelphia in Game 4 of the 2009 World Series

"[Jeter's] always been a really tough out. He never gives away an at-bat. He's always trying to take the ball the other way, and he does the little things very well at a pretty high rate. Having him in those Yankees lineups was tough, because you'd face him early and then have some big boppers behind him. He's just trying to get on base. He's a very solid player and not a fun at-bat at all."

—Cliff Lee, Philadelphia left-handed starter, who won Games 1 and 5 for the only two Phillies victories in the 2009 World Series

"The New York Yankees beat the Philadelphia Phillies 7–3 in Game 6 on Wednesday night to win the World Series at Yankee Stadium. The Yankees won their 27th World Series and first since 2000. They're the first team to win a World Series to start and finish a decade. . . . In Game 6, Jeter moved into a tie for third on the all-time World Series doubles list (nine, one behind Yogi Berra and Frankie Frisch), moved ahead of Lou Gehrig into fourth place on the all-time World Series runs list (32, behind Mickey Mantle with 42, Yogi Berra with 41, and Babe Ruth with 37) and into fifth on the all-time WS hits list (50). He's also second on the all-time WS list for strikeouts (39, behind Mickey Mantle with 54). Jeter had his second three-hit game of the World Series on Wednesday (Game 1 as well). Jeter hit safely in all six World Series games and, with 11 hits, fell one hit shy of the WS record for a six-game Series. His career World Series average is now .321 (50-for-156)."

—ESPN.com, after Jeter's final World Series game, November 5, 2009

"They stood together, arms around each other's shoulders, on a makeshift podium in the middle of a still-packed stadium as euphoria rained from the sky. Mariano Rivera. Derek Jeter. Andy Pettitte. Jorge Posada. . . . Behind the four of them, the scoreboard told the tale of the final World Series game, the final baseball game of 2009: Yankees 7, Phillies 3. . . . The Great Mariano got the final five outs. Derek Jeter slapped three hits. Andy Pettitte won the clinching game of a postseason series for the *sixth* time. Jorge Posada was the man catching that first pitch by Pettitte and that final pitch by Rivera. There was something fitting about that—the four of them finding their names in this particular box score—because they are the men who connect all the dots in the Yankees' universe."

—Jayson Stark, about how the Gang of Four, or Core Four, was pivotal in the Game 6 victory over Philadelphia that gave the Yankees their 27th world title, ESPN.com, November 4, 2009

"It's special. We've played together for what—17 years, 18 years? We were together in the minor leagues coming up. And you don't see that too often, especially with free agency. You don't see guys staying together. We're like brothers. And to get an opportunity to spend all these years together and win another championship, it really feels good."

—D.J., about his longtime friends and teammates Rivera, Posada, and Pettitte, November 4, 2009

"WE ALL HAD THE SAME MINDSET. WE HAD THAT MINDSET FROM THE MINOR LEAGUES COMING UP. WE ENJOYED WINNING. WE WERE SPOILED EARLY ON, BUT WE WORKED REALLY HARD, AND NONE OF US MADE EXCUSES."
—D.J., ABOUT WHAT UNIFIED THE CORE FOUR—JETER, RIVERA, PETTITTE, AND POSADA, 2014

"On those teams [that won in the '90s], those guys were young. They weren't veteran guys like they are now. They had different roles. Derek Jeter wasn't a leader back then. Jorge Posada wasn't a leader then. They were the guys looking to the David Cones, the Paul O'Neills, the Scott Brosiuses, the veterans around them. But now this is those guys' team. They've taken over that leadership role. And they've proved they can deliver a championship with a whole new cast."

—Brian Cashman, Yankees GM, about the team not having won a world title since 2000, back when Jeter, Rivera, Posada, and Pettitte were young ballplayers, November 4, 2009

"These guys are very classy individuals—Jeter, Mariano, Pettitte, and Posada— especially for me, in my first year here, being a pitcher. They're guys who really showed you how to be a New York Yankee. And they do that by being themselves. By showing class. And being the most humble human beings I've ever been around."

—A.J. Burnett, Yankees pitcher, November 4, 2009

"It's good to be back. This is right where it belongs."

—D.J., while holding the championship trophy above his head during the Yankees' post–World Series award presentation after defeating the Phillies, November 4, 2009

"It feels better than I remember it. It's been a long time."

—D.J., November 4, 2009

"Probably not as bad as you."

—D.J., in response to David Letterman asking him, and fellow guests Andy Pettitte and Jorge Posada, how hung over they were after celebrating the Yankees' 2009 World Series victory, *Late Show with David Letterman*, November 5, 2009

"You could do this every day, and you wouldn't get tired of it."

—D.J., during the Yankees' ticker tape parade in New York City to honor their 2009 world championship

"Derek Jeter has won his fourth Gold Glove at shortstop, joining New York Yankees first baseman Mark Teixara among the American League players honored for fielding excellence. . . . Jeter and Teixara helped lead the Yankees past Philadelphia last week for the team's 27th World Series championship."

—*Associated Press*, **November 10, 2009**

"The American League and National League honor rolls chosen include eight incumbents from the 2008 teams, led by Yankees shortstop Derek Jeter and the Phillies second baseman Chase Utley, who both claimed their fourth Silver Sluggers. . . . The New York captain excelled not with the long ball or even in run production—with modest totals of 18 homers and 66 RBIs—but responded to being asked to lead off by hitting .334, scoring 107 runs, and posting 200-plus hits for the seventh time."

—Tom Singer, about Jeter winning the Silver Slugger Award for being the best hitter at the shortstop position, MLB.com, November 12, 2009

"No, Derek Jeter hasn't blown through his fortune already; he's playing a bedraggled bum in a movie . . . a fictionalized version of himself in the upcoming Will Ferrell flick *The Other Guys*, which was being filmed yesterday at Nathan's Famous in Coney Island. . . . In the comedy Ferrell, and notorious Red Sox fan Mark Wahlberg play cops who . . . are permanently benched after Wahlberg's character wrongly shoots Jeter in the leg after seeing him walking around with a bat. . . . It's not the first time Jeter's played himself on the silver screen; he also had a cameo in the 2003 Adam Sandler–Jack Nicholson comedy, *Anger Management*."

—Rich Calder and Lukas I. Alpert, *New York Post*, November 13, 2009

"IT'S UNBELIEVABLE. IT WAS COMPLETELY UNEXPECTED. IT CAME OUT OF THE BLUE. WHEN I HEARD IT, WHAT CAN YOU SAY? IT'S ONE OF THE GREATEST HONORS YOU CAN ACHIEVE IN SPORTS."
—D.J., ABOUT BEING THE FIRST YANKEE SELECTED AS *SPORTS ILLUSTRATED'S* SPORTSMAN OF THE YEAR SINCE THE AWARD WAS FIRST GIVEN OUT IN 1954, NOVEMBER 30, 2009

"This verifies my idea that he is on the level of Ruth and Gehrig. He's the greatest shortstop in the history of the game."

—Terry McDonell, *Sports Illustrated* group editor, November 30, 2009

"You celebrate for a short amount of time, and then it's back to preparing for next season. Last year was a wonderful year, but last year is over with."

—D.J., at a pre–spring training workout in Tampa, February 9, 2010

"It was fun. None of us would be here if it wasn't for [Mr. Steinbrenner]. The stadium would not be here if it wasn't for him. To present him with the ring, you know how much winning means to him, that's the only thing he cares about."

—D.J., after presenting Yankees owner George Steinbrenner the 2009 championship ring before the 2010 home opener at Yankee Stadium, April 13, 2010

"I got the chance to tease [Mr. Steinbrenner] because he had an Ohio State ring, and I told him to take it off now and replace it with the Yankees ring. That's what you remember, those intimate moments."

— D.J., about presenting Yankees owner George Steinbrenner the 2009 championship ring on April 13, 2010

"We gather to honor two men who are both shining stars in the Yankee Universe. They'll be forever remembered in baseball history and in our hearts."

—D.J., speaking at a memorial service for Yankees owner George Steinbrenner and Yankees iconic public-address announcer Bob Sheppard, who died a few days apart, July 16, 2010

THE BOSS AND HIS TRUE YANKEE

"He respected George Steinbrenner like a second father. And it meant the world to Derek that George respected him back."

—Dorothy Jeter, to Meredith Marakovits, YES Network, 2014

"[This] defines Derek in my book. He always showed up [in street clothes] to see my dad and tell him how he would do the best job that he could. I always cherish how respectful [he] was with my dad."

—Jennifer Steinbrenner Swindal, Yankees general partner and vice chairperson, recalling Jeter's annual visit to her late father George Steinbrenner at the Yankees facility in Tampa, prior to spring training, to Christian Red, New York *Daily News*, September 28, 2014

"I've known [Mr. Steinbrenner] since I was 18 years old. There's a respect factor because he's the owner, and I work for him, but we were more friends than anything. I'd go visit him in the off-season because we both live in Tampa. We would have bets on Ohio State–Michigan football games. I've been in trouble a couple of times. We've filmed commercials with him dancing. It's tough because he's more than just an owner to me. He's a friend of mine."

—D.J., about rarely seeing Yankees owner George Steinbrenner because of his declining health since presenting him with his final championship ring prior to the 2010 home opener on April 13, 2010

"There's not a better shortstop in the game today than Derek Jeter."

—George Steinbrenner, Yankees owner, on his rookie star, 1996

"I don't know anyone I'd take ahead of him. He's as good as [Alex Rodriguez and Nomar Garciaparra]. If I had my choice of those three, I'd take Jeter."

—George Steinbrenner, Yankees owner

"He's a father figure to anyone in his organization, past or present."

—D.J.

"He expected perfection, and that rubbed off on the organization; whether it was the players, the front office, people working at the stadium, it didn't make a difference. . . . He expected a lot."

—D.J., July 13, 2010

"I'm very proud of Derek Jeter. He's a great leader and a great captain, and he deserves every honor he wins. He truly works hard for the Yankees and for our fans."

—George Steinbrenner, Yankees owner, 2005

"The name Derek Jeter is made for stardom. He's got an infectious smile, and he's so handsome and well-behaved. He's just a fine young man who does everything right. He's like Jack Armstrong and Frank Merriwell, guys I grew up rooting for. Some guys come along who just measure up."

—George Steinbrenner, Yankees owner

"The Boss and I always had such a good relationship. I always felt the same way he did when it came to playing and doing your job and being accountable and leading by example."

—D.J., who believed he got along so well with George Steinbrenner because while he was respectful of him he wasn't intimidated by him

"WHETHER IT WAS THE PLAYERS, THE FRONT OFFICE, THE PEOPLE WORKING AT THE STADIUM, IT DIDN'T MAKE A DIFFERENCE. HE EXPECTED PERFECTION."
—D.J.

"His biggest thing was accountability. . . . If we didn't win, it was somebody's fault. Who didn't do their job? Why didn't they do it?"

—D.J., to Brandon Steiner, Steiner Sports event

"You're the best, Jetes."

—George Steinbrenner, Yankees owner, when on Opening Day 2010 he received his seventh and last World Series ring from his captain, April 13, 2010

"It is no revelation to call Derek Jeter the face of the Yankees, now more than ever after the passing of George Steinbrenner, the franchise's dominant figure for more than a third of a century. . . . The more interesting question is whether the Yankees captain is not merely the front man for the Yankees but whether he is the current face of Major League Baseball itself. Overstatement? Consider a *Sports Business Daily* poll released yesterday in which more than four dozen business executives and journalists named Jeter the most marketable player in baseball. By a lot. Jeter was named first on 39 of 49 ballots."

—Neil Best, *Newsday*, July 20, 2010

"Derek Jeter passed Babe Ruth on the career hits list and drove in three runs . . . [helping lead] the New York Yankees to a 7–2 victory over the Boston Red Sox on Sunday night. . . . Jeter broke a tie with The Babe for 39th place on the career hits list with an RBI single in the second inning, his 2,874th hit. Jeter waved his helmet to an exuberant crowd and [Alex] Rodriguez retrieved the milestone ball that was rolled toward the Yankees dugout as fans [at Yankee Stadium] chanted 'Der-ek Je-ter!'"

—*Associated Press*, August 8, 2010

"It's part of the game. My job is to get on base."

—D.J., offering no apology when instant replay proved he conned umpire Lance Barksdale with dramatic acting into believing he'd been hit on the wrist by an inside pitch from Tampa Bay's Chad Qualls that actually hit his bat, September 14, 2010

"If our guys had done it, I would have applauded that performance. If our guy does it, I'm very happy if we end up getting the call."

—**Joe Maddon, Tampa Bay manager, not criticizing Jeter's gamesmanship, September 14, 2010**

"The incident [in which Jeter was granted first base by feigning he was hit by a pitch] opened up the whole concept of what constitutes cheating and what constitutes, for lack of a better term, gamesmanship. . . . Raising the whole thing to another level was the identity of the perp. *Derek Jeter?* . . . The Yankee shortstop is regarded by many as Mr. Purity, the man Who Plays the Game Right. . . . He is the closest thing we have to baseball royalty, sainthood even. Shouldn't this man be honor-bound to play the game above reproach? No one who has watched him play for the Yankees these past 16 years should feel that way."

—**Bob Ryan, *Boston Globe*, September 17, 2010**

"Jeter has a very well-defined style of play, and it certainly involves borderline chicanery. Take for example, his infuriating habit of jackknifing away from pitches on the inside corner. He absolutely flings his body backward in a violent manner, even on pitches that have as much chance of hitting him as they do John Sterling and Suzyn Waldman up in the broadcast booth. But this selling job has gained him countless balls that should have been strikes. . . . In the field, he is the master of the elaborate swipe tag, a maneuver designed to sell safes into outs."

—**Bob Ryan, explaining why Jeter's pretending to be hit by a pitch was consistent with other ways he misled umpires, *Boston Globe*, September 17, 2010**

"The first time we went to Yankee Stadium [in 2010], I screamed at Derek Jeter from the dugout. Our guys are thinking, 'Wow, he's screaming at Derek Jeter.' Well, he's always jumping back from balls just off the plate. I know how many calls that team gets—and yes, he [ticks] me off."

—**Buck Showalter, Baltimore manager, *Men's Journal*, April 2011**

"Overnight, the ageless wonder at short had devolved into the picture of Dorian Gray."

—**Ian O'Connor about Jeter's disappointing 2010 season in which he hit a career-low .270, had career lows in on-base and slugging percentages, and saw his sabermetric fielding numbers tumble, *The Captain*, 2011**

"They hit better than us; they pitched better than us; they played better than us."

—D.J., on how the Yankees, who had swept the ALDS from Minnesota, were dominated by Texas in the six-game 2010 ALCS

"It's a tremendous honor to receive the Gold Glove award, especially since this recognition comes from managers and coaches for whom I have a great deal of respect. It is particularly gratifying to be recognized for defense, as it is something I take a lot of pride in and am constantly working to improve."

—D.J., after winning his fifth Gold Glove, to the consternation of sabermetricians, for a season in which he made just six errors and had a career-high .989 fielding percentage, both best among full-time American League shortstops, November 9, 2010

"The desire to be the greatest can never be turned down by Father Time. . . . I still think the sky's the limit for Derek."

—Jason Riley, Jeter's fitness trainer, who was championing Jeter because his client needed to negotiate a new long-term contract after coming off a bad year

"WE'VE ENCOURAGED HIM TO TEST THE MARKET AND SEE IF THERE'S SOMETHING HE WOULD PREFER OTHER THAN THIS. IF HE CAN, FINE. THAT'S THE WAY IT WORKS."
—BRIAN CASHMAN, YANKEES GM, PLAYING HARDBALL WITH THE UNSIGNED JETER AND HIS AGENT, CASEY CLOSE, AFTER THEY REJECTED THE YANKEES' INITIAL CONTRACT OFFER, TO WALLACE MATTHEWS, ESPNNEWYORK.COM, NOVEMBER 2010

"I was the one who said, 'I didn't want to [test the free-agency market].' I was the one who said, 'I wasn't going to do it.' To hear the organization tell me to go shop it, when I just [said] I wasn't going to, yeah, if I'm going to be honest, I was angry about it."

—D.J., at a press conference announcing he had re-signed with the Yankees for $51 million over three years and an $8 million player option for a fourth year, December 7, 2010

"The thing that bothered me the most was how public this became. This was a negotiation that was supposed to be private. It was an uncomfortable position I felt I was in. It was not an enjoyable experience because throughout the years I've prided myself on keeping things out of the papers and out of the media. This turned into a big public thing. That is something I was not happy about. I let my feelings be known."

**—D.J., after contentious negotiating between Jeter
and the Yankees, December 7, 2010**

"On three occasions during the negotiations, Jeter [and his agent, Casey Close] met with Yankees co-owner Hal Steinbrenner and Yankees general manager Brian Cashman. While the Yankees and Jeter have agreed to reconcile, Cashman had no regrets about speaking publicly about Jeter."

—Andrew Marchand, ESPNNewYork.com, December 8, 2010

"I was angry I was put in the position to have to respond [to Close's comments]. Anger met anger. You get past it, and you move forward."

—Brian Cashman, Yankees GM, December 7, 2010

"We were all upset and a little bit angry that it reached the level that it did. You always had unnamed sources making this comment or that comment, but that is what sells papers. But that is why we sat down together face-to-face. It was a difficult three, four weeks, but we got it done, and everyone is ready to move on."

**—Hal Steinbrenner, Yankees principal owner following the death of his father
George Steinbrenner on July 13, 2010, putting on a happy face along with Jeter,
Cashman, and Girardi at the press conference announcing Jeter would
remain a Yankee, December 7, 2010**

"We are a big happy family."

—D.J., December 7, 2010

"I'm a little partial, but knowing how he feels about the Yankees, I'm just glad it worked out for both [sides]."

—**Joe Torre, Los Angeles Dodgers manager, December 7, 2010**

"In my mind, it's over with; it's done with. . . . I don't want any distractions."

—**D.J., to Seth Mnookin, *GQ*, April 2011**

"Jeter is as mature a star as we are ever going to see. If he resents the Yankees' working on him in public, he is not going to share that, by word or by body language. We all got caught up in it. The manipulative Yankees. The Jeter camp. Everybody took sides. Somebody wrote that it might be good for Jeter's socialization to make new chums on another team, but I was being facetious, mostly. Jeter was always coming back to the Yankees because he knows what is good for him. He has one of the most supportive family structures of any athlete, and he has surely been told that it is in his best interests to take the high road and finish his career in New York—not as an icon but as a great player."

—**George Vecsey, *New York Times*, December 5, 2010**

"He can play shortstop for us right now; there is no doubt in my mind about that. If I have to move him from shortstop, if we believe that is the case, if he plays himself off the position, we will adjust."

—**Brian Cashman, Yankees GM, about concerns the newly re-signed Jeter might continue to slow down in the field, December 7, 2010**

"You would like to think that last year was a hiccup. It is my job to prove that it was."

—**D.J., December 7, 2010**

"The Boss's oldest son, Hank . . . in 2011 said, 'I think maybe they celebrated too much last year. Some of the players, too busy building mansions and doing other things, and not concentrating on winning.' The reference was clearly to Jeter, who had just concluded the construction of a 30,000-square-foot mansion on Davis Island in Tampa, known locally as 'St. Jetersburg.'"

—**Marty Appel, *Pinstripe Empire*, 2012**

"Owners can say anything they want to say. They're owners. They're entitled to their opinion. You don't have to necessarily agree with their opinion, but they can say what they want to say. I have no problem with it."

—D.J., about supposed criticism from Hank Steinbrenner that was in the mode of his late father George Steinbrenner, to reporters, February 22, 2011

"It certainly isn't Derek. Derek's got five rings. You don't win five rings by being complacent. So, it was definitely not Derek I was talking about, and it wasn't, obviously, a few other players, either. But in the end, we've got to win."

—Hank Steinbrenner, Yankees co-owner, telling everyone he wasn't referring to Jeter or any other player when he criticized "some of the players" for not having the hunger to win in 2010

"I think every time it seems like you don't win, people say that you don't have the hunger. We got beat by a team that was better than us in that series; that was the bottom line. I wouldn't say there was a lack of hunger. I just think we didn't play as well. That's why we lost. But any time teams lose, you always hear that."

—D.J., February 22, 2011

"Shortstop Derek Jeter was named the greatest New York athlete of all time, besting fellow Yankee Babe Ruth, according to a Siena College poll. Two other Yankees, outfielders Joe DiMaggio and Mickey Mantle, and Jets quarterback Joe Namath filled out the top five in the polling of 801 New York state residents."

—Mason Levinson, Bloomberg News, March 15, 2011

"Derek Jeter's No. 2 is No. 1 with fans. Major League Baseball and the players union announced Wednesday the 20 best-selling jerseys from last season, and the Yankees captain's top headed the list."

—*Associated Press*, March 23, 2011

"Today, Jeter is one of the most famous athletes the world has ever known. . . . Even today, after earning hundreds of millions of dollars in salary and endorsements . . . Jeter comes across as a genuine, down-to-earth good guy."

—Seth Mnookin, *GQ*, April 2011

"My focus is always one year at a time. I don't go into 2011 thinking about 2010. I haven't met a person who can change what's happened in the past, and I haven't met a person who can tell the future, so my job is 2011. That's the only thing I'm focused on. That's the only thing I'm concerned with."

—D.J., to Seth Mnookin, *GQ*, April 2011,

"I THINK IT'S THE WRONG MIND-SET TO PREPARE FOR THE END. I THINK YOU KNOW WHEN YOU GET THERE. BUT I DON'T SIT HERE AND MAP IT OUT AND SAY, 'OKAY, FIVE YEARS FROM NOW I'M DONE'—'CAUSE WHAT IF YOU DON'T FEEL THAT WAY WHEN YOU GET THERE?"

—D.J., TO SETH MNOOKIN, *GQ*, APRIL 2011

"Eight games into a new season, Derek Jeter's new batting approach was dead. . . . Hitting coach Kevin Long confirmed what your eyes have seen lately. Jeter had abandoned his stride-less approach [which was] an attempt to shorten and speed up his swing, hopefully eliminating the inordinately high number of ground balls he hit last season."

—Wallace Matthews and Andrew Marchand, ESPNNewYork.com, April 10, 2011

"People always say I was changing my swing. I wasn't changing my swing; I was changing my set-up. I worked on it for six months in spring training, and it just didn't work. About a week into the season, I said, 'I'm not comfortable. I can't be thinking about this. I've just gotta hit.' So that's when I just went back to striding. But then it's trying to re-find [your] timing all over again."

—D.J., HBO's *Derek Jeter 3K*, July 2011

"Derek Jeter on Saturday set a major league record for the most games played at shortstop for one team. Jeter played in his 2,303rd game at shortstop for the New York Yankees on Saturday night at Texas. It was his 2,324th career game overall since his major league debut in 1995. Cal Ripken Jr. played 2,302 games at shortstop during 21 seasons for Baltimore. Only three players have played more games at shortstop than Jeter and Ripken, all playing for multiple teams."

—*Associated Press*, May 7, 2011

"If he said he needed a day to clear his mind, there's no need to apologize. I think everybody understands that. I think everybody in here [the clubhouse] understands that sometimes this game can be tough on you mentally."

—D.J., defending his upset friend Jorge Posada, who was hitting just .165 as a DH and was penciled in as the number nine hitter, for telling manager Joe Girardi he was taking that day off rather than playing, to reporters, May 14, 2011

"It's hard to believe. Rickey was only here what? A year-and-a-half?"

—D.J., joking after stealing his 327th base against the Mariners to pass Rickey Henderson, who played 596 games for the Yankees from 1985 to 1989, as the team's all-time stolen base leader, May 28, 2011

"Just one thing has reduced Jeter to human scale, and it is not surprising what it is: age. On June 26, he turns 37, which makes Jeter a decade older than Einstein was when he published the special theory of relativity, a decade older than Lindbergh when he set the Spirit of St. Louis down in Paris and 15 years older than Ted Williams when he batted .406 in 1941. Even more to the point, Jeter is a dozen years past the best baseball version of himself—the 25-year-old who in 1999 played a sprightly shortstop and also functioned as a slugger."

—Michael Sokolove, prematurely thinking Jeter was finished, *New York Times Magazine*, June 23, 2011

"Scouts are sort of the undercover agents of baseball and will rarely consent to be quoted by name. I asked the scout I visited with in Florida about Jeter, and his answer was succinct. 'His hands are not as quick,' he said. 'His feet are not as quick. His overall strength is diminished.' The scout summed it up by saying, 'Father Time catches up with all of us.'"

—Michael Sokolove, *New York Times Magazine*, June 23, 2011

"He's not the same player he used to be. . . . But I think he's above average at that position, despite his age."

—Brian Cashman, Yankees GM, on why Jeter wasn't asked to vacate the shortstop position

"I was approached about the opportunity of doing this documentary [about his quest to 3,000 hits]. I said, 'I've never done this before. I don't know if I'm comfortable with it.' But I'm always jealous of the other players with their kids coming down to the clubhouse and on the field. If and when I have kids, they wouldn't be part of this. They wouldn't have ever had the opportunity to see it. So at least I'll have it for my kids, because they may not believe me when I tell them."

—D.J., about the one-hour documentary that would premiere in late July on HBO titled *Derek Jeter 3K*, July 27, 2011

"Derek Jeter's 3,000th hit will be cause for celebration, marketing, and—not the least of all—digging up dirt. After the game, a groundskeeper will tote a shovel and bucket onto the field to scoop five gallons of dirt from the batter's box and shortstop's pouch. In baseball's version of preserving the chain of evidence, the bucket will be sealed with tape and verified as the dirt beneath Jeter's feet with tamper-proof holograms."

—Richard Sandomir, *New York Times*, June 22, 2011

"DJ 3K"

—The campaign name for merchandise marked with a logo associated with Jeter's reaching 3,000 hits

"I've been here for 13 years. And other than the home run race in 1998, this is the most significant business we've done for a hot market player."

—Howard Smith, senior vice president of licensing for Major League Baseball

"Between the New York market and how revered Jeter is, it's going to be a huge event."

—Michael Johnson, spokesman for Majestic, which was producing jerseys and T-shirts to commemorate Jeter's 3,000-hit day

"WE HAVE TO BE READY. HE COULD GO 5 FOR 5."
—COSMO LUBRANO, AUTHENTICATOR FOR MAJOR LEAGUE BASEBALL, MAKING
AN INCREDIBLE PREDICTION ABOUT JETER'S UPCOMING 3,000-HIT DAY

"Derek Jeter limped off the field with a sore right calf four innings after getting his 2,994th hit, and Carlos Carrasco escaped early trouble to pitch the Cleveland Indians past the New York Yankees 1–0 Monday night. There was no immediate word on the severity of Jeter's injury. He was noticeably hurt as he jogged toward first base during a flyout in the fifth and left the game, stalling his pursuit to become the 28th big leaguer to reach 3,000 career hits."

—Associated Press, **June 13, 2011**

"Actually, I got hurt before that at-bat. I was on the field for defense, [and] when I went to go run in, my leg tightened up, and I felt like a ball in my calf. So I just thought I had a cramp. So I was leading off the next inning. After my swing, it just locked up."

—D.J., about a calf strain that put him on the disabled list when he was only six hits shy of 3,000, *Derek Jeter 3K*, **July 2011**

"I never like to go on the disabled list, but especially at this time. . . . I felt I was disappointing people . . . who were coming out to see something special."

—D.J., *Derek Jeter 3K*, **July 2011**

"I had the opportunity to work out some [hitting] kinks . . . a blessing in disguise."

—D.J., about getting to work with Kevin Long and Gary Denbo at the Yankees rehab center in Tampa while on the disabled list, *Derek Jeter 3K*, **July 2011**

"Now the 2–2 to Jeter. Hit on the ground toward third and into left field, a base hit. Jeter is aboard to start things off."

—Jay Burnham, Trenton Thunder broadcaster, on Jeter's getting a leadoff single to begin his rehab assignment with the Yankees' Class AA affiliate, July 3, 2011

"You know I haven't played in three weeks. So there was some nerves. I didn't sleep much (Friday night). It feels good to get going because you can't simulate anything you do in a game. You can try to do it on the field, but until you get in a game and you actually have to move, you won't know until then."

—D.J., expressing happiness at the postgame press conference that he hit well and his defensive play was flawless and varied, because that meant his return to the Yankees was imminent, July 3, 2011

"Ever since I was younger, I always liked to be with a lot of friends. Going to a movie, I wanted everybody to come. At the house, I wanted everybody to come over. And when I do things like [getting 3,000 hits], I want everyone to experience it. I have a good mix of friends: black, white, male, female; they come in all sizes and shapes, races, religions. . . . You want to share experiences with the people that you love. If you don't get the opportunity to share these experiences, then I think it's a waste."

—D.J., *Derek Jeter 3K*, July 2011

"I felt pressure to do it at home. Everywhere I'd go, everyone was telling me, 'Oh, you have to do it at home; you have to do it at home.' I didn't want to disappoint anyone."

—D.J., about the pressure to get his 3,000th hit at Yankee Stadium before the All-Star Game and the road trip that followed, *Derek Jeter 3K*, July 2011

"I didn't know what it would be like, but I wanted to experience it with Yankees fans."

—D.J., *Derek Jeter 3K*, July 2011

"Talk about a lucky catch. The fan who manages to catch the ball off Derek Jeter's historic 3,000th hit could pocket as much as $250,000, experts said."

—Paul Thorp, *New York Post*, July 7, 2011

CLASSIC MOMENT:
JULY 9, 2011, YANKEE STADIUM, NYC

"Take it easy on me today, will ya?"

**—D.J., to catcher John Jaso prior to his first at-bat on Saturday, July 9, when he'd
single off Tampa Bay ace David Price, for his 2,999th career hit,
two games before the All-Star break**

"And now the crowd is pumped because the crowd is thinking, 'We can be here for
this milestone.' In his family box on the first base side, everyone is pretty excited."

—Michael Kay, Yankees broadcaster

"Everyone is standing; it's a fabulous sight."

**—John Sterling, Yankees radio broadcaster, when Jeter came
to the plate for the second time**

"Derek Jeter since we saw him break in in '96, has always risen to the occasion."

—John Sterling, Yankees radio broadcaster

"He knows how to relax in those situations, and he's not going to get caught up in
the moment, and he's going to be disciplined in his approach."

—Joe Girardi, Yankees manager

"He could have thrown it in the dugout, and I would have swung."

—D.J., about being nervous when going for his 3,000th hit against David Price

**"I WANTED TO HIT THE BALL HARD. I DIDN'T WANT TO HIT A SLOW DRIBBLER
THAT I HAD TO BEAT OUT. I DIDN'T WANT A JAM SHOT THAT'S PLAYED OVER
AND OVER AGAIN. WHERE IT WENT, I DIDN'T CARE, JUST AS LONG AS I MADE
GOOD CONTACT."**

—D.J.

"HE HUNG A BREAKING BALL. AND I HIT IT GOOD."

—D.J.

"That one's driven deep to left field. Going back Joyce."

—**Michael Kay, Yankees broadcaster, watching Tampa outfielder Matty Joyce retreating to the fence on Jeter's long fly**

"I knew he wasn't going to catch it, but I wasn't exactly sure where it was going to go."

—**D.J.**

"That ball's outta here! That ball's outta here!"

—**Mike Kelleher, Yankees first base coach, watching the flight of the ball**

"Looking up! . . . See ya!"

—**Michael Kay, Yankees broadcaster, making his home run call**

"What a way to join the 3,000 hit club. Derek Jeter has done it in grand style."

—**Michael Kay, Yankees broadcaster**

"The first thing I felt—a sense of relief. And then you can't believe what just happened."

—**D.J., who had only two homers all year and none in his last 100 at-bats**

"There were a lot of emotions running around the bases. It's amazing how many things you can think about when you're running around. You think about your family and friends that have all been part of it. I thought of my mom and sister that couldn't be there because my sister just had a baby. So I was happy my mom could be there with my sister. But on a selfish side, I wish they could have been there."

—**D.J.,** *Derek Jeter 3K*

"Jorge [Posada] is the first to greet Derek, and he wraps him up in a massive bear hug, and I am next. Derek is on his way to a 5-for-5 day as we win, 5–4, and even for someone who supposedly doesn't care about milestones, I am filled with joy at this whole experience, seeing a guy Jorge and I have played with for almost 20 years get to a place that even players such as Babe Ruth, Joe DiMaggio, and Mickey Mantle never got to."

—**Mariano Rivera, Yankees reliever,** *The Closer*, **2014**

"In many ways, the Yankees' 2011 season will be remembered for what Derek Jeter accomplished on July 9. In the third inning, he joined the 3,000-hit club with a home run on a 3–2 pitch from the Rays' David Price, an exclamation point to his incredible career. Jeter became only the 28th player to reach 3,000 hits [the second to homer, joining Wade Boggs] and amazingly, the first Yankee to hit that magic number. Jeter went 5-for-5 that day, including the game-winning single. It was amazing in every way."

—**Kevin Kernan,** *Girardi: Passion in Pinstripes*, **2012**

"This is already movie-ready. His 3,000th hit is a homer, and 3,003 is a game winner."

—**Joe Girardi, Yankees manager**

"The only thing important to Derek was winning. . . . Well, without his go-ahead single later that led to a win, Derek would not have been able to smile after the game."

—**Joe Torre, Yankees manager from 1996 to 2007**

"It would have been really, really awkward to do interviews on the field and wave to the crowd if we'd lost."

—**D.J., July 9, 2011**

"I was pretty relieved. I've been lying to you guys for a long time, saying I wasn't nervous and there was no pressure; there was a lot of pressure to do it here while we were at home."

—D.J., after becoming the 28th member in the 3,000-hit club, to reporters, July 9, 2011

"If I was tied to the record books with any player in baseball, it's definitely hands down Derek Jeter. With the way he's conducted himself on and off the field, on the biggest stage and in the biggest city for baseball, his character speaks for itself. He's a different breed."

—David Price, Tampa Bay pitcher

"You don't ever want to be on the losing side of any game. But being behind the plate that day and seeing him do what he did, that's a day I'll never forget. It was a pretty awesome seat. And how can you not be impressed with the way he hits?"

—John Jaso, Tampa Bay catcher

"What a way to do it, too."

—Jay-Z, famed rapper, to his friend Jeter after the game

"I saw the ball roll in front of me, and I jumped on it. It was instinct. I was like, 'Wow, this is it, it's my chance.'"

—Christian Lopez, cell phone salesman who picked up Jeter's 3,000th hit in the left field bleachers and gave it to him without compensation, although the ball would have a six-figure value

"You worked so hard for it that I'm not going to take that away from you."

—Christian Lopez, to Jeter when they met, July 9, 2011

"He got his ticket from his girlfriend so he owes her quite a bit after this one. He's going to be paying her back for quite some time."

—D.J., at the postgame press conference about Christian Lopez, who retrieved and gave him the 3,000-hit ball

"To our captain, leader, and friend. Congratulations on a great achievement, from your teammates."

—Inscription on 225-pound, mirror-polished stainless steel sculpture commissioned by Jorge Posada and CC Sabathia to commemorate Jeter's 3,000th hit

"New York has a greater baseball tradition than any other city, but we've never had a player get all 3,000 hits in a New York uniform until today. Congratulations, Derek. You've made all of New York City proud."

—Michael R. Bloomberg, mayor of New York City

D.J. DATA: Visitors to the Baseball Hall of Fame in Cooperstown, New York, can find batting gloves and a helmet from when Derek Jeter recorded his 3,000th hit at Yankee Stadium on July 9, 2011. There are numerous other Jeter items at the HOF, including a Yankees jersey from his rookie season, 1996; a bat from the 1997 American League Division Series; spikes and a bat from the 1998 World Series; a bat he used in the 2000 All-Star Game when he was named Most Valuable Player; a batting helmet from the 2000 World Series, when he was named Most Valuable Player; a Team USA jersey from the 2006 World Baseball Classic; spikes worn when he broke Lou Gehrig's hit record at Yankee Stadium on September 16, 2008; a bat he used during the Yankees' final home stand of 2008, their last season at the first Yankee Stadium; batting gloves he wore on September 11, 2009, when he recorded his 2,722nd hit at Yankee Stadium, surpassing Lou Gehrig's Yankees' record; a bat he used during Game 6 of the 2009 World Series; a baseball cap from the 2014 All-Star Game; scorecards from his last home game at Yankee Stadium on September 25, 2014; and scorecards from his final major league game at Fenway Park on September 28, 2014.

"I do believe, as a ballplayer, if you have no injuries, you should be here. The fans are the ones that vote for you and want to see you here."

—Carlos Beltran, San Francisco Giants outfielder, about Jeter's controversial decision to skip the 2011 All-Star Game because of his mental exhaustion from pursuing 3,000 hits

"Everybody would want a piece of him here [if Jeter did attend], and sometimes you need a little mental break. I'm not going to say anything about him because I'm probably his biggest fan."

—Troy Tulowitzki, Colorado Rockies outfielder, who wore number 2 in honor of his favorite baseball player

"Let's put the Derek Jeter question to bed. There isn't a player that I'm more proud of in the last 15 years than Derek Jeter. . . . I know why Derek Jeter isn't here. I respect that. And I must tell you I think I would have made the same decision Derek Jeter did."

—Bud Selig, MLB commissioner

"After Jeter collected his 3,000th hit on July 9, 2011, he went from being a .260–.270 hitter to a .325 hitter the rest of the 2011 season and ended up with a .297 batting average. Jeter admitted that the pressure of trying to get his 3,000th hit at home was on his mind, and it was like a weight off his shoulders once he got it."

—Doug Rush, *Bleacher Report*, April 24, 2012

"When you first come up, you're just trying to keep your job and stay as long as you can. So this one was something I never looked at."

—D.J., about playing in his 2,402nd game against the Baltimore Orioles to pass Mickey Mantle as the Yankees' all-time leader in games played, August 28, 2011

"It's very satisfying. You can't sit down and figure out what's going to happen before a season starts. You have to go out there and play the games. We know how good the other teams are in our division and in baseball, but we had confidence in our own team."

—D.J., after the Yankees swept Tampa Bay in a day-night doubleheader to clinch their 12th AL-East title in 16 years with him as their shortstop, September 20, 2011

"With his teammates pacing so much they were practically colliding in the dugout, [Jose] Valverde set down Curtis Granderson on a fly ball to left field, Robinson Canó on a lineout to center and Alex Rodriguez on a swinging strike three to seal a 3–2 Detroit victory. . . . Jeter went 1-for-5 in Game 5 with an infield single in the seventh that seemed like it was going to spark a rally. The Yankees eventually loaded the bases and seemed on the verge of a big inning. But Alex Rodriguez and Nick Swisher sandwiched strikeouts around Mark Teixeira's RBI walk, stifling the rally. He also hit a deep fly to the warning track in right with one out in the eighth. If it went out, it would have given the Yankees a one-run lead. Jeter would say afterward that he thought it had a chance."

—Jerry Crasnick, about the Yankees' frustrating loss in the ALDS that ended their championship run, ESPNNewYork.com, October 7, 2011

"Disappointed. Dejected. Somber. Subdued. At times, Derek Jeter was all of the above when talking to reporters after the Yankees' Game 5 loss."

—Ian Begley, ESPNNewYork.com, October 7, 2011

"I don't know if you can put it into words. . . . You play all year to get to this point, and we lost. It's extremely disappointing. We had some opportunities, and they pitched out of them. . . . We came here to try to win, and we didn't get it done."

—D.J., who batted .250 in the division series against Detroit

"It's a true honor to be recognized in this way by the Louisville Slugger Museum and Factory. Louisville Slugger is synonymous with baseball. I've used the same model [P72] throughout my career, and it's a privilege to have such a tribute in this great museum devoted to the skill and history of hitting."

—D.J., about having a new lifelike sculpture of him become a permanent exhibit at the museum

"I always looked at this as my field. Now I can actually say, 'This is my field.'"

—D.J., when attending a ceremony at Kalamazoo Central High at which its baseball field was named in his honor, December 2011

"I WOULD LIKE TO OWN A TEAM. I WOULD LIKE TO BE THE ONE TO CALL THE SHOTS. I WOULD LIKE TO BE LIKE THE BOSS."
—D.J., TO BARBARA WALTERS, *10 MOST FASCINATING PEOPLE OF 2011*, DECEMBER 14, 2011

"It was a night of firsts for Derek Jeter and the New York Yankees. Jeter went 4 for 4, Ivan Nova gave up two runs in seven innings, and New York got its first win of the [2012] season, 6–2 over the Baltimore Orioles on Monday night. Jeter singled and scored in the first inning, singled in the third, hit an RBI double in a three-run fourth, sacrificed in the sixth, and singled in the eighth. . . . New York began the season by losing three straight to Tampa Bay and was in danger of going 0–4 for only the fourth time in franchise history."

—*Associated Press*, April 9, 2012

"A lot of times, the first of everything is the most difficult to get in a season. Whether it's the first hit, first RBI, first win."

—D.J., after leading the Yankees to their first victory of the season, April 9, 2012

"Remember when everyone said that Derek Jeter looked finished? I bet not too many people are saying that right now. Not after the start he's having to the 2012 season. Entering Tuesday night's game, Jeter is hitting an amazing .411 with four home runs and 13 RBIs and an on-base percentage of .436. Those aren't just good numbers, those are All-Star quality numbers for the Yankees captain."

—Doug Rush, *Bleacher Report*, April 24, 2012

"I think a lot has to do with that Derek has been pretty healthy this year. And the part of the year where he really struggled last year was when he was in pursuit of his 3,000th hit. After that, he hit about .320 the rest of the year. And he's kept hitting."

—Joe Girardi, Yankees manager

"I don't think I'm doing anything different this year than I did before. I just took that one year off."

—D.J.

"It's like there's no way you can pitch him that will stop him from hitting balls to right field. I've seen him take balls that are 6 inches off the plate, inside, and inside-out them to right. Trying to keep the ball off of his barrel is as challenging as it gets for a pitcher. . . . He just knows how to get base hits"

—**John Jaso, Seattle catcher, on how Jeter, who was hitting .316, already had more hits up the middle and to right field than in all of 2011, quoted by Jeff Bradley, *Newark Star-Ledger*, August 4, 2012**

"Jeter's current assault on the record books has not only mesmerized and astonished everyone, but it has also given credence to the notion that he is one of the most consistent and durable hitters to have ever played the game. Anytime that a ball player's name can rest comfortably next to Hank Aaron and Willie Mays, they must have accomplished something that is beyond extraordinary. Currently, Jeter and Mays are the only two men in baseball history to have accumulated at least 3,000 hits, 250 home runs, 300 stolen bases, and 1,200 runs batted in during their careers. Jeter also shares a unique distinction with Aaron as being the only two men in baseball history to have at least 150 hits in a season for 17 years. To add to an already exemplary resume, Jeter has had seven seasons in which he has exceeded 200 hits, and an eighth will be added by the first week of October."

—**Wayne G. McDonnell Jr., *Forbes*, August 31, 2012**

D.J. DATA: On September 14, 2012, Derek Jeter got his 3,284th hit to move past Willie Mays into 10th place on the all-time major league hit list. The single came off David Price, the victim of Jeter's 3,000th hit.

"It's a lot of hits. I've always felt that if I was healthy and I go out there and play every day, it's something I'd have a chance to do."

—**D.J., recording his 200th hit in a season for the eighth time, tying Lou Gehrig's Yankees record, in a 2–1 win over Toronto, September 20, 2012**

"I always try to stay consistent. If you're consistent throughout the course of the year, then you have a chance to do it."

—D.J., upon becoming the fourth player in history to have 200 hits in a season 14 years after doing it the first time, September 20, 2012

"I don't judge a year until it's finished, and we haven't finished yet. Hopefully we're a long way from that happening."

—D.J.

"Jeter . . . returned to shortstop for the first time in a week in Wednesday's night game, the second of a doubleheader against the Blue Jays. A bothersome ankle injury has relegated him to being the team's primary designated hitter. Jeter aggravated his left ankle last Wednesday in Boston. Since then, manager Joe Girardi has used him as the team's DH. Jeter did not play . . . during the day portion of the doubleheader. Prior to Wednesday's matinee opener, the Yankees had not played since Sunday because of an off day Monday and a rainout Tuesday, so Jeter had a chance to rest the injury. 'Physically, I was fine,' Jeter said after playing nine innings on Wednesday. 'I was nervous [about being out of synch].' Added Girardi: 'I never saw him limp once today. It's been a while since we've seen that.'"

—Ian Bagley, ESPNNewYork.com, September 20, 2012

"In . . . 2009, after working with Yankees infield coach Mick Kelleher on 'aggressive defensive positioning,' Jeter posted a plus-3 DRS, the first time he'd ever cracked positive territory. . . . But that was as good as it got: The next year he fell back to minus-9, and then minus-15, and then [in 2012] minus-18. So this is the tragedy of Derek Jeter's defense: Just when he finally found out how to play shortstop, he began to get old [and] . . . lacks the speed to take advantage of his improved positioning. All of which makes Jeter's defensive evolution one of baseball's best might-have-beens."

—Ben Lindbergh, Grantland.com, August 27, 2013

"With that knock, Jeter broke Ty Cobb's record for the most hits in a season by a player who entered the year with 3,000 or more career hits. Cobb had 211 hits under those circumstances in both 1922 and 1924. Jeter's 212th hit of the season was also the 3,300th hit of his career. Among the 10 players who've reached that milestone, only Cobb (age 36 in 1923) got there at a younger age than Jeter (38 years, 96 days)."

—**ESPN, statistics from Elias Sports Bureau, September 30, 2012**

"I don't pay attention to prognostication, prediction. One of the worst phrases in sports is 'on pace for.'"

—**D.J., when asked if he could play long enough to pass Pete Rose's major league record of 4,256 hits**

"If one were to construct the Mount Rushmore of Yankees icons, Jeter's name would prominently appear in the discussion as to who should be included on the monument. With or without his famous face being carved into granite, Jeter is unquestionably in the same company as Ruth, Gehrig, DiMaggio, Mantle, Berra, and Ford as the gold standard for the New York Yankees."

—**Wayne G. McDonnell Jr.,** *Forbes,* **August 31, 2012**

"So much for Derek Jeter being over the hill; the New York Yankees shortstop finished 2012 with the most hits in baseball at the ripe old age of 38 with 216, which was 11 more than the Triple Crown–winning Miguel Cabrera, who finished with 205. As if he needed another bullet point on his Hall of Fame resume."

—**Timothy Rapp,** *Bleacher Report,* **October 3, 2012**

"DEREK'S GREATEST ACCOMPLISHMENT HAS BEEN HIS CONSISTENCY. TO BE ABLE TO PUT UP BIG NUMBERS FOR AS LONG AS HE HAS IS EXTREMELY DIFFICULT. HE'S BEEN CONSISTENTLY GREAT BECAUSE OF HIS RELENTLESS DRIVE. NO ONE GOES ABOUT THEIR BUSINESS WITH MORE OF AN UNWAVERING DESIRE TO BE THE BEST THAN DEREK."

—DAVID CONE, YANKEES BROADCASTER AND FORMER PITCHER, *YANKEES MAGAZINE'S HOMESTAND BLOG,* JULY 29, 2014

"Two Maryland state troopers who were at Camden Yards as part of the game's security detail [for Game 1 of the ALDS between Baltimore and New York] asked Derek Jeter and Nick Swisher for autographs in the Yankees dugout during the top of the ninth inning, the *New York Post* reports. The troopers violated a (very spoken) rule of professional sports, where everyone from team staff to writers to local cops are expected to do their job and refrain from fan-like activities such as asking for autographs or photos. But they also did it at the worst of times as Jeter and Swisher were both due up in the inning, during which the Yankees staged a five-run rally to put themselves ahead for a 7–2 win. The out-of-line request was poorly timed, and the troopers weren't even hitting up their own team. . . . The *Baltimore Sun* reported Monday that the Maryland State Police will be reminding officers how they're supposed to be acting when they do security at the park."

—Jen Slothower, NESN.com, October 9, 2012

D.J. DATA: Batting leadoff for the Yankees in their 7–2 Game 1 win over Baltimore in the ALDS on October 7, 2012, Derek Jeter went 2-for-4, scoring both times after he singled. He finished his career in opening games of division series with 26 hits in 58 at-bats for a .448 average, reaching base in 15 of 16 openers. Overall, Jeter batted .343 in division series with 92 hits, 10 of them home runs.

"We'll enjoy this one for a few minutes, and then get ready for tomorrow."

—D.J., after the Yankees' 3–1 victory over the Orioles in Game 5 of the ALDS—the
final postseason triumph he would experience—catapulted the team
into the 2012 ALCS, October 12, 2012

"For a moment, it felt like nobody could breathe; nobody could move. This baseball basilica, which shook with life and energy barely an hour before, was suddenly silent. . . . Because the captain was on the ground . . . Jhonny Peralta hit a ball to Derek Jeter in the top of the 12th. Jeter dove for the ball. And never got up. He rolled on the ground, flipped the ball aside. And was in pain. Real pain. . . . Jeter couldn't put any weight on his leg."

—Mike Vaccaro, about Jeter injuring his ankle in a 6–4 loss to Detroit in the first game of the 2012 ALCS, *New York Post*, October 14, 2012

"DO NOT CARRY ME."
—D.J., INSTRUCTIONS HE GAVE TO MANAGER JOE GIRARDI AND TEAM TRAINER STEVE DONOHUE, PROMPTING THEM TO HELP HIM TO WALK OFF THE FIELD ON ONE FOOT BY SUPPORTING HIS SHOULDERS, A GESTURE JETER FELT WAS IMPORTANT FOR THE MORALE OF THE TEAM

"He's tough. That's the only way I can describe it. He's tough."

—Joe Girardi, Yankees manager

"Prior to Sunday's 3–0 loss to the Tigers in Game 2, Yankees manager Joe Girardi said it appeared the byproducts of a previous injury or injuries had affected Jeter's footwork on the play Saturday night in which he broke his ankle. Girardi also acknowledged, without verbally addressing it, that his 38-year-old shortstop had received a cortisone shot to allow him to keep playing after he originally suffered a bone bruise in early September. Jeter suffered a bone bruise in his left foot in Game 3 of the AL Division Series. . . . The injury . . . first troubled him during a road trip against the Tampa Bay Rays on Labor Day. He aggravated it later by fouling a ball off it in Boston in mid-September and injured the same ankle, in a different place, in the last game of the regular season against the Red Sox."

—Wallace Matthews, ESPNNewYork.com, October 14, 2012

"Losing Derek, especially in the postseason, it stinks. It's the last guy you want to see go down."

—David Robertson, Yankees reliever

"We probably feel worse for him than anyone else who could go out."

—Mark Teixeira, Yankees first baseman, on how Jeter lived for the postseason

"We didn't hit. Jeter was hitting, and then his replacement [Nunez] hit. We lost because a number of guys didn't hit, and it wasn't at the shortstop position."

—Brian Cashman, Yankees GM, on why the team was swept by the Tigers in the 2012 ALCS, which would turn out to be Jeter's final trip to the postseason

D.J. DATA: According to Wikipedia, in 2015 "Jeter . . . earned the titles of 'Captain Clutch' and 'Mr. November' due to his outstanding postseason play. He has a career .309 postseason batting average, and a .321 batting average in the World Series. Except for 2008, 2013, and 2014, the Yankees [went] to the postseason every year since Jeter joined the team. Jeter holds MLB postseason records for games played (158), plate appearances (734), at-bats (650), hits (200), singles (143), doubles (32), triples (5), runs scored (111), total bases (302), and strikeouts (135). Jeter is also third in home runs (20), fourth in runs batted in (61), fifth in base on balls (66), and sixth in stolen bases (18)."

"I'm hopeful that [Derek's] going to come back 100 percent. And I know he's going to do everything in his willpower to get back to 100 percent. Let's hope that he can come back."

—Joe Girardi, Yankees manager, after Jeter has ankle surgery performed by Dr. Robert Anderson in Charlotte, N.C., and it was announced that his recovery should take four or five months, October 19, 2012

"Louisville Slugger® . . . proudly announced the 2012 Silver Slugger Award winners. . . . Ten of the 18 team members were recognized as Silver Sluggers for the first time. . . . Two players made the team for the fifth time—the American League's shortstop, Derek Jeter of the Yankees, and the National League's Ryan Braun, leftfielder for the Milwaukee Brewers."

—Louisville Slugger, bat company, announcing Jeter's final Silver Slugger award, news release, November 8, 2012

"Derek Jeter called the mother of Victoria Soto, a young teacher killed while protecting her first-grade students at Sandy Hook Elementary School in last week's Newtown tragedy. Jeter telephoned Donna Soto on Wednesday, the same day she laid her daughter to rest. Carlee Soto, Victoria's sister, tweeted the family's excitement about hearing from Jeter. 'Derek Jeter just called my mom!!!!! Thanks Vicki, she needed it thank you @yankees this meant a lot to my mother and all of us,' the tweet read. James Wiltsie, a cousin of Victoria Soto, said she had been a huge Yankees fan, according to the New York *Daily News*. 'Vicki loved the Yankees; that was part of her eulogy,' Wiltsie said Wednesday night. 'No one in the family reached out, so [Jeter] must have read about it and . . . reached out.'"

—Andrew Marchand, ESPNNewYork.com, December 20, 2012

"I just ran out of days. When is Opening Day, Monday? I just ran out of time."

—D.J., realizing that a setback with his ankle recovery meant he would start the 2013 season on the disabled list

"When you have doubt, that's when you're in trouble. I've been told this bone will heal, and when it heals, I'll be ready to go. It's frustrating that I can't magically make it heal sooner than it's taking, but I have no doubt I'll be back."

—D.J., at a press conference after it was revealed he had a small fracture in his left ankle and his return had been delayed, April 2013

"New York Yankees captain Derek Jeter has been diagnosed with a small crack in his surgically repaired left ankle, a setback that will keep him sidelined until after the All-Star break. For once, the Yankees' charmed captain has taken the kind of blow only mere mortals expect."

—Wallace Matthews, about the latest chapter in the story of the worst injury of Jeter's career, ESPNNewYork.com, April 18, 2013

"The Yankees' Derek Jeter has defied the impact of the two most influential elements of his time: the institutional shift toward quantitative analysis and the cynical lust for home runs, fueled by performance-enhancing drugs."

—William C. Rhoden, recognizing Jeter's career is winding down, *ESPN The Magazine*, May 13, 2013

"Jeter played his first rehab game with Triple-A Scranton/Wilkes-Barre on July 6, going 0-for-2 with a walk. More importantly, nothing in the vicinity of his left ankle was smarting. Nothing happened in any of the next three games Jeter played, either."

—Zachary D. Rymer, *Bleacher Report*, September 11, 2013

"People! It feels so good to be back."

—Eminem, lyrics in "Square Dance," which Jeter had played when he returned from his severe ankle injury and made his first plate appearance of the season—and beat out an infield hit against Kansas City, July 11, 2013

"It's not frustrating yet. We'll see. They MRI everything around here. I'm going to get an MRI, and we'll find out, but I hope it's not a big deal. I don't ever think anything is a big deal, so I'm hoping for the best."

—D.J., after exiting during his first game back with tightness in his right quadriceps, which would put him back on the disabled list, July 11, 2013

"He returned to the lineup on July 28 and, in typical dramatic fashion, Jeter hit a home run in his first at-bat against Tampa Bay Rays young lefthander Matt Moore. . . . Jeter later singled . . . in a 6–5 Yankees victory."

—Phil Pepe, *Core Four*, 2013

"He's a movie."

—Joe Girardi, Yankees manager, about Jeter homering in his return

"Now *that* was vintage Jeter. It's also the only time in 2013 that vintage Jeter made an appearance. Following his big triumphant return game, Jeter collected just one hit in 11 at-bats in his next three games, with only one walk mixed in. And along the way, he got hurt. Again. This time, it was a strained right calf. And once again, the Yankees decided to play it cool at first, hoping a couple of days off would do the trick. But on Aug. 5, they had to give in and put Jeter back on the DL for a third time [until August 11]."

—Zachary D. Rymer, *Bleacher Report*, September 11, 2013

"Derek Jeter moved into ninth place on the all-time hits list with an infield single during the third inning of Tuesday's New York Yankees game against the Chicago White Sox. With the 3,314th hit of his career, Jeter surpassed Eddie Collins. . . . Jeter, 39, picked up the hit off White Sox starter Chris Sale on a ground ball toward the middle. Second baseman Gordon Beckham made a diving stop on the ball, but Jeter was too quick to first. In the eighth, Jeter added another single during the Yankees' five-run eighth inning in their 6–4 comeback win over the White Sox."

—Andrew Marchand, ESPNNewYork.com, September 7, 2013

"Jeter has been shut down until 2014. He ends his season with 17 games played, 12 hits, one home run, one double, and four trips to the DL. Now what? Should we cue up The Doors? Is this the end?"

— Zachary D. Rymer, *Bleacher Report*, September 11, 2013

"Derek is one of the most driven people I have ever known. It's what makes him great. But I also think in this case his drive just blinded him, and maybe everybody else, too. To me, it was obvious he wasn't ready, and yet somehow he kept pushing and pushing and nobody stopped him—or protected him from himself. . . . With a healthy Derek Jeter, I can't see our season ending in September."

—Mariano Rivera, Yankees pitcher, on finishing his career-ending 2013 season
without Jeter, *The Closer*, 2014

"It's very disappointing not to be able to play, especially this time of year. This is when I want to play the most. Unfortunately, that's not the case. The entire year has been pretty much a nightmare for me physically, so I guess it's fitting that it ends like this."

—D.J.

"I'LL BE HERE TO ROOT THE TEAM ON. I'VE HAD POM POMS ON FOR A LOT OF THE YEAR ALREADY. YOU JUST TRY TO HELP OUT AS MUCH AS YOU CAN, IN ANY WAY THAT YOU CAN. MY TEAMMATES HAVE ALWAYS BEEN THERE FOR ME, SO NOW IT'S MY TURN."

—D.J.

"Andy . . . and Derek keep walking, and now they are on the mound. Andy holds out his left hand, and I put the ball in it. I won't be needing it anymore. Andy wraps his arms around me, and I put mine around him and now the dam finally bursts, the emotions flooding me, overwhelming me, the finality of it all descending on me like an anchor. . . . It's okay, Derek says. It's okay. The embrace lasts a long time, and then I hug Derek, and I don't want any of this to end. . . . "

—Mariano Rivera, Yankees reliever, on being taken out not by manager Joe Girardi but by retired former Yankee Pettitte and current teammate Jeter with two outs in the ninth inning of his 1,115th and final career game on September 26, 2013, *The Closer*, 2014

"Only Derek was left [of the Core Four]. He was Paul without John, George, and Ringo; Jerry without George, Elaine, and Kramer. He was Theodore Roosevelt alone on Mount Rushmore."

—Phil Pepe, about Jeter without the retired Andy Pettitte, Jorge Posada, and Mariano Rivera, *Core Four*, 2013

"Despite coming off an injury-plagued season, the New York Yankees chose to reward captain Derek Jeter for his years of good service by re-signing the shortstop Friday to a $12 million contract for 2014. The new contract is $2.5 million more than the player option Jeter could have picked up for next year. A source with knowledge of the negotiations told ESPN New York that the talks were largely held between Jeter and team owner Hal Steinbrenner, who both live in Tampa, Fla. Jeter's agent, Casey Close, handled the details of the contract."

—**Andrew Marchand, ESPNNewYork.com, November 1, 2013**

"It's a mutual respect factor. We know he wanted to be a Yankee and stay with the Yankees, and we respect what he's done for this organization and particularly last year when he worked so hard and went through so much to try and come back, and going all the way back to two years ago when he literally left it all on the field in the playoffs. We felt this was the appropriate thing to do."

—**Brian Cashman, Yankees GM, October 31, 2013**

"I run the show. CEO. I call the shots. I understand how important content is [in] this day and age and [to] share people's stories. It doesn't necessarily have to be baseball. It could be any walk of life I find interesting. I'm happy to get the opportunity to do it."

—**D.J., about publishing house Simon & Schuster creating a book imprint for him, Jeter Publishing, November 14, 2013**

"If I put my name on something, I'm going to be involved. I'm not just going to put my name on it and not pay attention."

—**D.J., about Jeter Publishing, for which Jeter would publish his own books and be hands-on with books by other authors, November 14, 2013**

"The whole last year has been sort of a blur. Being away from it for so long gave me the opportunity to think about what the future may hold after baseball."

—**D.J., about becoming a book publisher, November 14, 2013**

— SEVEN —

Into the Sunset

"I want to start by saying thank you.

"I know they say that when you dream, you eventually wake up. Well, for some reason, I've never had to wake up. Not just because of my time as a New York Yankee but also because I am living my dream every day.

"Last year was a tough one for me. As I suffered through a bunch of injuries, I realized that some of the things that always came easy to me and were always fun had started to become a struggle. The one thing I always said to myself was that when baseball started to feel more like a job, it would be time to more forward.

"So really it was months ago when I realized this season would likely be my last. As I came to this conclusion and shared it with my friends and family, they all told me to hold off saying anything until I was absolutely 100 percent sure.

"And the thing is, I could not be more sure. I know it in my heart. The 2014 season will be my last year playing professional baseball."

—D.J., who posted a 14-paragraph retirement announcement with this beginning, Facebook, February 12, 2014

"The year he was hurt, he realized there were other things in life he wanted to do."

—Dorothy Jeter, 2014

"Jeter is known for keeping things close to the vest, and his retirement announcement came as a shock to nearly all. Yankees owner Hal Steinbrenner said Jeter called him Wednesday morning to break the news, but the team at large was left in the dark. Setup man Shawn Kelley has been working out alongside Jeter all week, and said none of the players had any clue that Jeter would announce his retirement. . . . Kelly said the players are still in shock, only starting to digest the idea of life without their captain."

—**Daniel Barbarisi**, *Wall Street Journal*, **February 12, 2014**

"He said nothing to us. Since I can remember, baseball has always had Derek Jeter, so I imagine baseball without Jeter would be comparable to basketball without Jordan or boxing without Ali, just not the same. As for the Yankees, I can't even imagine what it will be like without him."

—**Shawn Kelley, Yankees pitcher**

"In the 21-plus years in which I have served as commissioner, Major League Baseball has had no finer ambassador than Derek Jeter. Since his championship rookie season of 1996, Derek has represented all the best of the national pastime on and off the field. He is one of the most accomplished and memorable players of his—or any—era."

—**Bud Selig, MLB commissioner, making a statement in response to Jeter's retirement announcement**

"Late last August, here at ESPN.com, we took a poll. . . . We commissioned our friends at Turnkey Intelligence, one of America's most prominent sports polling firms, to ask people . . . Who's the Face of Baseball? Guess who won? Yep. When Turnkey gave 1,028 baseball fans a list of players . . . Jeter pretty much squashed the rest of the field. He was chosen by 38 percent of those polled. . . . So here's a serious question, one that everyone inside Major League Baseball should be asking themselves today: Is Derek Jeter irreplaceable?"

—**Jayson Stark, ESPN.com, February 13, 2014**

> "YOU REALLY CAN'T SAY 'IRREPLACEABLE,' BECAUSE THERE'S ALWAYS SOMEONE WHO COMES ALONG WHO HAS GOT SOME OF [DEREK JETER'S] ATTRIBUTES, ON AND OFF THE FIELD. BUT I WILL SAY THIS: HE'LL BE VERY, VERY TOUGH TO FOLLOW. . . . YOU CAN CREATE THE IMAGE. BUT YOU CAN'T CREATE THE AUTHENTICITY."
> —STEVE SEIFERHELD, TURNKEY INTELLIGENCE SENIOR VICE PRESIDENT

A PERSON OF HIGH CHARACTER

"Obviously, you're known for what you do. But you still want to be known as a good person. You're a person a lot longer before and after you're a professional athlete. People always say to me 'Your image is this; your image is that.' Your image isn't your character. Character is what you are as a person. That's what I worry about."

—D.J., *Men's Health*, April 2008

"I've said this for years, and it's still true: He's a better person than he is a ballplayer."

—Don Zomer, Jeter's Kalamazoo Central High varsity baseball coach, 2010

"Derek wants to set a good example. He wants to be a role model. Seeing that, as his father, I'm extremely proud."

—Charles Jeter, 2005

"He will never ever embarrass the Yankees. [I know] because I met his parents. Special. He will never embarrass them, the Jeter name, or the New York Yankees organization."

—Buck Showalter, Yankees manager, to Yankees radio broadcaster Michael Kay, 1995

"I've always tried to treat people with respect, the way I've been treated. I've always been cautious with what I do."

—D.J.

"One mistake could be the end of things how you know it. So I'm very conscious of how I act and what I do."

—D.J., to Yankees broadcaster Michael Kay, February 2003

"I'm in high school the first time I see him on the scene, and he's Derek Jeter. You see the commercials, and all the people he's dated, and it's like this man has it all. But when he puts on that uniform and you're on the field and you come over to talk to him [for the first time], he makes you feel like he knows you."

—Jimmy Rollins, Phillies shortstop, to Sweeny Murti,
SportsNet New York, September 22, 2014

"I had a lot of animosity toward Derek Jeter early on in my career. He beat me in two World Series [in 1996 and 1999], and I didn't know him. I sat across the field from him so many times, saw all the accolades he was getting, and was a little green with envy. Then I got a chance to play with him [at the 2006 World Baseball Classic]. In the clubhouse, in the dugout, off the field at dinner, this is the best dude I have ever met."

—Chipper Jones, Atlanta Braves third baseman

"He's always been—the word I feel like is presidential. You feel like you've known him for a while, he's one of those people that is real easy to talk to, he kind of draws people to him I think, and he has that certain star quality about him that is only evident in people that are in a class like him. I just remember the first time [I played against him his] being real approachable. And over the years, he's never changed, always been very gracious."

—Evan Longoria, Tampa Bay third baseman, to Sweeny Murti,
SportsNet New York, September 22, 2014

"He's the poster child for what a baseball player should be. He's a guy that obviously has been readily accepted as an ambassador of the game through his career. Just a class act on the field and off the field. Always a classy guy with the media. Competing against him, he was always a guy that has respected everybody he played against and done everything the right way. . . . If you could have a movie script of how somebody is supposed to handle their profession in a baseball career, he'd be the prototypical guy for it."

—**Tim Hudson, pitcher for Oakland, Atlanta, and San Francisco**

"I have two sons, Jeremy and Chris, and they were with me in Minnesota during one series with the Yankees when Derek came walking by on the way to the team bus. My boys were just in awe. I called him over, introduced them, and Derek talked to them for five minutes, not too long. But he never forgot their names. Any time I was working at second or third base after that, he'd come up and say, 'How are Jeremy and Chris doing?' I'm talking years and years later. A lot of players have met my sons, and a lot of them were nice, but I can honestly tell you that nobody but Derek Jeter ever remembered their names."

—**Chuck Meriwether, umpire**

"When a superstar goes out of his way, that makes you feel good. It makes you feel like you did something right."

—**Mike Lowell, Marlins third baseman, about how he played with the Yankees for only one month in September 1998 as a rookie, yet Jeter called him after he was diagnosed with testicular cancer in February 1999**

"I got drafted in 2005, so probably the first time I really ran into him was around January 2006. I was down in the minor league complex (in Tampa) working out. I don't want to say he necessarily went out of his way to say hi to me, but he introduced himself to me at a time when he didn't have to. He could have just kept walking by. He obviously didn't know who I was. But I just remember at the time thinking, wow that's cool that he said hello."

—**Brett Gardner, Yankees outfielder, to Sweeny Murti,** *SportsNet New York*, **September 22, 2014**

"For most home games, the Yankees take the field just before the national anthem. Jeter stands at shortstop, on the edge of the outfield grass. He looks toward the Yankee Stadium video board while the music plays. When the anthem ends, Jeter bends at the knees, crouches into a solitary bubble, says a prayer, and crosses himself. He said he's offered a prayer before every game since Little League."

—Chad Jennings, writer for the Westchester, NY, *Journal News*,
APP.com, September 24, 2014

"Everyone has their beliefs. I don't try to push my beliefs on anyone. I've just always done that. I don't necessarily want to tell you what I say, but it's just something that is important to me, so I always do it."

—D.J., who was raised a Catholic and prayed after the National Anthem to thank God and ask that the Yankees play to the best of their abilities, that no one gets hurt, and for a little heavenly help if the team was struggling

"I've always tried to be accountable and responsible, and I try to do that every day."

—D.J., to Brandon Steiner, Derek Jeter Day Steiner Sports event,
December 6, 2014

"I'm inspired to be as good as I can be. You're never gonna be perfect, but I think everyone strives to be perfect. . . . You can never be satisfied with anything you've done, because once you do that, it's time to go home. No one's perfect . . . and you gotta work extremely hard day in and day out, and you get a chance to reflect on everything when you're finished."

—D.J., May 11, 2008

"I'm a perfectionist. A lot of times I don't enjoy things as they're going on, because I'm looking forward to *what else?* What else can you do? Sometimes you gotta enjoy things. I think I'm always looking forward to the next thing."

—D.J., about what he thought was his worst trait, to Steve Serby,
New York Post, May 16, 2004

"He's got a little Joe DiMaggio in him. You look at a player for what he does, for what he represents. That's the awe we had for Joe D."

—Bobby Doerr, Boston Hall of Famer, 2006

> **"HE HAS A BIT OF THE DIMAGGIO GRACE AND RESERVE AROUND HIM. THERE IS SOMETHING ABOUT HIS PRESENCE AND PERSONALITY WHERE YOU COULD SEE HIM FIT IN 1949 AS WELL AS 1999."**
> **—BOB COSTAS, QUOTED BY JOHN DELCOS, *DEREK JETER: A YANKEE FOR THE NEW MILLENNIUM*, 2000**

"They have the same kind of mannerisms. Joe never walked to the outfield . . . he always ran on the field, he always ran off, just like Jeter. [Players] all looked up to Joe. Joe did everything perfect like Jeter does. I knew Jeter as he came along; he's a loner a little bit; he likes to be private. But all the girls go after him. With Joe, it was the same thing."

—**Yogi Berra, Yankees Hall of Famer, 2006**

"It wasn't like I molded myself after [Joe DiMaggio]. You can't be something you're not, or you aren't going to be believable."

—**D.J.**

"He's rather unique for a young man in the 1990s. Endowed as he is with all that talent, all that money, and such impeccable manners—that makes him an anachronism. In this era of boorish athletes, obnoxious fans, greedy owners, and shattered myths, here's a hero who's actually polite, and that has to have come from good parenting. You can't compare him to Joe DiMaggio, for DiMaggio didn't have bad manners—he had no manners. Where have you gone, man with manners? Here you are, Derek Jeter."

—**Gay Talese, writer**

"I stay out of trouble because I surround myself with good people. These are friends I've had going back to school in Michigan. Much of the time, it's the people who hang out with you who get you into trouble. So when you have good people who've known you for so long, you can still live some kind of life and not worry about these things."

—**D.J., 2010**

"As an athlete, he's unusual, extraordinary—not unique, perhaps. But beyond that is the way he deports himself. He has enough of a small boy in him to make him charming, but he is at all times civil, well mannered, living by the obvious manners."

—Mario Cuomo, former New York governor and former minor league outfielder

"He's basically shy. And I know most people don't see him that way. He's so fluid among people. He knows what he is as far as the matinee idol stuff, and he wears it well. He has no pretenses. He's real. He enjoys himself and makes it easy for others to enjoy him."

—Joe Torre, Yankees manager

"Jeter is a testament to consistency and character and the way he's been brought up."

—Don Mattingly, former Yankees teammate and coach

"It says a lot about his character that he cares about the game . . . about his willingness to work. He has a love and a passion and respect for the game."

—Cal Ripken Jr., Orioles former shortstop and current third baseman, quoted by John Delcos, *Derek Jeter: A Yankee for the New Millennium*, 2000

"I trusted him more than any other player I ever managed. I trusted him to be prepared mentally and physically every day and to prioritize winning above all else. I trusted his instincts and his calm under the greatest pressure. I trusted he would never tell me if he were hurting, even when he was, because he thought the right thing for the team was to play."

—Joe Torre, Yankees manager

"He's the first guy to pop out of the dugout to congratulate someone who's hit a home run; he does many little things like that."

—Phil Rizzuto, Yankees Hall of Fame shortstop and broadcaster, to Dan Schlossberg, *Derek Jeter: A Yankee for the New Millennium*, 2000

"He doesn't try to make himself stand out. It just happens naturally because he has such a good sense of the game—how to play it and how to carry himself."

—Joe Torre, Yankees manager, to Marty Noble, *Derek Jeter:*
A Yankee for the New Millennium, 2000

"I think it takes me a long time before I trust someone. But I think that's a good trait to have."

—D.J.

"I wish I trusted people more. But when I meet someone, the first thing is, 'What does this person want?' And I put up a defense mechanism. But I've always been that way."

—D.J., to Ed Bradley, *60 Minutes*, September 25, 2005

"He can definitely be one of the players people point to when they list the things that are right about baseball."

—Bob Costas, broadcaster, to John Delcos, *Derek Jeter:*
A Yankee for the New Millennium, 2000

"Derek Jeter is every bit the professional and abidingly decent person you would like to think he is."

—Peter Abraham, *Boston Globe,* September 26, 2014

"Jeter is unique. He's a gentleman, but there's a standoffish way about him. I've known him for a long time, and he doesn't show a lot of emotion. But the right things are important to him, the things a manager knows are important."

—Joe Torre, Yankees manager, *The Yankee Years,* Joe Torre and Tom Verducci, 2009

"I'm not squeaky clean."

—D.J., to Barbara Walters, *10 Most Fascinating People of 2011*,
December 14, 2011

"What also endeared Jeter to his Yankees teammates, but not the team's medical personnel, was his near maniacal desire to play, no matter how hurt he might be. Fact is, the Yankees medical people often didn't know the extent of Jeter's injuries because he would refuse to even admit he was hurt."

—Tom Verducci, *The Yankee Years*, Joe Torre and Tom Verducci, 2009

"What's the difference? I'm playing anyway."

—D.J., to the Yankees' medical personnel when they wanted to take X-rays after he was hit by a pitch and possibly had a fracture on his hand or wrist

"IF YOU'RE LOOKING FOR COMPLAINTS, YOU'RE TALKING TO THE WRONG GUY." —D.J.

"I always get a kick when people say, 'Oh, he's worried about his image.' If I was worried about a so-called 'image,' people would have figured that out a long time ago. I am who I am. I try to be the same every day."

—D.J., to Meredith Marakovits, YES Network, 2014

"I thought it was a little strange that he announced (his retirement) before the season started. I thought for sure he would test himself physically in the course of spring training and actually get into the season to see where he was. A short time ago, he had 200 hits. You almost feel like he's got a lot left in his tank. Somewhere along the lines, he made a decision that this was going to be his last season. I like that decision because it gives him a chance to say goodbye but more importantly gives baseball fans a chance to say goodbye to him."

—Cal Ripken Jr., broadcaster and Orioles Hall of Famer

"The greatest compliment we can give Derek Jeter, as he prepares to leave the grandest stage in baseball, is that he never let us down. He has made thousands of outs and hundreds of errors and finished most of his seasons without a championship. Yet he never disappointed us."

—Tyler Kepner, *New York Times*

"For those choosing to believe the shortstop that he was, is, and always has been a clean ballplayer, the monument to his fidelity and greatness lies in his old-school bona fides. Jeter, along with possibly Ken Griffey Jr., is the only player in the modern game whose iconic moments were generated by all five tools—not just by standing in the batter's box and hitting another home run in a game that encouraged nothing but. Like Jackie Robinson, Jeter is pure baseball."

—William C. Rhoden, *ESPN The Magazine*, May 13, 2013

"He is the greatest player I've ever seen that was not great at any one thing. So it's just the sum of the parts that makes him awesome."

—Michael Kay, Yankees broadcaster

"Now he begins another victory lap, across one more baseball summer, the one during which he somehow turns 40."

—Mike Lupica, New York *Daily News*, February 12, 2014

"I'm already looking forward to an exciting final chapter of his storied career."

—Brian Cashman, Yankees GM

"Why would I be emotional and sentimental? We haven't even started the year."

—D.J.

"I haven't gone through it yet, so I can't tell you."

—D.J., about how approaching retirement will feel during his final season,
to reporters, April 2014

"I WANT TO SOAK IN EVERY MOMENT OF EVERY DAY THIS YEAR, SO I CAN REMEMBER IT FOR THE REST OF MY LIFE."
—D.J., FROM HIS RETIREMENT ANNOUNCEMENT, FACEBOOK, FEBRUARY 12, 2014

"I'm still looking forward to opening day. But I'm looking forward to things being over as much."

—D.J.

"This is a 12-month job, I've always approached it [like that]. I've always taken a lot of pride in working and staying in shape and doing everything I could to make sure I'm on the field. And that starts in November. The one thing I'm looking forward to [is] not having to . . . go out there and pretty much every day, even when you may be on vacation and you don't have any games, [still think] about what you have to do in order to get ready for a season. So I won't miss that."

—D.J., April 2014

"I get the fact that I have to play a game, I have to play a season. I think not enjoying it is not the right way to put it. I think balancing it is the better way to put it."

—D.J., on his last Opening Day, 2004

"They partied like it was 1999. Well, for a few moments at least. Derek Jeter's scheduled season-long farewell party began Wednesday night at Minute Maid Park [in Houston], where the retiring Yankee captain was feted by his former Yankees teammates Andy Pettitte, Roger Clemens, and Mike Stanton—all of whom were together for the '99 season when the Bombers swept the Braves in the World Series."

—Christian Red, New York *Daily News*, April 2, 2014

"He had to do it. I know that it's probably a little bit of torture for him, to be going through this. Fans here, fans all over deserve to celebrate it, show him how much they appreciate what he's done in this game."

—Andy Pettitte, former Yankees pitcher, about Jeter's discomfort celebrating his retirement in every visiting ballpark during the 2014 season, April 1, 2014

"Derek Jeter tied Paul Molitor for eighth place on the all-time hit list with a third-inning single and then passed the Hall of Famer one inning later with another hit Sunday afternoon against the Blue Jays. Jeter started the day with 3,318 career hits, one behind Molitor, a former Blue Jay. He got both singles Sunday off Toronto starter Drew Hutchison, bringing his career total to 3,320."

—**Anthony McCarron, on Jeter's historic hits in the Yankees' 6–4 victory over the home Blue Jays, New York** *Daily News*, **April 6, 2014**

"Aparicio! Everyone knows how great he is. I guess it's ironic that we're here. It's hard to believe when you think about the history of the game and there is only one guy who has played more games."

—**D.J., after a 6–5 Yankees loss to Chicago in which he tied Hall of Famer and former White Sox great Luis Aparicio by playing his 2,583rd game at shortstop, which was behind only Omar Vizquel's 2,709 games, May 22, 2014**

"I think he's the greatest Yankee of all time. That's because of the position he plays and the era he plays in. . . . As a manager, I don't want him coming up late in the game to win it. He is still that kind of player."

—**Robin Ventura, Chicago White Sox manager**

"Jordan Brand released a new, star-studded tribute on Monday to pay homage to Derek Jeter, one of the company's longest sponsored athletes. Titled 'RE2PECT,' the spot shows a veritable army of athletes, coaches, and pop culture icons tipping [and raising] their caps to the 40-year-old New York Yankee, who will retire this year after wrapping up his 20th season in the MLB. Tiger Woods, Michael Jordan, and Jay Z are just a few of the many familiar faces paying tribute to the Yankees captain in the ad. . . . He has 12 signature cleats to his name—more shoes than any other athlete besides Jordan, per Nike's official site. The ad will make its television debut Tuesday night, during Jeter's final All-Star Game."

—**Dan Carson, about a moving ad campaign that would become a nationwide sensation,** *Bleacher Report*, **July 14, 2014**

"Mr. Met might have to go into witness protection after doffing his cap for Jeter."

—Dan Carson, about a surprise cap-tipper in Nike's RE2PECT ad for Jeter, *Bleacher Report*, July 14, 2014

"Derek Jeter got the full monty at the All-Star Game, all right: a thunderous ovation that included both dugouts, the unveiling of a powerful Jordan-brand commercial before his first at-bat, two hits, and a sendoff that stopped the game dead-cold when the Yankees' captain came off the field in the fourth inning. It wasn't just great theater, it was an event that, even as it was happening, was destined to stay with you forever. Jeter made history as the oldest player to have a multi-hit performance in the Midsummer Classic, reason enough to memorialize it."

—Bob Klapisch, on Jeter's final All-Star appearance in which he got a double and a single in his two at-bats to up his lifetime average in the Midseason Classic to .481, *Bergen Record*, July 16, 2014

"I was going to give him a couple of pipe shots. He deserved it. I didn't know he was going to hit a double, or I might have changed my mind."

—Adam Wainwright, Cardinals pitcher and NL All-Star Game starter, about grooving pitches on Jeter's double to begin the game, a comment that would cause controversy about the integrity of the game, July 15, 2014

"If [Wainwright] grooved it, thank you very much. You still have to hit it. But I appreciate it if that's what he did."

—D.J., laughing off reporters who considered the incident worthy of controversy, July 15, 2014

"HE JUST WANTED TO THANK US. YOU KNOW, WE SHOULD BE THANKING HIM."
—MIKE TROUT, ANGELS OUTFIELDER, ABOUT JETER'S PREGAME MESSAGE TO ALL HIS AMERICAN LEAGUE TEAMMATES AT HIS FINAL ALL-STAR GAME, JULY 15, 2014

"On Friday night, Jeter started his 2,610th game at shortstop. That moved him past Omar Vizquel for the most in the major league history. It might not be Lou Gehrig or Cal Ripken stuff, and it came without confetti or fanfare. But you do not start that many games in the middle infield—all those double-play pivots, etc.—without a sense of responsibility, reservoir of pride, and steely constitution. The day-after-day mental and physical grind ultimately defeats every athlete. But some endure better than others. And Jeter is at the top 1 percent."

—**Joel Sherman,** *New York Post,* **July 19, 2014**

"Derek Jeter made major-league history, and Brett Gardner made personal history, but none of it was enough to get the Yankees back in the win column Monday night. The Bombers lost their third straight game as David Phelps couldn't hold an early lead, giving up four runs in the fifth inning that propelled Yu Darvish and the Rangers to a 4–2 win. Gardner had his first career two-homer game, while Jeter moved past Carl Yastrzemski into seventh place on baseball's all-time hits list with three. Jeter moved within one of Yastrzemski with his first-inning single, then tied him on the all-time list with a two-out double in the third. Jeter grabbed sole possession of seventh place with a seventh-inning single off Darvish, hit No. 3,420 for his career."

—**Mark Feinsand, New York** *Daily News,* **July 28, 2014**

"It's quite an accomplishment. It's tough to enjoy it when we lost the game. But I'm pretty sure when this season's over and done with, I'll look back and get a chance to realize how special it is."

—**D.J., about moving past Carl Yastrzemski into seventh place on the all-time hit list, July 28, 2014**

"Last night (Aug. 8), runners on first and second, and he lays down a bunt. Are you kidding me? This guy is playing in his last year, with all those hits, and he's still about the team."

—**Nick Swisher, Indians outfielder and Jeter's former Yankees teammate, August 9, 2014**

"Derek Jeter has passed Honus Wagner on the career hits list with 3,431, getting an infield single in the sixth inning Saturday against the Cleveland Indians. Jeter led off the inning with a soft grounder off Corey Kluber that shortstop José Ramirez charged but failed to pick up with his bare hand. Jeter tied Wagner on Friday night with a grounder that Ramirez made a nice play on, but the throw went off first baseman Carlos Santana's glove as the Yankees captain crossed the base."

—*Associated Press*, **August 9, 2014**

"It is one of those 'wow' moments . . . something I'll be able to tell my kids one day. Honus Wagner, he is the last one on the [all-time hit] list who has played shortstop. That one hits home a little bit. Anytime you pass guys that have had the [great] careers that they've had, it is kind of overwhelming."

—**D.J., upon passing Honus Wagner to become the all-time hit leader for shortstops, August 9, 2014**

D.J. DATA: Derek Jeter moved into sixth place on the all-time major league hit list when he passed Honus Wagner with his 3,431st hit. When he retired at the end of the 2014 season, he was still in sixth place, and the leaderboard looked like this: 1. Pete Rose, 4,256; 2. Ty Cobb, 4,191; 3. Hank Aaron, 3,771; 4. Stan Musial, 3,630; 5. Tris Speaker, 3,515; 6. Derek Jeter, 3,465; 7. Honus Wagner, 3,430; 8. Carl Yastrzemski, 3,419; 9. Paul Molitor, 3,319; 10. Eddie Collins, 3,314.

"Any time that you're mentioned with some of the greats, and [they] say you've done things only a few people in our organization have done, it makes you feel good."

—**D.J.**

"Not saying I don't think I could play longer. . . . I mean—who knows if they'd want me to come back."

—**D.J., almost acknowledging that at the age of 40 he was having a poor statistical 20th season, 2014**

"I've never taken it for granted, but it goes a lot quicker than you can imagine."

—D.J., reflecting on his long career

"Derek Jeter accepts the #ALSicebucketchallenge and nominates [his girlfriend model] Hannah Davis, [actor and director] Kevin Connolly, and Michael Jordan! Thanks Jenny Steinbrenner, Mickey Rourke, and Roger Clemens for nominating him. And a special thank you to Pete Frates for starting this movement."

—D.J., accepting the challenge to have a bucket of ice poured on him as part of a national craze to raise money to fight ALS/Lou Gehrig's disease, Facebook, August 19, 2014

"Grateful to his parents, humble, well-mannered—this is the kind of role model we want for our kids."

—Decker Communications, explaining the reason Jeter ranked second, behind only the late actor Robin Williams, on its 19th annual Top Ten Best Communicator list

JETER'S PARENTS: STILL HIS BIGGEST INFLUENCES

"My parents and I were very close while I was growing up, but I think we've grown even closer as I've gotten older, as it is with my sister, Sharlee, and them. They treat us like adults now, but they're still our parents, and they're going to tell us what they feel is right and wrong. And that's good to know. They are at a lot of games and get a lot of TV time now, and they still get on me. If I'm struggling at the plate, my mom will be in the stands yelling at me. It's good to have people that you can go to for honest advice, because a lot of times when you're in a situation where people look up to you, they're only going to tell you what you want to hear. But my parents don't care; they'll tell me the truth. They've been honest with me ever since day one when I told them I wanted to play for the Yankees."

—D.J., *Tim McCarver Show*, May 9, 2000

"Early in his career, Jeter believed his parents would serve as auditors of his personality. He couldn't change and get away with it around Charles and Dorothy Jeter."

—Buster Olney, *The Last Night of the Yankee Dynasty*, 2004

> **"THE FIRST THING THAT JUMPS OUT AT YOU IS VERY OBVIOUSLY WHAT A QUALITY JOB HIS MOM AND DAD HAVE DONE WITH HIM."**
> **—BUCK SHOWALTER, YANKEES MANAGER IN 1995**

"The thing that stuck out to me was his mom and dad and his sister and watching him interact with them, and I felt like a lot of things that challenge players off the field, especially in New York, were not going to be as much of a challenge for Derek. His upbringing was the thing that stuck out to me, how he interacted with people. He had good people skills."

—Buck Showalter, Yankees manager in 1995, to Sweeny Murti, *SportsNet New York*, September 22, 2014

"In 1996, we were like The Beatles in New York. For 60 days, I was the king of New York because Jeter was my best friend. . . . I'm setting up every place we'd go after games. . . . I'm setting it up, and he's just riding along. Darryl Strawberry and Dwight Gooden were on that '96 team. And *60 Minutes* did a special on their downfall (due to drugs). His parents are watching it in Michigan, and we're watching it in New York. As soon as that show is over, the phone rings. It's his parents, and they basically say, 'We're not liking what we see between you and R.D. You guys are partying too much.' . . . This is a kid who listened to his parents. He just won a World Series, and his parents are telling him who he can and cannot live with. It made me a casualty."

—R.D. Long, Jeter's Greensboro teammate

"I remember he was rushing out to the field, and he was in a panic about his [apartment], because it had not been cleaned. Here's the Rookie of the Year that season, playing on a team that [would win] the World Series, and he's worried about his mother coming over to his [apartment] that wasn't clean."

—Jennifer Steinbrenner Swindal, Yankees general partner and vice-chairperson and daughter of Yankees' late owner George Steinbrenner, remembering meeting Jeter for the first time when he was a rookie in 1996, to Christian Red, New York *Daily News*, September 26, 2014

"Derek is a perfect example of what his parents taught him. He's very humble. Even with all the fanfare, he's still on an even keel. You always get the true Derek when you meet him, and that tells a lot about a person. And you can see how much he appreciates his parents."

—Jorge Posada, Yankees catcher, to Tara Sullivan, *Bergen Record*

"My dad, mom, and sister are the first people I look for after we win. . . . It's so wonderful to have my family there to cheer me on. They know what my dreams have been, and they've seen me through the whole journey—from my Little League and high-school days to the major leagues. I have always had my family's support, and that's why I want to share our victories with them first."

—D.J., *Game Day*, 2001

"We communicate [during the game]. Sometimes, you know, he'll just stick up his head and [glance up]. It means he's going to try to hit a home run. I shouldn't give that away, should I?"

—Dorothy Jeter, to Ed Bradley, *60 Minutes*, September 25, 2005

"My parents have always joked that they've played every game with me; that's why I've said they're ready to retire as well."

—D.J., 2014

"My parents are baseball fans so I'm sure they'll miss coming here and having the opportunity to watch me play."

—D.J., 2014

"I thank my parents by not embarrassing them. I think that would be the worst thing I could do, if I embarrassed them and did something stupid. If I mess up, obviously, it's going to be on TV. I show my respect for them by not messing up."

—D.J.

"I started at a young age. . . . I guess that fear is still there."

—D.J., about how his scandal-free career was the result of his never wanting to embarrass his parents, to Matt Lauer, *Today*, September 30, 2014

"I hope they're proud. They've been supportive through the good times, more importantly through the bad times. When things are on your mind and you're struggling, they're the first people that I called. So I wouldn't have been able to last so long without them."

—D.J., 2014

"It's been fun for me to be back on the field. Missing all of last year, you realize how much you miss competing and playing the game. The way the fans have treated me at home and on the road has been something that's overwhelming, to say the least. It's been fun, but at the same time we're trying to win games and in that sense it's been the same. . . . Up until this point . . . the thing that I'll remember most about this year [is] the way fans in opposing stadiums have treated me. Especially some of the places I'm used to getting booed in. They've always been respectful, but obviously they're cheering for their team, and this year has been completely different."

—D.J.

"Tampa Bay Rays manager Joe Maddon doesn't seem to be enjoying Derek Jeter's farewell tour. The New York Yankees' longtime captain, who is retiring at the end of the season, was cheered at Tropicana Field throughout a three-game series over the weekend. That didn't sit well with Maddon. 'Yeah it's great. It's great that it's sold out. And I understand that the people like Derek Jeter. But you've got to come out and root for the Rays, too, you understand,' Maddon said on Sunday after a 3–2 loss. 'I mean, I totally understand what's going on. But I'm not going to sit here and defend all of that noise in the Yankees' favor in our ballpark. I'm not going to defend that. So we're going to come out and root for the Rays. We'd appreciate that.' Maddon wasn't the only one who noticed the Jeter love at the Trop. After the game on Saturday, Yankees manager Joe Girardi said he hasn't seen an away stadium cheer for Jeter as much as the fans did at Tropicana Field."

—**Michael Klopman,** *Huffington Post***, August 18, 2014**

"Yankee fans made their pilgrimage to the Bronx Sunday, young and old, to celebrate the man who had given them a lifetime of chills and thrills over the last 20 years. It was their turn to say thanks and goodbye to a Yankees legend, the way past generations did with Babe Ruth and Lou Gehrig and Mickey Mantle and Joe D. But when Derek Jeter took the microphone following his pregame ceremony honoring him, it was the captain who took the opportunity to thank the people he believes helped him become the player he is: the fans."

—**Mark Feinsand, about Derek Jeter Day at Yankee Stadium,**
New York *Daily News***, September 7, 2014**

"It's kind of hard to believe that 20 seasons have gone by so quickly. There are so many people I want to thank, and I'll have the opportunity to do that over the next few weeks both publicly and privately. I want to take a brief moment to thank the Steinbrenner family and Mr. George Steinbrenner for giving me the opportunity to play my entire career for the only organization I ever wanted to play for. . . . I love what I've done, I love what I do, and more importantly, I've loved doing it for you. So from the bottom of my heart, thank you very much. We've got a game to play."

—**D.J., concluding his speech to the fans at Derek Jeter Day at Yankee Stadium**
three weeks before playing his final game, September 7, 2014

"Many know that Jeter and [Michael] Jordan have a close relationship, with No. 2 having a contract with No. 23's brand that includes a whole slew of customized cleats for his final season, and by now just about everyone has seen some part of the 'RE2PECT' campaign that Jordan unleashed."

—**Lou DiPietro, after Jordan showed up unexpectedly at Derek Jeter Day,**
YESNetwork.com, September 8, 2014

"Kalamazoo community members tipped their caps Thursday to one of their own. A 'Community Hat Tip' honored Derek Jeter, the Kalamazoo Central graduate whose skill on the baseball field, and his graciousness off it, has earned him respect across the country, but especially in his hometown. Filmed in the lobby of the Radisson Plaza Hotel & Suites, about 200 people raised their hats to Jeter in unison for a video that was then quickly edited and then previewed to the crowd. Thursday's hat tip is part of a larger video that will be sent to the New York Yankees star. The video is a local response to Nike's 'RE2PECT' commercial that honors Jeter through celebrity cameos and cap-tipping fans. Homewatch CareGivers of Southwest Michigan and ImageStream conceived and produced the local video, which has been in production since July and features Kalamazoo Central teachers who had Jeter in class, former classmates, long-time friends, local dignitaries, and others all tipping their caps to the five-time World Series champion."

—**Katie Alaimo, *Kalamazoo Gazette*, September 9, 2014**

"The problem is, along with his many other virtues, Jeter has been so *companionable*. He's always been so reassuringly *there*. On summer nights, and autumn nights, maybe especially autumn nights, it was a pleasure to turn on the TV and know he'd be at short, tugging the bill of his cap, doing that dancery thing he did every pitch, that half-step toward the hole or the plate just as the pitcher went into his windup. If you walked into any bar, from Midtown to Montauk, between, say 7 p.m. and 11, Jeter would be above the bartender's head, stepping lithely into the batter's box, waggling his helmet, that dainty way he does, with the pointer finger in the ear hole, then holding his right palm to the ump, begging, *Wait, please, wait, just a little more time.* For 20 years, he's been more than a great player, he's been great company, and so he'll be missed, not like a limb, not like a friend—but something like. And no one can truly gauge how much he'll be missed until he's gone."

—**J.R. Moehringer, *ESPN The Magazine*, October 13, 2014**

"Derek Jeter scored the 1,920th run of his career in the Yankees' 6–3 loss to the Blue Jays on Saturday, breaking a tie with Alex Rodriguez for sole possession of ninth place on baseball's all-time list. Jeter reached base with a third-inning infield single off starter Marcus Stroman and moved to second base on a wild pitch before sliding home safely on Brian McCann's single to left field, tying the game at 1. . . . Rodriguez has missed all of this season due to a suspension [for purchasing steroids] and will have the opportunity to move past Jeter when he rejoins the Yankees next year. Stan Musial is in eighth place on the all-time list with 1,949 runs scored."

—**Bryan Hoch, MLB.com, September 20, 2014**

"With the crowd chanting his name in the bottom of the ninth, Jeter ripped a one-out double to plate Brett Gardner and cut the Yankees' deficit to three runs. The RBI was Jeter's 1,303rd, lifting him past Miguel Tejada and into 100th place alone on the career RBIs list."

—**Bryan Hoch, MLB.com, September 20, 2014**

"He's turned it around again. You're seeing it again. The guy never stops fighting and believing in himself. Obviously, it's an attitude that's infectious. It's an attitude that you want in your players."

—**Joe Girardi, Yankees manager, about Jeter scoring his 1,920th run and driving in his 1,303rd run against Toronto, September 19, 2014**

"Nothing he does surprises you anymore. Obviously, what he's accomplished in his career is pretty special, and he's definitely a guy you don't ever want to count out."

—**Brett Gardner, Yankees outfielder, after Jeter's big day against Toronto, September 19, 2014**

> "WHEN I WAS A KID, AS I REMINISCED THE OTHER DAY, MY FAVORITE PLAYER WAS JOE DIMAGGIO. WHAT JOE D. MEANT TO MY GENERATION, DEREK JETER HAS BEEN TO HIS. . . . HE IS A GREAT CHAMPION IN EVERY WAY."
> —BUD SELIG, MLB COMMISSIONER, AT A NEWS CONFERENCE ABOUT AWARDING JETER THE COMMISSIONER'S HISTORIC ACHIEVEMENT AWARD AND ANNOUNCING MLB HAS DONATED $222,222.22 TO JETER'S TURN 2 FOUNDATION, SEPTEMBER 23, 2014

"It's almost like you're at your own funeral. Everyone had great things to say, which I really appreciate. But it's very, very odd to be out there and hearing about yourself as if you're about to die."

—D.J., about an unusual aspect of his farewell season, *Tonight Show Starring Jimmy Fallon,* October 3, 2014

CLASSIC MOMENT: SEPTEMBER 25, 2014, YANKEE STADIUM, NYC

"In anticipation of Jeter's last game [at Yankee Stadium], fans have been buying tickets for far more than the normal price. Currently, tickets on StubHub range from about $300 to as high as $15,225 for infield grandstand tickets."

—Gillian Mahoney, via *Good Morning America,* September 24, 2014

"Jeter turned what should have been a meaningless game at the end of a lost Yankee season into one of the greatest sports nights we have ever had around here."

—Mike Lupica, New York *Daily News,* October 2, 2014

"He seemed nervous, just getting ready. . . . He actually almost walked out without his cleats on. I've never seen him do that."

—CC Sabathia, Yankees pitcher

"Fifty thousand people. I've never been an actor on Broadway, but it feels like you're on a stage when you play at Yankee Stadium. And that's the feeling I've always had. To have everyone there standing up and cheering for you, and saying 'thank you,' I just never wanted to play another game out there."

—D.J., on his last home game

"I've done a pretty good job of controlling my emotions. I try to hide them. I try to trick myself into not feeling those particular emotions. Today, I wasn't able to do it. . . . I was honestly out there saying, 'Please don't hit it to me.' I was thinking to myself, 'Get me out of here before I do something that costs us the game.'"

—D.J.

"Certainly, the script was completely altered on the fly. The game plan was to remove Jeter from the game in the top of the ninth inning with the Yankees leading 5–2. Yet, before anyone knew it, closer David Robertson coughed up three runs, the last on Steve Pearce's home run. Never did a blown save look so beautiful."

—Bob Nightengale, *USA Today*, September 26, 2014

"You've always been the best set-up man in the game."

—Mariano Rivera, former Yankees pitcher, to David Robertson after his successor as the Yankees' closer blew a three-run lead in the top of the ninth inning for the only time to allow Derek Jeter to have one more at-bat in the bottom of the ninth inning, September 25, 2014

"GOD, IF YOU HAVE ANY MORE MAGICAL MOMENTS IN YOU, CAN IT PLEASE BE RIGHT NOW?"

—D.J., PRIOR TO HIS LAST AT-BAT AT YANKEE STADIUM, *TONIGHT SHOW STARRING JIMMY FALLON*, OCTOBER 3, 2014

"Now batting for the Yankees, Number 2, Derek Jeter, Number 2."

—Bob Sheppard, Yankees' late public address announcer, has his recorded introduction play for the last time as Jeter bats for the final time at Yankee Stadium, September 25, 2014

"Don't cry."

—D.J., to himself as he stepped into the batter's box for the final time at Yankee Stadium

"Well, the script is there, the last page is in Derek's hands. Meek deals. Base hit to right field! Here comes Richardson! Here's the throw from Markakis! Richardson is safe! Derek Jeter ends his final game with a walk-off single. Derek Jeter, where fantasy becomes reality. Did you have any doubt?"

—Michael Kay, Yankees broadcaster, on Jeter's final Yankee Stadium at-bat in the bottom of the ninth inning with the score tied 5–5, the Orioles' Evan Meek on the mound, and Antoan Richardson on second base representing the winning run, YES Network, September 25, 2014

"It was sort of an out-of-body experience. It was a weird range of emotions. I was just trying not to cry."

—D.J.

"Jeter has got God on speed dial."

—Zach Britton, Orioles reliever

"It was already written. Could it have happened any other way?"

—Nick Hundley, Orioles catcher

"Not surprised. I knew it was going to happen. It sounds weird. You expect it of him. It's crazy."

—CC Sabathia, Yankees pitcher

"Everyone in the dugout, and the stadium knew it was going to happen."

—David Robertson, Yankees reliever

"Jeter, after celebrating with his current and former teammates, slowly then walked around the infield, waving to the crowd. He stopped at the shortstop position. He kneeled down, lowered his head, and prayed."

—Bob Nighengale, *USA Today*, September 26, 2014

"I BASICALLY JUST SAID, 'THANK YOU,' BECAUSE THIS IS ALL I EVER WANTED TO DO. NOT TOO MANY PEOPLE HAVE THE OPPORTUNITY TO DO IT. IT WAS ABOVE AND BEYOND ANYTHING I DREAMED."

—D.J., SEPTEMBER 25, 2014

"It was a night when everything seemed to happen specifically to allow Jeter to be Jeter in front of the home fans for the last time."

—David Waldstein, NYTimes.com, September 25, 2014

"I don't think there was a more fitting way for it to end."

—Joe Girardi, Yankees manager, September 25, 2014

"I don't know what to tell you. Write what you want, and put my name on it."

—D.J., feeling too emotional to express himself at the postgame press conference

"The last time I packed my locker I was 20 years old. So I never had to do it."

—D.J., Steiner Sports event, 2014

CLASSIC MOMENT:
SEPTEMBER 28, 2014, FENWAY PARK, BOSTON

"If I couldn't finish my career here [in New York], it's only fitting I guess that it's in Boston. It will be fine. I enjoy playing in Boston."

—**D.J., at Derek Jeter Day Steiner Sports event, December 6, 2014**

"During a pregame ceremony, Derek Jeter, initially standing alone at short, was greeted by a parade of Boston stars from Carl Yastrzemski to the Boston Bruins' Bobby Orr, the New England Patriots' Troy Brown, and the Washington Wizards' Paul Pierce, who donned a Boston Celtics shirt. . . . Red Sox third-base coach Brian Butterfield—the minor league instructor who helped Jeter improve the most after his 56-error season in 1993—presented Jeter with customized L.L. Bean boots. The current Red Sox players then came out to visit Jeter, led by David Ortiz. Dustin Pedroia, the final one in the procession, gave Jeter a second base inscribed with No. 2. The Red Sox also donated $22,222.22 to Jeter's Turn 2 Foundation. Jeter received $599,888.88 in charitable donations during all his tributes this season. The Red Sox also gave Jeter a custom-made 'RE2PECT' Fenway placard."

—**Andrew Marchand, about the ceremony at Fenway Park prior to Jeter's final major league game, ESPNNewYork.com, September 28, 2014**

"This place is where we've been the enemy for a long, long time. For them to flip the script the way they did today for me extremely proud and happy that I was part of the rivalry."

—**D.J., who was thrilled by the fine treatment he received in Boston at his last game**

"I've had them stand and say some things, but it was never an ovation."

—**D.J., about the Boston crowd in Fenway Park giving him a standing ovation during his last game, to Matt Lauer, *Today*, September 30, 2014**

"Derek Jeter played his last game Sunday, ending his career with a play typical of his time in the majors, in which he hustled out an infield single for his 3,465th hit. As Jeter stood at first base, in the top of the third inning against Boston, Manager Joe Girardi made a slashing motion at his throat, asking with the hand signal if that was it for Jeter. Jeter nodded. The fans had been standing from the moment he had come to the plate, but the cheering and the 'Derek Jeter' chants grew louder. Jeter handed his arm and foot pads to the first-base coach, Mick Kelleher, and patted him on the helmet. He waited for Brian McCann, the pinch-runner, to arrive and gave him a heartfelt hug. Then he jogged across the diamond, stopping to shake hands with Clay Buchholz, the Red Sox' starting pitcher, and hugged each of his teammates before he sat down in the dugout. His 20-year career was over."

—**David Waldstein,** *New York Times*, **September 28, 2014**

"I FELT THE TIME WAS RIGHT. I WAS READY FOR MY CAREER TO BE OVER."
—D.J.

"And that's going to be it for Derek Jeter. His final hit an RBI single as Jeter says goodbye to baseball . . . and baseball says goodbye to him. . . . And one of the greatest careers in history has just come to an end. And what a perfect way to end it, with a base hit and an RBI. Twenty years of excellence ends on the field at Fenway Park."

—**Michael Kay, Yankees broadcaster, on Jeter's final career at-bat, an infield hit on a high chopper to third off Boston's Clay Buchholz, to give the Yankees a 3–0 lead in the third inning, YES Network, September 28, 2014**

"Jeter's last hit did not go far, but it nudged his career average up a point, to .310, where it will sit forever. He finished with 1,923 runs scored—an evocative number in the history of the Yankees, who won their first title in 1923—and nobody ever started more games at shortstop than Jeter's 2,660."

—**Tyler Kemper,** *New York Times*, **September 28, 2014**

"I never played the game for numbers. So why start now?"

—D.J., to Yankees manager Joe Girardi that morning about how he wanted to come out of his final game after two at-bats even if he was one hit away from tying Ty Cobb's major league record of 150 hits in 18 seasons, September 28, 2014

D.J. DATA: After he had played his last game on September 28, 2014, Derek Jeter led the Yankees in all-time plate appearances (12,602), at-bats (11,195), hits (3,465), singles (2,595), doubles (544), stolen bases (358), hits-by-pitch (170), and strikeouts (1,840). Additionally, Jeter finished second all-time in runs scored (1,923), ninth in home runs (260), sixth in RBIs (1,311), and fifth in extra-base hits (870). This is where he stood on career batting average:

1. Babe Ruth, .349; 2. Lou Gehrig, .340; 3. Earle Combs, .325; 4. Joe DiMaggio, .325;

5. Wade Boggs, .313; 6. Bill Dickey, .313; 7. Bob Meusel, .311; 8. Derek Jeter, .310;

9. Robinson Canó, .309; 10. Don Mattingly, .307

"I'll miss it, but I won't play again. I've played my last game. That's 100 percent."

—D.J., to Matt Lauer, *Today*, September 30, 2014

"It feels good. I don't know if will necessarily hit me until when I would normally start working out for the next season."

—D.J., to Matt Lauer, *Today*, September 30, 2014

"Someone mentioned to me that I went from an old man in baseball to a young man in life. I liked how that sounded, so I consider myself young again."

—D.J., to Matt Lauer, Today, September 30, 2014

"First and foremost, I want to rest. I don't want to have a schedule. You know I've been doing this professionally for 23 years, and I've been playing baseball since I was four or five, so I really haven't had much time off. I'm not complaining, but I'm looking forward to having some time off."

—D.J., to Brian Williams, *NBC Nightly News*, September 25, 2014

"I look forward to having a family. I just don't think personally I would have been able to juggle a family and my career at the same time."

—D.J., to Brian Williams, *NBC Nightly News*, September 25, 2014

"I want to own a team one day. You know, that's my next goal."

—D.J., repeating a goal he stated to Barbara Walters in 2011 and to others after, to Matt Lauer, *Today*, September 30, 2014

"I've already heard him talk about possibly owning a team. He has a great reputation, and he's put himself in a position financially, and I promise you he's going to give it the same type of effort as he did in the game of baseball. I wish him the best."

—Michael Jordan, basketball Hall of Famer and owner of the NBA's Charlotte Hornets, September 9, 2014

"I'm not there anymore."

—D.J., to a reporter on the street who asked him about the current Yankees, TMZ.com, 2015

"*Tampa Bay Business Journal* reported Jeter entered a proposal to open The Players' Tribune Bar & Grill in a 3,439-square-foot space inside the Tampa International Airport. Come beyond the velvet rope to enjoy the VIP atmosphere,' Jeter's proposal said. 'Not a sports bar . . . a sports lounge.' No prices were included in the menu that features everything from chicken wings to the Jeter Burger. The restaurant will have iPads at 'virtually every seat' so diners can explore The Players' Tribune website while they enjoy a meal."

—Travis Durkee, SportingNews.com, March 26, 2015

"The Yankees will start training at George M. Steinbrenner Field in Tampa, and Jeter—the guy who holds as many franchise records as Babe Ruth does—will not be among the players in pinstripes on the field. No doubt it will be weird."

—Jim Baumbach, before the Yankees pitchers and catchers reported to spring training in 2015, *Newsday*, February 15, 2015

"FOR TWO DECADES [DEREK JETER] WAS THE YANKEE THAT KIDS WANTED TO BE."
—MIKE LUPICA, NEW YORK *DAILY NEWS*, FEBRUARY 12, 2014

"His grace and elegance in everything he does, and his ability to be the same exact guy today that he was the day he stepped into the big leagues, is just incredible."

—Billy Beane, A's GM, 2009

"He sets the bar for the way guys go about their game."

—John Farrell, Boston manager

"They created the Hall of Fame for players like him. Never a doubt. Totally earned. He may be the first 100 percenter."

—Joe Maddon, Tampa Bay manager

"I've enjoyed watching him play, seeing him perform, seeing him perform in the postseason. I'm a little happy, and I'm a little sad at the same time that Derek is going. Wonderful, long, long career with the same team. Not a lot of people get to enjoy that."

—Cal Ripken Jr., Baltimore Hall of Famer

"I always had an eye on him. He was a guy that you look at and keep an eye on to see what he's doing because you want to be doing the same things. What was kind of nice [seeing him at All-Star Games] is it kind of reinforces the things that you do. I like the way he went about his business. It'll be different not to see him out there. You appreciate what he's done as a player, and he's a pretty good guy too."

—**Joe Mauer, Twins catcher and first baseman, to Sweeny Murti,**
SportsNet New York, **September 22, 2014**

"He's the way you want kids to grow up. There's nobody perfect on this Earth. Only Jesus was perfect, but he's pretty close to being that perfect guy."

—**Albert Pujols, Angels first baseman**

"It's hard to put into words what he's meant to the game. I've watched this guy since I was a kid, since I was eight or nine. . . . It's remarkable what he's accomplished, not only the hits and the accolades, but (also) the timely hits and the big moments he's had. It's a great career that you're sad to see come to an end, but at the same time, it's been a really good one and a long one."

—**Buster Posey, Giants catcher, 2014**

"I'm going to tell you right now, playing against the Yankees and not seeing D.J. is going to be a totally different feeling. Not being able to see him is going to feel kind of weird."

—**David Ortiz, Boston Red Sox designated hitter**

"No one can replace the captain. I know I'm going to miss him tremendously."

—**Alex Rodriguez, Yankees third baseman, February 24, 2015**

"He was a kind of prince in baseball cleats, George Clooney in pinstripes, the guy every woman wanted to bring home to Mom, and very few did. He was humble and handsome yet hard to hate. He was like a good magician. You could never figure out how he did it. He was the best player in baseball for a good 10 years straight, and yet he never won a batting title, never won an MVP, never was the highest-paid player in the game. The only thing he did better than anybody else was excel: five rings, 13 [soon to be 14] All-Star Games, the greatest Yankee since Mickey Mantle. He spoke to the media every day, yet managed to say nothing. He dated the most traffic-stopping women, yet he never seemed to wind up on Page Six or TMZ or 'Extra.'. . . . If there was a better man in sports, I never met him."

—Rick Reilly, ESPN.com, May 28, 2014

"I believe Derek Jeter is the most important baseball player of our age. I don't mean the best player—although he might be that, too—but the most important. That's because during a time period that has been characterized by upheavals that might have capsized baseball, most especially the problem of PEDs [performance enhancing drugs], he has provided the image of a leader above reproach, every-day excellence on the field balanced with personal modesty and strong personal values."

—Walter Harrison, University of Hartford president

"I can't see how he won't be unless somebody beats him to the punch. I've thought about it; Jeter should be the one. What can you say he hasn't done. He has every credential imaginable—great player, good citizen. He plays the game properly, respects the game and his predecessors. He's done it in the big city, for one team that wears a uniform of greatness. He has no marks against him. He has the numbers. And he wins."

—Tom Seaver, New York Mets pitching great, who received the highest percentage of Hall of Fame votes, 98.84 percent, on why he expects Jeter to be the first player elected unanimously for induction, July 24, 2014

"THEY SHOULD PUT HIM IN THE HALL OF FAME NOW. WHY WAIT?"
—MITCH LUKEVICS, TAMPA BAY'S DIRECTOR OF MINOR LEAGUE OPERATIONS,
QUOTED BY DANIEL CARP, *USA TODAY*, SEPTEMBER 4, 2014

"I live for this."

—**D.J., promoting MLB by expressing how much he loved playing
for the Yankees and their fans,** *ESPN*

"He wasn't the all-time home run king, and he didn't hit in 56 straight games, and
he never won a Triple Crown the way Mantle did. Still: You add it all up today,
you remember everything he has done on the field and everything he has meant off
it, how much he did to make the Yankees the Yankees again, and you know there
has never been a Yankee who mattered more. Or will ever matter as much again."

—**Mike Lupica, New York** *Daily News*, **February 12, 2014**

"I know you're going to miss the game, but as far as I'm concerned, the game is
going to miss you more."

—**Chili Davis, A's hitting coach and former Yankees outfielder,
congratulatory video message to Jeter, 2014**

"You can't replace a Derek Jeter."

—**Joe Torre, Yankees manager from 1996 to 2007, September 26, 2014**

"For him to remain a Yankee was the utmost compliment that Major League
Baseball gave to Derek."

—**Dorothy Jeter, 2014**

"I've lived a dream since I was four or five years old, and now the dream is over."

—**D.J.**

D.J. DATA: Jeter never cared about his personal statistics, but they are impressive.

YEAR	TEAM	LG	LEVEL	G	AB	R	H	TB	2B	3B	HR	RBI	BB	IBB	SO	SB	CS	AVG	OBP	SLG	OPS	GO/AO
1992[+]	2 teams		Minors	58	210	23	44	66	10	0	4	29	26	0	52	2	3	.210	.311	.314	.626	-
1993	GBO	SAL	A (Full)	128	515	85	152	203	14	11	5	71	58	1	95	18	9	.295	.376	.394	.770	-
1994[+]	3 teams		Minors	138	540	103	186	250	27	11	5	68	58	3	61	50	8	.344	.410	.463	.873	-
1995	COL	INT	AAA	123	486	96	154	205	27	9	2	45	61	1	56	20	12	.317	.394	.422	.816	-
1995	NYY	AL	MLB	15	48	5	12	18	4	1	0	7	3	0	11	0	0	.250	.294	.375	.669	-
1996	NYY	AL	MLB	157	582	104	183	250	25	6	10	78	48	1	102	14	7	.314	.370	.430	.800	-
1997	NYY	AL	MLB	159	654	116	190	265	31	7	10	70	74	0	125	23	12	.291	.370	.405	.775	-
1998	NYY	AL	MLB	149	626	127	203	301	25	8	19	84	57	1	119	30	6	.324	.384	.481	.864	-
1998	COL	INT	AAA	1	5	2	2	4	0	0	0	0	0	0	2	0	0	.400	.400	.800	1.200	-
1999	NYY	AL	MLB	158	627	134	219	346	37	9	24	102	91	5	116	19	8	.349	.438	.552	.989	1.30
2000	TAM	FSL	A (Adv)	1	3	2	2	3	0	0	0	0	0	0	0	0	0	.667	.667	1.000	1.667	-
2000	NYY	AL	MLB	148	593	119	201	285	31	4	15	73	68	4	99	22	4	.339	.416	.481	.896	1.43
2001	NYY	AL	MLB	150	614	110	191	295	35	3	21	74	56	3	99	27	3	.311	.377	.480	.858	1.77
2002	NYY	AL	MLB	157	644	124	191	271	26	0	18	75	73	2	114	32	3	.297	.373	.421	.794	1.76
2003	TRN	EAS	AA	5	18	2	8	11	1	1	0	5	3	0	0	0	0	.444	.545	.611	1.157	-
2003	NYY	AL	MLB	119	482	87	156	217	25	3	10	52	43	2	88	11	5	.324	.393	.450	.844	2.14
2004	NYY	AL	MLB	154	643	111	188	303	44	1	23	78	46	1	99	23	4	.292	.352	.471	.823	1.43
2005	NYY	AL	MLB	159	654	122	202	294	25	5	19	70	77	3	117	14	5	.309	.389	.450	.839	2.33
2006	NYY	AL	MLB	154	623	118	214	301	39	3	14	97	69	4	102	34	5	.343	.417	.483	.900	2.74
2007	NYY	AL	MLB	156	639	102	206	289	39	4	12	73	56	3	100	15	8	.322	.388	.452	.840	1.86
2008	NYY	AL	MLB	150	596	88	179	243	25	3	11	69	52	0	85	11	5	.300	.363	.408	.771	1.98
2009	NYY	AL	MLB	153	634	107	212	295	27	1	18	66	72	4	90	30	5	.334	.406	.465	.871	2.66
2010	NYY	AL	MLB	157	663	111	179	245	30	3	10	67	63	4	106	18	5	.270	.340	.370	.710	2.91
2011	NYY	AL	MLB	131	546	84	162	212	24	4	6	61	46	0	81	16	6	.297	.355	.388	.743	2.54
2011	TRN	EAS	AA	2	4	1	2	2	0	0	0	0	0	0	1	0	0	.500	.667	.500	1.167	0.00
2012	NYY	AL	MLB	159	683	99	216	293	32	0	15	58	45	1	90	9	4	.316	.362	.429	.791	3.16
2013	NYY	AL	MLB	17	63	8	12	16	1	0	1	7	8	1	10	0	0	.190	.288	.254	.542	4.00
2013	SWB	INT	AAA	7	18	4	4	5	1	0	0	1	5	0	3	0	0	.222	.391	.278	.669	11.00
2014	NYY	AL	MLB	145	581	47	149	182	19	1	4	50	35	0	87	10	2	.256	.304	.313	.617	2.18
MLB Totals				2747	11195	1923	3465	4921	544	66	260	1311	1082	39	1840	358	97	.310	.377	.440	.817	2.08
Minors Totals[+]	7 teams			463	1799	318	554	749	83	32	16	219	213	5	270	90	32	.308	.386	.416	.803	5.50

Bibliography

Appel, Marty. *Pinstripe Empire: The New York Yankees from Before the Babe to After the Boss*. New York: Bloomsbury, 2012.

Araton, Harvey. *Driving Mr. Yogi: Yogi Berra, Ron Guidry, and Baseball's Greatest Gift*. Boston: Houghton Mifflin Harcourt Publishing, 2012.

Barra, Allen. *Yogi Berra: Eternal Yankee*. New York: W.W. Norton & Company, 2009.

Buscema, Dave. *Game of My Life: 20 Stories of Yankees Baseball*. Champaign, Ill: Sports Publishing, LLC, 2004.

Bush, George W. *Decision Points*. New York: Crown Publishers, 2010.

Craig, Robert. *Derek Jeter: A Biography*. New York: Pocket Books, 1999.

Damon, Johnny, and Peter Golenbock. *Idiot: Beating "The Curse" and Enjoying the Game of Life*. New York: Crown Publishers, 2005.

Dewan, John. *The Fielding Bible: Break-Through Analysis of Major League Baseball Defense—by Team and Player*. Chicago: Acta Publications, 2006.

Dobrow, Larry, and Damien Jones. *Derek Jeter's Ultimate Baseball Guide 2015*. New York: Jeter Children's, 2015.

Francona, Terry, and Dan Shaughnessy. *Francona: The Red Sox Years*. Boston: Houghton Mifflin Harcourt, 2013.

Giles, Patrick. *Derek Jeter: Pride of the Yankees*. New York: St. Martin's Press, 1999.

Jeter, Derek, and Christopher Anderson. *Jeter Unfiltered*. New York: Jeter Publishing, 2014.

Jeter, Derek, with Jack Curry. *The Life You Imagine: Life Lessons for Achieving Your Dreams*. New York: Random House Children's Books, 2000.

Jeter, Derek. *Game Day: My Life On and Off the Field*, ed. Kristin Kiser. New York: Three Rivers Press, 2001.

Kepner, Tyler, ed. *Derek Jeter: Excellence and Elegance (The* New York *Times Collection)*, Chicago: Triumph Books, 2014.

Kernan, Kevin. *Girardi: Passion in Pinstripes*. Chicago: Triumph Books. 2012.

Kiner, Ralph, with Danny Peary. *Baseball Forever: Reflections on 60 Years in the Game*. Chicago: Triumph Books, 2004.

Madden, Bill. *Steinbrenner: The Last Lion of Baseball*. New York: Harper, 2010.

Massarotti, Tony, and John Harper. *A Tale of Two Cities: The 2004 Yankees-Red Sox Rivalry and the War for the Pennant.* New York: Lyons Press, 2005.

McCarver, Tim, with Danny Peary. *The Perfect Season.* New York: Villard, 1999.

McCarver, Tim, with Jim Moskovitz and Danny Peary, eds. *Tim McCarver's Diamond Gems: Favorite Baseball Stories from the Legends of the Game.* New York: McGraw-Hill, 2008.

Nauen, Elinor. *So Late Into the Night.* New York: Rain Mountain Press, 2011.

New York Post. *Derek Jeter: Born to Be a Yankee.* Rosen, R.D., ed. New York: HarperCollins, 2014.

New York Daily News, with Claudia Mitro and Joseph J. Bannon, Jr., eds. *Jeter: Hero in Pinstripes.* New York: Sports Publishing, Inc., 2001.

O'Connor, Ian. *The Captain: The Journey of Derek Jeter.* Boston: Houghton Mifflin Harcourt, 2011.

Olney, Buster. *The Last Night of the Yankee Dynasty.* New York: HarperCollins, 2004.

O'Neill, Paul, with Burton Rocks. *Me and My Dad: A Baseball Memoir.* New York: William Morrow, 2003.

Pepe, Phil. *Core Four: The Heart and Soul of the Yankees Dynasty.* Chicago: Triumph Books, 2013.

Rappaport, Ken. *Super Sports Star: Derek Jeter.* Berkeley Heights, New Jersey: Enslow Elementary, 2004.

Rivera, Mariano, with Wayne Coffey. *The Closer.* New York: Little, Brown and Company, 2014.

Rizzuto, Phil, and Cal Ripken Jr., Roger Clemens, Ozzie Smith, Bob Costas, and Joe Torre. *Derek Jeter: A Yankee for the New Millennium.* Dallas, Texas: Beckett Publications, 2000.

Roberts, Selena. *A-Rod: The Many Lives of Alex Rodriguez.* New York: Harper, 2009.

Robinson, Tom. *Derek Jeter: Captain On and Off the Field.* Berkeley Heights, New Jersey: Enslow Publishers, 2006.

Schnakenberg, Robert E. *Derek Jeter: Surefire Shortstop.* Minneapolis: Lerner Publications, 1999.

Sheehy, Harry, with Danny Peary. *Raising a Team Player: Teaching Kids Lasting Values on the Field, on the Court, and on the Bench.* North Adams, MA: Storey Publishing, 2002.

Slovak, Richard, ed. *Derek Jeter: From the Pages of the New York Times.* New York: Abrams, 2011.

Stout, Glenn, and Matt Christopher. *On the Field with . . . Derek Jeter.* Boston: Little, Brown Books for Young Readers, 2000.

Tan, Celia. *The 50 Greatest Yankee Games.* New York: John Wiley & Sons, Inc., 2005.

Torre, Joe, with Tom Verducci. *Chasing the Dream: My Lifelong Journey to the World Series.* New York: Bantam Books, 1997.

Torre, Joe, and Tom Verducci. *The Yankee Years.* New York: Doubleday, 2009.

Wells, David, with Chris Kreski. *Perfect I'm Not: Boomer on Beer, Brawls, Backaches, and Baseball.* New York: William Morrow, 2003.

Williams, Bernie, with Dave Gluck and Bob Thompson. *Rhythms of the Game: The Link Between Musical and Athletic Performance.* Milwaukee, Wisconsin: Hal Leonard Books, 2011.

Zimmer, Don, with Bill Madden. *A Baseball Life.* Kingston, New York: Total Sports Publishing, 2001.

Acknowledgments

I didn't need a village to help me with this book because I had a few exceptional individuals who turned my idea into reality. First, I wanted to express my gratitude to the two people who got this project off the ground: my formidable agent and ideal lunch companion, Al Zuckerman, and my enthusiastic and creative publisher, Will Kiester, whose love of baseball matches my own. I was in good hands.

I also was very fortunate that Sarah Monroe was my editor. I trusted her instantly because of her savvy choices and insights. Thank you for keeping my anxiety to a minimum. I also want to express my appreciation for my copyeditor, Ruth Strother, as well as Meg Palmer, Harriet Low, Laura Gallant, Meg Baskis, and everyone else at Page Street Publishing. I also thank Mickey Novak and everyone else at Writers House.

For his help in providing me with research material, I want to acknowledge Matt Rothenberg, the manager of the Giamatti Research Center at the National Baseball Hall of Fame and Museum. I also thank Bill Francis at the HOF, Tim Wiles, Marty Appel, Dave Sims, and Bill Ames. Everyone needs a personal researcher, and I had the best, Carol Summers. Thank you for playing detective and tracking down a number of key articles from Derek Jeter's pre-Yankee years.

I also applaud all the people I have quoted, particularly sports figures and journalists, including those I have never met. If you are quoted, then obviously I appreciate what you have said or written. There are a number of instances when I was unable to confidently attribute quotes by Derek Jeter and others to the correct original sources. Often several journalists were present when something quotable was said and, understandably, they all took credit; also journalists often repeated words said to other journalists without identifying the original sources. I apologize to any journalist slighted and encourage journalists, baseball historians, and fans to help me fill in the blanks.

Of course, I salute Derek Jeter himself for providing a career and exhibiting a personality that made him, in my opinion, worthy of a tribute such as this. He was, in my lifetime, right up there with Willie Mays, Hank Aaron, Roberto Clemente, Rickey Henderson, and Cal Ripken as the embodiment of baseball in its purest form, playing and thinking the game as it was meant to be.

Finally, thank you, Suzanne, my cheerleader.

About the Author

DANNY PEARY is a sports and film historian who has published 24 books. He collaborated on the biographies of Roger Maris and Gil Hodges, the autobiographies of Ralph Kiner and Shannon Miller, and three books with Tim McCarver. He also edited the anthology *Cult Baseball Players*, the oral histories *Super Bowl: The Game of Our Lives* and *We Played the Game: Memories of Baseball's Greatest Era*. He is the writer-researcher of *The Tim McCarver Show*. Danny lives in New York City and Sag Harbor, New York.

Index